THE PERFECT SALESFORCE

THE PERFECT
SALESFORCE

THE 6 BEST PRACTICES
OF THE WORLD'S
BEST
SALES TEAMS

Derek Gatehouse

PORTFOLIO

PORTFOLIO
Published by the Penguin Group
Penguin Group (USA) Inc., 375 Hudson Street, New York, New York 10014, U.S.A. • Penguin Group (Canada), 90 Eglinton Avenue East, Suite 700, Toronto, Ontario, Canada M4P 2Y3 (a division of Pearson Penguin Canada Inc.) • Penguin Books Ltd, 80 Strand, London WC2R 0RL, England • Penguin Ireland, 25 St. Stephen's Green, Dublin 2, Ireland (a division of Penguin Books Ltd) • Penguin Books Australia Ltd, 250 Camberwell Road, Camberwell, Victoria 3124, Australia (a division of Pearson Australia Group Pty Ltd) • Penguin Books India Pvt Ltd, 11 Community Centre, Panchsheel Park, New Delhi - 110 017, India • Penguin Group (NZ), 67 Apollo Drive, Rosedale, North Shore, 0632, New Zealand (a division of Pearson New Zealand Ltd.) • Penguin Books (South Africa) (Pty) Ltd, 24 Sturdee Avenue, Rosebank, Johannesburg 2196, South Africa

Penguin Books Ltd, Registered Offices: 80 Strand, London WC2R 0RL, England

First published in 2007 by Portfolio, a member of Penguin Group (USA) Inc.

10   9   8   7   6   5   4   3   2   1

Copyright © Derek Gatehouse, 2007
All rights reserved

ISBN 978-1-59184-178-4

Printed in the United States of America

Designed by Chris Welch • Set in Dante
Charts by John Del Gaizo

This book is dedicated
with eternal love and gratitude
to my wife, Linda.

CONTENTS

Foreword   ix

INTRODUCTION   1

1 *THE PERFECT SALESFORCE*   5

2 THE 6 BEST PRACTICES OF
   THE PERFECT SALESFORCE   19

3 BEST PRACTICE #1: THE 10 SELLING TALENTS   33

4 BEST PRACTICE #2: SORTING SALES
   STAGES FOR TALENT   55

5 BEST PRACTICE #3: THE TALENT-BASED
   HIRING PROCESS   77

6 BEST PRACTICE #4: THE PAY PLAN AND QUOTAS   101

7 BEST PRACTICE #5: SALES BEHAVIOR TRAINING   159

8   **B E S T   P R A C T I C E   # 6 :   R E S U L T - B A S E D   M A N A G E M E N T**   181

9   **G R O W I N G   *T H E   P E R F E C T   S A L E S F O R C E***   201

Acknowledgments   209

Appendix: Case Study   211

Perfect SalesForce Online Support   265

Index   267

FOREWORD

Derek Gatehouse begins his book with the words, "This is not a book about selling." That's an odd way to start one of the most interesting books about selling to appear for a long time. What's behind this astonishing disclaimer? After all, Gatehouse has spent the last thirty years in selling, in running sales forces, and in improving sales performance. Can he hate the field *that* much, I wondered? When you read a little further, things start to become clear. He's out to attack conventional books on how to sell, arguing that they make the assumption that anyone can sell, provided—of course—that they adopt the author's success formula. Not so, argues Derek Gatehouse. There is no silver bullet. Neither the advice in books nor sales training, he argues, will generally result in sustainable improvement. In fact, he says, most of the billion dollars or more spent every year in this country on sales training is money down the drain. This is where I start to twitch a little. "He's writing about *bad* training," I think hopefully, knowing how many sales training programs have inadequate models, mediocre instructional technology, or a pitiful lack of reinforcement. But no. It's a much more controversial point that he's making.

He starts with a startling fact. Top salespeople, often with no sales training of any kind, can sell up to four times as much as their average counterparts—many of whom have been extensively trained. This, Gatehouse argues, suggests that salespeople may be born rather than made, that sales ability may be baked into some people's DNA. It's an unfashionable position to take; I would dispute some details of his conclusions. But it's good to have such an articulate challenge to the conventional wisdom. Predictably, the author says that his ideas have met strong resistance from both the vendors of silver-bullet solutions and the well-meaning HR crowd, who would like to believe that all salespeople are created equal. Yet he argues his case persuasively. You could perhaps train a dog to behave like a cat, he says, but it would be a long, difficult road. And, even if you succeeded, your dog still wouldn't be as convincing as a real cat.

So, if training isn't the answer, what is? One obvious candidate is sales process. Most large companies have spent multiple millions of dollars designing, installing, and enforcing sales process systems. What's more, the vendors who have grown rich in the sales process boom have not been shy about taking the credit for massive increases in sales that they claim have resulted from their efforts. Again, Gatehouse takes an interestingly contrarian view. "Sales," he writes, "is about people, not process." He argues that process, at best, is a safety net that gives mediocre performers a pedestrian and inflexible path to follow. Stacked against him here are the many claims that sales process has transformed sales figures and boosted profits. Who is right? I put much of my money on Gatehouse. I've studied a number of these extravagant claims for the power of process. In the sales field, they generally turn out to be voodoo science. I remember one claim from a famous consulting firm that, after adopting their sales process, a client company's sales doubled in a single year. No mention that the company made three acquisitions in the same year. These acquisitions alone were enough to almost double their sales revenues. Don't get me wrong: process has its place. When it's well designed it can codify experience and accelerate learning. However, it's no panacea, and Gatehouse does an excellent job of exposing the dangers of overreliance on sales process as a performance tool.

I could say much more about how this book cheerfully steps on the toes of many widely held beliefs about sales. For that quality alone, it makes interesting and satisfying reading. I've stepped upon some of the same toes myself and have always enjoyed hearing the squeals of protest from the entrenched interests I've offended. However, it's all too easy to deride the conventional wisdom. The hard thing is to put something better in its place. The real reason why I like this book is less for its thoughtful criticism of popular beliefs; it's more for the well-reasoned alternatives it offers.

In The Perfect SalesForce you'll find a comprehensive set of blueprints for building high performance. There are 6 best practices described in detail. The first three are about how to hire the best talent. What makes these best practices noteworthy is that they focus on how to assess your type of sale and how to identify the specific qualities and characteristics required for success. This may not seem an unusual approach but, believe me, it is. As Gatehouse rightly points out, the typical specification for the perfect salesperson is for a self-starter with strong communication skills, a team player who is aggressive and highly motivated. These qualities are so lacking in specificity that they are one standard deviation better than useless as guidelines for selection. Is there *any* job in the organization where these would not apply?

In the place of these conventional platitudes, Gatehouse proposes a framework based on 10 selling talents. Six of these talents are hardwired, four depend on your type of sale. It's an interesting framework and it should make you rethink the way you define sales talent. Throughout the book there are work sheets to let you assess your own sales performance issues and to help you move forward toward building a better sales force. I hope you read *The Perfect SalesForce*. Sales is a field better known for its hype than its thought, so it has been a real pleasure for me to read such a well-reasoned and practical contribution to our profession.

—Neil Rackham, *author of* SPIN Selling,
Visiting Professor of Sales and Marketing
Portsmouth University
Portsmouth, England
and
Visiting Professor in Selling
Cranfield School of Management
Cranfield, England

THE PERFECT SALESFORCE

INTRODUCTION

This is not a book about selling. It does not feature some arbitrary selling formula to be taught to salespeople in order to increase their sales. In fact, this book advocates that to a large degree, you can't actually teach salespeople to sell very much more than they currently do.

This book will talk instead about "natural born" salespeople. You've met them: those men and women who sell circles around all the rest. Top-producing salespeople consistently sell at least *four times* more than their average counterparts—measured across all industries and sale types—and without ever having cracked open one of those books on selling that promise the world. Think about that. Without training, very often without previous sales experience, naturals just go out and sell four times more than everyone else. How can it be?

If you have been fortunate enough to witness these gifted stars in action, you will agree it is usually difficult to identify exactly what things they do differently. What exactly are their "gifts"? How might we find and hire these people on a consistent basis? Do they know they're four times more productive than the rest? Is it their conscious plan to be that productive or does it just turn out that way? How come when I ask them why they sell so much more, their answers are so inconsistent? Their responses vary so wildly that it leads one to believe that they don't actually know what makes them so effective.

Why did my top salesperson fail so badly when I promoted him to be the sales manager? Why couldn't he just teach everyone to do what he's doing? What is he doing, anyway?

How is it that my two top salespeople have such different selling styles? They sell so much more than everyone else, and yet they have completely different approaches and work ethics. If I *could* identify what they're doing differently, which of their approaches would I teach to the others? Which one is right? And can those things even be taught to others?

Why doesn't sales training seem to work? If it did, the vast majority of salespeople would not revert back to their old way of doing things. Maybe I should try a different sales training program; there seem to be so many. Which one is the best?

Am I paying my people enough? Would more money motivate them to perform better? How much is enough? How much is too much? I don't want them to make so much that they stop trying to make more.

How can I get my salespeople to do the things I want them to be doing, without watching over them constantly? I am told that micromanaging is wrong, but what do I do instead? My experience tells me that if I'm not as involved as I am, productivity will surely drop.

This book will answer these questions once and for all, and provide a process that will build a sales force of top performers. It is an extensively field-tested approach to identifying, hiring, organizing, and motivating a sales force comprised of people who possess the natural talents for specific types of sales. The majority of America's sales forces today produce only a fraction of their potential (this includes the successful ones, not only those that may be floundering), and if you ask ten different sales "experts" what to do to increase productivity, you will likely get ten completely different action plans—which is wrong. There shouldn't be such contradiction, so many different approaches, each claiming to be the best. Your company's sales are far too important to leave to today's seemingly hit-or-miss approach to building a sales force.

I have spent thirty years in the trenches of corporate sales. I find it fascinating and more than a little disturbing that the correct answers to these questions—the proven conditions and practices that must be present for top sales force performance—are so contradictory to what most companies currently embrace. A shocking sum of money is thrown away every year on training and consulting and motivating and processes that appear to be valid—certainly logical—but that end up doing nothing at all to produce a sustained increase in performance. Over one billion dollars is spent each year for sales training in the United States alone, and every study on the topic suggests that 80 percent of those companies will realize no sustained increase in performance. And make no mistake—a sustained increased in performance is the only measure of success that counts in this profession.

This book will explain what a *Perfect SalesForce* looks like, give the 6 best practices required to build one, and provide step-by-step instructions for implementation in any company. But beware: to build such an environment you will have to do certain things differently than you might be used to. This book shatters a fair amount of conventional sales "wisdom," as there are a great many misconceptions running rampant in the corporate sales world. This is a curious thing, given that the findings that led to the 6 best practices in this book are among the most substantiated in the world. As you will read, they include the results of the Gallup Organization's thirty-year study of top performance, which includes more than three million people to date, Huthwaite's famous twelve-year study of over ten thousand salespeople, eighty years of research in behavior analysis, and my own thirty years of experience with top salespeople, including interviews with more than two thousand business owners and executives.

So take your time and enjoy the read. Everything in this book has been implemented by me and by my salespeople a great many times in the last decade. I promise that if you adopt the mind-set described in this book—if you follow the 6 best practices and create the resulting culture—you will have the answers to all of the sales force questions that have plagued you, and you will transform your sales force into a top-performing one.

After reading this book, I hope you never look at your salespeople the same way again.

THE PERFECT SALESFORCE

S ales is about people, not process. *The Perfect SalesForce* is a return to people—different types of people that excel very naturally at different types of sales jobs. It's about how to find such people, what conditions and tools they will require from you, and how they need to be managed on a daily basis to be kept happy, motivated, and productive.

Most companies try to teach their salespeople how to become top performers, but in the vast majority of cases this is simply not possible. There is a fine but very definite line between the things people are and are not capable of learning and repeating. Unfortunately, most companies regularly embark on training their salespeople in practices that actually have no chance of ever becoming their new habitual behavior. Just think of those salespeople you have worked with who outsold everyone else, but who never learned any selling process or received any sales training. In fact, most top producers have their own process, their own way of doing things.

Companies that have amassed top sales teams have learned how to hire these natural born salespeople. They have learned what things to look for in candidates—for all different sale types.

They have learned how top salespeople are programmed, what makes them happy, productive, motivated, unmotivated, and so on—and then they turn them loose to do their thing. There are books and consultants and Web sites that suggest you study what it is that your top salespeople do differently so that you may then teach these behaviors to your other salespeople. It seems logical: study exactly what behaviors produce certain results, and then copy them. The problem is that it just doesn't work. A good analogy would be trying to teach an introvert to be an extrovert by simply saying, "just watch the things an extrovert does in a typical day and then copy that." Well, the very things that make an introvert introverted will make it pretty difficult for one to mimic the behavior of an extrovert. The sales talents needed for different sale types discussed in chapter 3 are just as inherent and untrainable.

Many of you have tried this approach. You have trained your salespeople to use the sales techniques and practices of other top performers, whether those top performers came from within your company or elsewhere, and found there was no resulting sustained increase in performance.

The Perfect SalesForce advocates that studying top-performing salespeople *is* a good idea—not so you can copy them, but instead to better understand just what type of people they are, so that you can hire more of that type. Instead of trying to teach a dog how to behave like a cat, you will have much more success finding more cats. A cat will always perform like a cat far better than a dog that you've trained to be like a cat. You *can* train the dog—it is doable—but you'll always have superior performance from a natural cat. The only reason that companies continue to try to create top sales performers through training is they have had very little success in their attempts to hire natural top performers on a regular basis.

There are several reasons for this. The first is that, unfortunately, there isn't only one type of top salesperson. The recipe of talents, characteristics, and personality traits that you will look for differs depending on the type of sale you need them for. Secondly, even if you know exactly what to look for, determining whether your candidates truly possess these qualities is challenge number two. The huge majority of interview methodologies used today do absolutely nothing to reveal a candidate's true performance potential.

And the final obstacle: *most top performers do not even know they are top performers.* Many come from past sales jobs where they were miscast and produced only average results, but then go on to become top salespeople at a new position that ends up being a perfect fit for their particular talent set. This is most common, as people do not understand how to match natural talents to different sale types.

To address this, most companies train processes. We have seen a huge increase toward process in recent years—a natural byproduct of increasing advancements in technology—and I am the first to admit that process has its purpose and its benefits. But there is a growing and largely unrecognized problem with the "process-izing" mentality when it involves human interaction on a daily basis. The more management moves toward process, the more it simultaneously moves away from human interaction. As more and more sales departments become process-ized in the noble quest for constant betterment, they all too often end up creating processes for functions that ultimately shouldn't have them—functions that should be closely monitored and coached and developed through human interaction and in-the-moment judgment, not through a computer program or a flowchart or an e-mail report.

Process-izing removes the need for in-the-moment human

judgment—this is largely its intended function—so that every eventuality throughout a process has been considered and has been prescribed a predetermined action that must be adhered to. Again, process is necessary for a great many jobs. I would not want to trust my fate to a nuclear power plant worker who makes an in-the-moment judgment call on what to do during a containment breach in the middle of the night. I think I prefer that he follow the established process for such an event.

But lines need to be drawn when it comes to working with people. It is realistic to assign a process to something that has a reasonable number of variables. There are really only a handful of variables, or choices that can be made, during a nuclear breach. But where human interaction is concerned, the variables are endless. Trying to establish a set of actions for every eventuality involved with managing people, or selling to someone, is ludicrous. Yet this is where so many companies are inadvertently heading.

A top-performing sales force is 100 percent about leading and influencing other people, about getting all the salespeople doing what you want them to do, at consistently high levels of performance. As you will read throughout this book, the process that your sales manager will need to employ to do this will actually end up being very different from one salesperson to the next. How then could you hope to process-ize one consistent approach?

The same thing can be said for the selling process itself. Isn't it true that clients and prospects rarely respond the way most sales training processes suggest they will? This leaves salespeople to make in-the-moment decisions and judgments—which is the very thing they should be doing. Top sales teams have returned to (or never strayed from) a mind-set of hiring salespeople based on their in-the-moment decision-making abilities—and then they let them do so, rather than overriding those natural talents with a rigid common process that must be used by everyone. Today's process-driven sales forces make me think of a professional football team spending great time and resources to hire the five best quarterbacks in the world—who all have their own unique style that works for them, honed over many years—only to then retrain all five to do things the same way.

You need only look at your own sales force. I'm willing to bet that you can easily find two very good salespeople whose approaches are quite different (different selling styles, different work ethics)—proof that there isn't only one right process, and that in fact each person finds their own process that works best for them.

The only feasible growth system for a sales force, and the only way to build a sales force comprised of top performers, is to learn the language of selling talents. This will let you cast the exact right talents into each stage of your particular sale type, and then gain an understanding of what specific conditions generate autonomous top performance from these gifted sellers. This is the essence of *The Perfect SalesForce*—and in fact the very definition of a top producer:

Natural talent operating under specific conditions

This definition has been distilled from decades of studying top-performing sales teams, and I hope you notice how different it is from the conventional "hire-experienced-salespeople-and-train-them" model. The reason for this disparity is that I asked a different question than other sales consultants; I was looking for something different. I did not go looking for a formula that would simply raise sales performance—I set out to find the formula for a top-producing sales force, one that is made up primarily of those salespeople that sell four times more than all the others.

Before I lay out the 6 best practices that will build such a team, it will help you to understand the three different fields of study that these best practices all stem from. They are areas that many of you have wondered about, as I have, because of the widely varying opinions that seem to be associated with them. Once I had what I felt were the indisputable facts on these topics, I tested them extensively in the field and only then assembled them into the *Perfect SalesForce* system. They are:

1. The study of **natural talent** or ability—that which you are born with, that which cannot be taught to another.
2. An understanding of **training** as performance enhancement—can you make someone better by a margin that sufficiently exceeds the effort and, if so, how?
3. An understanding of what external **conditions** affect performance.

1. NATURAL TALENT

Everyone would agree that talent is important. Well, if it's top performers you want, talent is not only important, it's essential. In the absence of the natural-born talents needed for a task, top levels of performance at that task are not possible. While this may sound obvious to many, I believe it is no exaggeration to say that 95 percent of American companies have no methodology whatsoever for identifying which natural talents their new hires possess or for identifying which natural talents might be needed for the job at hand. As essential as talent is to top performance—and as badly as everyone wants to hire top talent—most companies have no real system for accurately casting talent. They may know what skills are needed and what knowledge is required—and they generally test candidates quite well for these two criteria. But when asked what talents they look for in sales candidates, most executives' answers are extremely imprecise.

For our purposes, natural talent is best explained like this. If you tried to teach me to paint a landscape or a portrait, I tell you now you would be wasting your time. Certainly as I receive this training I will get better than I was before, but I will never approach top levels of performance. I have the desire, the intelligence, and the same "equipment" as anyone else, but I do not possess the natural talents required to be a great painter.

Now imagine spending that training time and budget on the six-year-old prodigy who lies on the kindergarten classroom floor and effortlessly sketches a picture that resembles a van Gogh. That six-year-old is already better on her worst day than I can ever hope to be—and she hasn't even received training yet. Another good example is having an ear for music. Can you train someone who is clearly tone deaf to sing opera or play the violin? Again, with training the person will develop, but only to a point—and that point will never be anywhere near the point reached when the same training is given to someone with natural born talent.

It seems obvious with painting and music examples, but the line between possessing and not possessing certain sales talents has been considerably harder to identify. This will be covered in chapter 5. For the moment, understand that the inbred talents we all possess are part of our DNA. They cannot be taken away from us and they cannot be taught to another person. Many sales courses claim they can teach anyone to be a top seller. This is simply not possible, as many of you have undoubtedly discovered. New skills and new knowledge can be taught, but natural talent cannot. You must learn how to identify which talents you need for your sale type, and then have a reliable interview methodology for identify-ing those talent sets in your candidates.

2 . TRAINING

Sales training is an ongoing distraction for a great many compa-nies. Does it work or not? Can it raise performance by a margin that sufficiently exceeds the effort for all trainees, or at least most of them, and can that enhanced performance sustain itself at the new, higher level? I have participated in a tremendous amount of training over the years on both the receiving and teaching ends—training that has *not* raised performance in a lasting way. How-ever, I have also seen sales training work phenomenally well at other times. The topic of training is a most elusive one, and it has taken me the better part of thirty years to understand and perfect the training formula.

The answer is training will raise performance to a new and last-ing level if and only if all three of the following criteria are met:

1. **The natural talents required for the tasks must be pres-ent.** In the absence of talent, even the best training will not raise performance significantly.

2. **The training curriculum must be well substantiated, and must be adoptable by all personalities and selling styles.** In other words, it must be presented as a series of practices that trainees can "mix and match" at will, rather than a rigid, step-by-step selling process. Sales training should be akin to offering tradespeople many different top-notch tools to per-form the various stages of their job; different tradespeople will opt to use different tools that they each feel comfortable with. This instead of giving tradespeople one step-by-step

repair process—with only one set of tools—that is to be used on every job.

3. **The training methodology must respect what we now understand about permanently altering habitual behavior.** Sales training is behavior training, as we are asking trainees to suddenly change the way they behave in certain situations—situations that many have approached a certain way for a very long time. Just like a new exercise regime or eating plan, the formula for permanently adopting new selling behaviors must include certain reinforcement practices.

3. CONDITIONS

There are eighty years of research available on human behavior, known as *behavior analysis*. The application of behavior analysis in the workplace is called performance management and when I was first introduced to it, I remember being struck with how ridiculous it is that this information is not mandatory learning at some point in our careers. If a manager's job is to get her people to do the things she needs them to do, then the only management training ever needed is an understanding of behavior analysis.

I have interviewed hundreds and hundreds of salespeople. I have worked personally in the field with many hundreds more. Some were top performers, most were average performers, and, of course, many didn't perform at all. My fascination has always been with the top performers, and it doesn't take very long to identify who is happy and who is frustrated. It is both surprising and sad how far off the mark most employers are when it comes to fostering a happy, productive work environment. There are certain very simple conditions required, but all must be present and they must be administered by the right manager.

There are hundreds of workplace conditions that can be examined, some personal, some communal, but the first distinction to understand is that only a few (thankfully) are true *performance influencers*. A performance influencer is one that affects people's ability to consistently perform at the pinnacle of their talent. For example, many company perks could be called influencers—and they certainly serve a purpose—but they are not performance influencers. Offering a new recruit a retirement or medical/dental plan or a company car may well influence their decision to join your company, but you must accept the reality that it will not affect their ability to consistently perform at the pinnacle of their talent. Giving your top performers a membership to that swanky executive club will certainly make them feel appreciated, but it will not affect their ability to consistently perform at the pinnacle of their talent.

As I observed and tested workplace conditions over the years, I noticed that most fall into this category. They may well have an influence on a candidate choosing your company, or on employee retention, but they do not generally have an influence on daily performance. When I speak of the "conditions" you must create for your sales team, I am referring to your arrangement of these performance influencers.

There is one group of performance influencers that we will not cover. There are certain logistical things—tools and technology and such—that can influence performance. For example, if a laptop computer would help your people be more productive in the field, then it must be considered a performance influencer. I call these *logistical influencers* and I believe they are pretty obvious to each company (and I can't do much about them anyway), so I will leave such things to you. If you have salespeople on the phone all day, and they sit in a filthy, dark, run-down setting, I think you know it can affect performance. This book discusses only *psycho-*

logical influencers, and only those that are true performance influencers. They are:

1. Your pay plan
2. Your quotas
3. Sales training
4. The salespeople's immediate manager (referred to hereafter as the *sales manager*)

The raw talent you hire is like a seed—it is the starting point of future performance—and a seed needs a variety of conditions in order to flourish: good soil, water, air, sunlight. If you plant your seed in bad soil and you rarely water it or expose it to sunlight, it will not flourish. Interestingly, it will not necessarily die, it will just not do as well as it would under the ideal conditions.

Salespeople too need the right conditions in order to flourish, and if the four conditions listed above are arranged correctly, according to behavior analysis, then they will flourish indeed. However, if they are not arranged just so, performance will remain at the status quo. Every company already has a pay plan in place, as well as some sort of quota system; most implement sales training, and everyone reports to an immediate manager. But these four conditions rarely respect the rules of behavior analysis. In addition, they are typically considered separately rather than as part of a master plan for performance. Chapters 6, 7, and 8 will teach you the correct way to structure these four performance influencers, thereby establishing the ideal conditions for your salespeople to flourish.

Where group performance is concerned, in any industry, sport, or activity there are always two possible management structures. One way is to tell each participant what to do, assigning them tasks and duties and telling them how to do each of their jobs, and then manage them by making sure they are doing those things properly. If that structure sounds familiar, it is because 90 percent of American companies do this. And if you're thinking that it doesn't sound particularly crazy, you're right, it's not.

The problem lies in the word "properly." With the best of intentions, managers adopting this structure spend the majority of their time trying to get people to do things a particular way. They are policing the activities of the job. And while the ensuing revenues might be good—even very good—they are nowhere near what they could be. This structure does not necessarily put a company into trouble (although it often does); it just limits growth, and by a significant margin.

The second way to structure group performance involves policing results instead of activities. This approach sets the stage for group participation by encouraging everyone to brainstorm creative and better approaches. If you dictate activities, you benefit from the knowledge and talents of only those managers who established your company's selling process. If you create a result-managed environment, you benefit from the pooled knowledge and talents of every member of your sales force, and before long you will sit back and watch in awe as that sales force takes your company in directions you never dreamed of.

I worked with a company called International Profit Associates in the mid-nineties. They are a management consulting firm and very much a result-managed organization. Their astonishing growth landed them at number eight on *Inc. Magazine*'s 500 Fastest Growing Companies list in 1996, and again in 1997 at number nine. In 1998, after only eight years in business, this privately held and debt-free company broke the $100 million revenue mark, and as of 2006 they had seventeen hundred employees, five divisions, and revenue of $249 million.

The thing that struck me most about IPA while I spent time at their Chicago headquarters was how autonomous everyone was. There were departments and teams that were busier and more driven than any I've seen, but there was no visible managing going on. The truth is there was managing, just not the kind most companies are familiar with.

Salespeople at IPA know exactly what results are expected of them each period, and these results must be met. These results are known to be fair and reasonable, based on the results of all the salespeople that have occupied these selling positions in the past. Each position has a "correct" result—that is, an amount known to be achievable as long as the correct talents have been cast in the position. In this way, the deliverables, or results, are yardsticks for identifying whether each new hire is correctly cast in the position.

A very aggressive pay plan motivates each salesperson to surpass these preset results—something that happens very regularly at IPA—and all resources and tools needed to reach goals are gladly supplied. But again, the most fascinating thing to watch is the autonomy and unity of purpose. IPA works like an ant colony and (hold on to your hats) everyone is *happy*. Everyone feels trusted, appreciated, and necessary, and everyone knows precisely what they are accountable for.

In this most fast-paced of environments, where a full half of every day's decisions come from new situations that require on-the-spot adaptation, everyone knows they have management's full and unconditional support, and they are encouraged to constantly break the old molds if a better way is suspected.

What I think I enjoyed most at IPA were the squabbles. Every company has its internal squabbles, but in a result-managed environment, squabbles seem to get resolved immediately and without the intervention of any manager or outside party. And it is simply because of the unified purpose, the bigger picture. "There's work to be done, deadlines to be met, results that we all agreed would be delivered. If we don't deliver 250 more leads by five o'clock, seventy-five salespeople will have only two appointments tomorrow and they need three. There's no time for squabbles, the company needs us." Believe it or not, these words were really spoken.

So let's get going with the 6 best practices and see just what it is that the world's best sales teams do differently.

THE 6 BEST PRACTICES OF
THE PERFECT SALESFORCE

PINPOINT
TALENT CASTING

1

The 10 Selling Talents

6

2

Result-Based Management

Sorting Stages for Talent

5

3

Sales Behavior Training

Talent-Based Hiring

IDEAL
PERFORMANCE
CONDITIONS

4

Positive and Negative Motivators
Pay and Quota

The 6 Best Practices of the Perfect Saleforce

To build your *Perfect SalesForce*, you must do these six things:

1. Understand what arrangement of **the 10 selling talents** applies to your sale
2. Sort the **stages** of your sale according to talent

3. Cast the different selling roles using a **talent-based hiring** process

4. Generate ultimate motivation with the perfect **pay plan and quota**

5. Conduct regular **sales behavior training**

6. Manage and develop your team using **result-based management**

BEST PRACTICE #1: Understand what arrangement of the 10 selling talents applies to your sale.

Selling half-million-dollar engineering software to Fortune 500 CEOs requires a very different talent set than selling office supplies to mid-market purchasers or selling cars to soccer moms. What about selling management consulting services or restaurant supplies or industrial chemicals or cellular network towers? What talent sets are needed for each of these sales?

The first step to building a top-performing sales force is to learn the language of *work ethic talents, communication talents*, and *influencing talents*, so that you may cast the exact talent set needed for your company's sale.

BEST PRACTICE #2: Sort the stages of your sale according to talent.

Lead generation. Prospecting. Developing need. Asking questions. Closing. Account penetration. Customer service.

With an understanding of the different inherent selling talents learned in step 1, your second step is to determine whether your current sales process involves tasks—or sales *stages*—that actually require different talent sets. Many companies have their salespeople wearing too many hats. Top sales teams have learned that their most talented salespeople may well outperform the others, but at certain sales stages only.

BEST PRACTICE #3: Cast the different selling roles using a talent-based hiring process.

With the exact talent sets pinpointed for each stage of your sale, you will need an interview process that sees beyond your candidates' answers. Talent-based hiring is an interview methodology designed specifically for identifying the presence—or absence—of the natural talents you seek to hire.

BEST PRACTICE #4: Generate ultimate motivation with the perfect pay plan and quota.

With the right talents cast into each selling role, your next task is to create the performance conditions known to be the most motivating to salespeople. In step 4 you will receive a crash course in behavior analysis and learn which components of a pay plan and quota system will generate autonomous top performance from every member of your sales team.

BEST PRACTICE #5: Conduct regular sales behavior training.

Step 5 is to learn once and for all how sales training fits into the performance equation. You will learn what type of curriculum to teach your people, how often, and to which team members. You will also learn when training should be optional versus compulsory, and when training is actually futile and the salesperson should be released.

**BEST PRACTICE #6: Manage and develop
your team using result-based management.**

With the perfect team in place, operating under perfect performance conditions, your final step is to understand exactly which things should and should not be managed and enforced, and by whom. The world's best sales managers police results, not activities, and have very particular relationships with their salespeople.

It is important that you understand exactly what you will be building when you follow this program, and why it is so effective. Most programs designed to increase the productivity of a sales force do so by teaching existing personnel a variety of selling practices, time management skills, management practices, and so on. The question posed by their creators was, "How do we increase productivity here?" and the answer is always some version of teaching existing people new ideas and new practices. While this is not a foolish approach, it is very much incomplete, and the results from such programs prove it. In my experience with many such programs, it is rare to see any overall, lasting increase in sales. If there is a lasting increase, 10 percent to 13 percent is considered a success story. There are in fact some very good consulting and training firms that you can hire and—following all the training, the change, and the effort—you can expect a productivity increase of 10 percent to 13 percent. I recently visited the Web site of a colleague of mine who boasts on his home page that his clients' overall increase in 2006 was 12 percent.

There is nothing wrong with such an increase. But these mediocre results have become the paradigm, the expectation, and I'd like you to know that there are companies out there that grow exponentially beyond these rates. They are run by executives who have learned and had the courage to implement a few practices that trample this model, and they are staffed by salespeople who sell four times more than everyone else.

Instead of asking how to increase productivity, I have asked two different questions since I was first bitten by the selling bug in 1975: "What makes a top salesperson a top salesperson?" and, "What do top sales teams do differently?" The answers have come from studying top-performing salespeople and teams in their natural environments over the past thirty years, approaching them with no preconceptions, just a desire to observe and learn. Very helpful to this lifelong study is the fact that I am not the only one asking such questions. Let me share some of the research and findings that are relevant to *The Perfect SalesForce*.

The Gallup Organization has been studying top performance in human beings for over thirty years now. To date they have conducted detailed interviews with over three million participants, looking for common denominators in the world's best teachers and nurses and managers and, yes, salespeople. Their definition of top performance dwarfs even my own. Gallup found that top-performing salespeople sold between six and ten times more than their average counterparts.

Appreciate what you would learn if you were to conduct detailed interviews with two hundred fifty thousand salespeople, in search of the common denominators of the top people. Gallup found unequivocally that selling is a natural-born talent. Business degrees are not relevant to sales performance—in fact, schooling of any kind is not relevant. Experience in your industry is also not relevant. Even past experience in sales is not a requisite—imagine! Only talent. And talent cannot be taught.

This is not a trivial finding. I'm willing to bet that just about every person reading this book who has hired salespeople in the past has listed as a job requirement experience in their industry or perhaps a certain minimum education, *certainly* sales experience. All irrelevant.

Mark is a salesman I worked with in a software company in 2001. He was in his early forties and, for reasons he called "internal politics," had taken a sabbatical from his teaching position in the public school system. He had never been in sales; he had been a teacher his entire career. Within his first few months selling high-end corporate software, he was selling four to six times more than the other seven salespeople, all of whom had been at the job much longer and had a lot more in the pipeline. *Four to six times more*, each and every month.

Mark never had any sales training or previous experience at a sales job. There are Marks in most every company, and you must understand that their ability to achieve such numbers comes from having the natural talents that happen to perfectly suit their type of sale. They may have received training—and that training may well have augmented their performance—but in the absence of the talents needed for the task, these higher levels of performance are simply not possible.

Acknowledging that selling is inherent changes everything. Like many of you, I have hired my share of salespeople based on past sales experience, industry experience, how they present themselves, and so on. And, like many of you, I have had my share of ensuing frustration when these people who interviewed so very well did not end up performing as anticipated once on the job. This all began to change for the better when I started hiring for talent in the mid-nineties, but it brought about a new challenge: *precisely what talents should I hire?* Every recruiting consultant and sales expert I sourced would list all the same "qualities" to look for when hiring a salesperson, without any acknowledgement of the many different types of sales there are. This means we were being told to find the same talents whether hiring a salesperson to sell private jets to oil sheiks, or ink cartridges to small businesses. They're all salespeople.

Saying that they're all salespeople is like saying football linebackers, baseball pitchers, and pro golfers are all athletes. While it's true, there are distinctions between these jobs, and the distinctions are critical ones. We are told that human beings and chimpanzees share 98 percent of the same DNA. Well, the distinctions between the two, while only 2 percent, are critical distinctions to be sure. It was clear to me that there was no language in place to distinguish sales talents.

It took me five years to create the 10 selling talents that you will learn about in chapter 3. There were numerous earlier versions that I tested, scrapped, refined, and renamed until I couldn't make them any more accurate. There were more than ten talents at first, until I saw that some were actually versions of others, already named. They address natural work ethic and tolerance levels, natural ability to influence others (or lack thereof), and talents regarding abstract explanation and communication.

Pinpointing these sales talents and observing their applications in all types of real world sales jobs helped me reach another important conclusion: top-producing salespeople are specialists. That is to say, they excel not only at certain sale types that perfectly match their talent sets, but also at particular stages of those sale types. The talents that make someone great at selling actually have nothing whatsoever to do with the talents that make a great prospector. And the talents that make a dynamite prospector have little to do with ongoing customer service. From a perspective of the talent sets needed, these are actually very different jobs, and yet most companies mix all of these duties into one great category called "sales."

This does not mean that a person can't possess more than one talent and actually be, for example, a great closer and a great prospector, but it is definitely more difficult to find individuals that will perform at top levels in multiple sales stages. How many of you know a top seller who doesn't prospect as much as you'd like? How about a dynamo prospector who doesn't sell very well? I have noted that sales teams that have a high percentage of top performers are more likely to have different people performing different sales stages, rather than the same salespeople performing multiple stages.

Earlier I stated that a top performer is someone with *natural talent operating under specific conditions.* Following this definition, and as the diagram at the beginning of this chapter illustrates, all 6 best practices fall within two categories: pinpoint talent casting and ideal performance conditions. The first three best practices will elaborate all you need to know about structuring your sale according to talent, and casting the needed talents with pinpoint accuracy. Practices 4, 5, and 6 create the specific conditions. *Both* categories are required if a sales force of top performers is your goal. (Note that the definition of a top performer does not include training, only talent and conditions. This is because sales training is included in the conditions half of the program—sales training *is* one of the conditions.)

Throughout the nineties, my career was spent almost entirely in sales and sales management of various business services to the owners and C-level executives of mid-size to Fortune 500 companies. Because of my obsession with sales performance issues, the face-to-face time I spent with these owners and execs inevitably ended up in a passionate discussion of their sales force performance, or lack thereof. Whatever I was there to sell always ended up taking a backseat to these "interviews."

Over the span of a decade I had heart-to-hearts with over two thousand business owners and executives about what works, what doesn't, and why. We talked about pay plans, management styles and systems, hiring practices, personality profiling tools, motivation, natural talent, team-building activities, and every training program there is. If it's related to the productivity of the sales force, we talked about it, and it may surprise you to learn that I don't think talent is the biggest challenge for most companies. Yes, talent is an essential part of the formula—it's just not the biggest challenge. Talent is what every owner and manager *thinks* is their biggest challenge but based on what I have witnessed in thousands of companies, it is performance conditions that are far less understood and have far more impact on productivity. I saw a tremendous number of very talented salespeople operating under conditions that were counterproductive to performance. This was not intentional of course but sadly, very few companies understand what true performance conditions are. With the sincerest of intentions, most managers miss the mark completely. Some pay well but then micromanage. Some pay *too* well without proper accountability in return. Others hold their people accountable, but expect very unrealistic results. Some introduce factors with the intention of motivating their salespeople, only to achieve the opposite. Most rely too much on sales training and ignore other factors that actually have far more impact. Some companies do everything perfectly but have the completely wrong manager running the show, which unfortunately is more than enough to sabotage all the good.

Other findings cited in this book include Neil Rackham's research conducted during his years with the sales performance consultancy Huthwaite. Where the Gallup Organization studied top performers in order to answer, basically, whether top performance could be trained or whether it was inherent, Rackham was looking for what *things* top salespeople were doing differently. Did they work harder? Were they closing more aggressively? Did they talk more or talk less? What things were they saying?

For twelve years Rackham and his team at Huthwaite followed

ten thousand salespeople into thirty-five thousand sales calls. It remains the most thorough study of its kind to this day. They witnessed the best salespeople in action, the worst, and everyone in between, and by the end of their study they had identified exactly what top salespeople do differently. The resulting book, SPIN Selling (McGraw-Hill, 1988) ushered in the "consultative selling" era with a sales process comprised of asking questions to the prospect, rather than making presentations—four different types of questions asked at various key points in the sale. For my money, the SPIN Selling research identified beyond any doubt the best selling methodology in the world, and although it is used by half the Fortune 100 and gains more readers each year, Professor Rackham told me that his original publisher canceled his contract when they first read the manuscript, stating that the findings conflicted with "generally accepted sales ideas."

This seems to be a constant in the human condition. Although there can be a tremendous amount of evidence for a better way, people fear the idea of straying from the widely accepted collective thinking. Neil Rackham's work clearly proved that these "generally accepted sales ideas" actually lowered closing ratios, but people were skeptical simply because it was different. Fortunately, when the proposed better way actually is a better way, change is inevitable, and SPIN Selling was a bestseller right out of the gate and for many years. I found many of the practices that you will read about in this book were met with similar skepticism because they contradict much of today's common thinking. Their practitioners, however, continue to sell circles around everyone else.

These types of unbiased, observation-based studies illustrate the scientific research behind The Perfect SalesForce. In the world of science, when a theory is put forth, everyone goes about trying to disprove it. If they can't, then that theory is accepted for the time being, but they continue to question it and continually look for better answers. They are in search only of the truth. In the world of sales consulting, I am sad to say, too many "experts" do the opposite; they spend their energy *defending* their own theories—very often in the face of overwhelming testimony to the contrary!

My goal in writing this book was to report the truth about what works best and why—regardless of what may or may not be popular today. It is a collection of practices derived from decades of observing and working with the best salespeople and the best sales teams (and many of the worst) in search of common denominators. Many popular practices will be absent from these pages—things like motivational speakers and team-building excursions—not because they were not considered, but because they showed no correlation with a sustained increase in performance. This does not mean that such practices are necessarily bad, only that they did not contribute to performance. All you really need to understand in order to build a sales force of top performers is the proper arrangement of these 6 best practices for your company—or stated more accurately, for your type of sale.

THE SUM OF ALL PARTS

There are two different reasons that these 6 best practices work as well as they do. The first of course is the practical application of each: how you hire and how you motivate and how you approach training and how you manage your people. But the second criterion is equally important to their effectiveness, and that is an understanding of how interrelated these 6 practices are. Think of them as your "Master Plan for Sales Force Performance."

As an example, a result-based management system is definitely a better way to manage a sales force, but its success depends on your understanding of quota. The talent-based interview is definitely a superior way to reveal talent in your candidates, but this will only serve you if you understand exactly which talents you need. Creating the perfect performance conditions is moot if you have a tyrannical manager. You could have the best manager in the world, the best pay plan, the perfect quota structure, separated sales stages, and the best sales training, but without the talent-based interview to drive your casting process, peak performance will not be possible. Each of the 6 practices must be understood, but for them to be effective, their relationship to each other must be understood as well.

No one has described this relationship in a sales force before now—or identified all the practices—but the phenomenon is actually no different than the relationship between other departments in your company. The success of people and systems relies on the efficiency of other people and other systems. It reminds me of a high performance engine with its many parts: pistons flying up and down, cogs and wheels precisely entwined. If you pull just one of those parts ever so slightly out of alignment, even though it is only one part out of many, its effect on the total engine's performance is significant.

I find it quite tragic that this interrelationship is not well understood in sales departments. In the sincere pursuit of better sales force practices, a great many managers end up hurting performance simply because they don't realize the impact their daily choices have on the other practices of their Master Plan for Sales Force Performance. Most don't even realize they *have* a Master Plan for Sales Force Performance, or what the ingredient practices are. And unless you can identify these practices *and* understand their interdependency, you will be powerless to improve performance.

This interdependency is elaborated throughout the book and will become clearer and clearer to you. It is not complicated, and the good news is you're already halfway there just by being aware of it. There are also checklists and work sheets that you will be encouraged to print from our Web site (see below), that streamline everything and focus you at the daily operational level. For now, simply be aware that the recipe for stellar group performance is like any other recipe. First, the outcome will always be better if each of the ingredients is superior. Second, if you alter even one ingredient you will certainly affect the overall outcome.

Let's get going with the first best practice and learn the recipe for top sales performance once and for all.

Note: There are work sheets and various other tools referred to throughout this book, which you can download from:

www.theperfectsalesforce.com/tools

They are free after a brief registering screen, and I recommend you begin by downloading the bookmark now—it has the 6 best practices on one side and the 10 selling talents listed on the other, which will be a very handy reference for the next chapter.

BEST PRACTICE #1: THE
10 SELLING TALENTS

Some salespeople love to prospect. Some salespeople hate it. Some salespeople love serving the same clients for years and years. Others need to win over new people all the time. There are those salespeople who excel at the long-term sale, where many meetings are needed to assemble many pieces of a solution with many participants from different departments—they love to orchestrate all of this. Then there are those who prefer the shorter sales cycle, which typically means many more sales, or "victories," per period.

Some salespeople thrive on selling "concepts," where others simply can't do it, excelling instead with the consistency of unchanging product features and benefits. Some people love to convince others; they thrill to the challenge of converting others to their way of seeing things. Others thrive on fulfilling (or surpassing) the predetermined needs of their clients, and simply cannot sway other people's opinions—they're too empathetic. They make great servicers, but terrible closers.

There are an almost infinite number of combinations of these and a few other sale characteristics. Keep in mind why you need to make these distinctions: because of natural-born talent.

Remember, if hiring a top salesperson was as easy as finding a known top producer and then training them to sell your product or service, well . . . everyone would just be doing it. We have established that selling is a natural-born talent. The problem is, with so many different combinations of the above sale characteristics, selling your product or service could be a *completely different job* than selling another product or service, thereby requiring a completely different set of talents.

The following list was compiled from job ads in various daily newspapers and career Web sites. It denotes the typical characteristics being sought for most sales jobs today.

- A self-starter
- Strong communication skills
- A team player
- Aggressive
- Highly motivated
- A relevant postsecondary degree
- Sales experience
- Industry experience

During interviews, recruiters will be looking for these and any number of other qualities that they feel are needed for the job. While this may seem a logical approach, there are two flaws.

First, the typical job interview does nothing to uncover whether your candidate truly possesses whatever talents you are looking for (which we address in chapter 5). The second flaw is with the identification of the talents themselves. Self-starter, communication skills, team player, highly motivated—these "qualities" are not nearly specific enough. It is probably accurate to say that we would want to hire these qualities for all of the different sales jobs—perhaps for any job at all! You need to be far more precise in naming the talents you seek. You must learn how to hire people that are naturally "wired" for your *exact* sale type.

For instance, different sales jobs require salespeople to interact with varying levels of executives or managers. Some salespeople have to work one-on-one with customers while others must influence and lead groups of people. Sometimes the sale calls for more listening than talking, while other times it calls for being persuasive, even forceful. Some sales require the salesperson to be very empathetic, while "tough love" is called for at other times. There are sales that require deep levels of conceptual or abstract brainstorming, while others are nothing more than a friendly chat.

All of these different levels of influencing and communicating require different talent sets. If you think that a top salesperson from one sale type can perform at top levels in another sale type, you are mistaken. Many of you have experienced the frustration and downright bewilderment of hiring someone you knew for certain was a top producer, only to watch him or her flounder in your company. Top salespeople *can* move successfully to completely new industries and product lines, but only as long as the new sale type requires the same talents as the old.

An analogy I like to use is the owner of a football team who also happens to own a basketball team. He is passionate about sports and has the money and connections to make him a good team owner.

He does not, however, have a very good understanding of natural talent. He thinks that athletes are athletes. And so, when he suddenly has a need for a new running back for his football team, and he knows he has a recently recruited basketball athlete waiting to get his start, he thinks, "I have an available athlete! We'll put him in that running back position."

How will the basketball player perform? Not well, most likely, but why not? Both positions require physical stamina, athletic skill, experience, determination, a competitive spirit, the ability to perform autonomously in the position while also being a "team player"—the list of traits that are common to both positions is actually quite a long one! Why *wouldn't* the basketball player do well?

The answer is, although there is a long list of common talents for these two athletes, the different talents needed for each position happen to be *key* talents. They are the "final touches" that we would install if we were building an athlete from scratch. The final touches must be specific to the daily activities, or requirements.

The same is true of salespeople. The common talents include things like people skills, communication skills, leadership qualities, determination, autonomy, team spirit—we would want these talents in just about every sales position. But the final touches we would install if we were building a salesperson from scratch would depend on the specific daily interaction activities.

Over the years I identified and refined ten different selling talents. After you read their definitions you may realize that you have several different sale types within your organization—each requiring different talents—that are currently being executed by the same salespeople. This usually explains why you have salespeople who seem to always sell the same few products or services, and rarely sell others.

Before we get to the 10 selling talents, the term "prospecting" warrants clarification, as it is a major factor in a great many sales jobs. It is also a most common source of misinterpretation and disappointment among sales managers and executives.

For our purposes, *prospecting* is the act of calling or visiting someone who did not know you were going to call or visit. Responding to a "request for information"—even though you do not know the prospect and have never spoken to them before—is not prospecting. The prospect would be expecting a call at some point—a very different thing for a salesperson than calling someone who is *not* expecting your call. Even though you could be prospecting on behalf of a billion-dollar industry leader, if the prospect is not expecting your call you are likely to be lumped into that horrible category called "telemarketer." This is where salespeople's reluctance to prospect, or cold call, comes from: being labeled without being given the slightest opportunity to explain.

An interesting study was done to try to establish why some salespeople hate prospecting and others like it. The surprising finding was that almost no one likes to prospect. The fact is prospecting champions have forced themselves to tolerate it—even embrace it—because of the substantial rewards. Some of you are thinking, so why don't *all* salespeople force themselves? Don't they all recognize that it will increase their earnings? Yes, they know. Fully aware that they could be earning more money, the majority of salespeople still avoid prospecting like the plague.

The explanation is a primal one: the instinct to avoid pain. We all have different tolerance thresholds, and the fact is, for some salespeople the pain of prospecting outweighs the pain associated with earning less money. To others, the opposite is true. This is almost always a subconscious thing; it is most definitely a prime example of how you are wired at birth, and the most important thing to realize is that it is next to impossible to teach a nonprospector to prospect, at least to anywhere near the degree you need. You must hire those who possess the combination of talents that make them born prospectors.

So let's get to the 10 selling talents, which dissect the selling process into its influencing components. Do not distract yourself at this point with how to use this information—we will be covering that soon enough. For now, simply note the distinctions.

THE 10 SELLING TALENTS

THE 10 SELLING TALENTS

1	**Work Ethic:**	Quality vs. Quantity
2	**Tolerance:**	High vs. Low
3	**Persuasion:**	Adviser vs. Pleaser
4	**Executive Rapport:**	High vs. Low
5	**Need:**	Create vs. Established
6	**Explanation:**	Obvious vs. Concept

Preferences

7	**Sale Cycle:**	Short vs. Long
8	**The Solution:**	Unique vs. Commodity
9	**Products:**	Many vs. Few
10	**Decision Makers:**	Many vs. Few

* Always

* Good Speaker	* Good Listener

The first six talents deal with how people are hardwired in terms of work ethic, tolerance levels, ability to influence, and aptitude for abstract communication and thinking. One person's idea of "working hard" can often put another person to sleep. Some people's idea of fun on the job can be hell to others. Top salespeople all influence other people very well, but their specific communication abilities vary greatly. We can all think of someone for instance who is very persuasive, but not particularly articulate.

These six talents are must-haves; your candidates *must* possess the exact needed arrangement of all six. Talents seven through ten, however, are more preference than talent, and with these you have some leeway. This will be explained when you learn the talent-based interview process in chapter 5. Let's get to our first talent.

1. Work Ethic: Quality Versus Quantity

The first talent relates to your candidate's work ethic. While elements of *The Perfect SalesForce* certainly address motivating people to higher levels, we are all nonetheless preprogrammed when it comes to what we consider "working hard."

Half of the world's top salespeople are wired for *quantity*—that is, they need to be busy and productive. They like their day filled; they are hardwired to make many calls and many sales. They thrive in a repetitive and structured sales job. The other half prefer *quality* over quantity—a number of client interactions that, though fewer in number, require a near-perfect performance every time. This is typically a higher priced, higher executive level sale.

Does your sale require your salespeople to accomplish many different tasks throughout the day, knocking on many doors or calling many people? Or do they see fewer prospects or clients, in situations where they must perform flawlessly every time, where a tremendous amount is riding on each and every meeting? Or perhaps your sale is somewhere halfway between.

What is important is that you become conscious of these distinctions, and learn to match them to your own requirements. Once you learn the interview process that uncovers just how your candidates are wired in these areas, you will know if you have a match sitting in front of you.

Robert is a top-performing salesperson I worked with in the automotive industry. Month after month he outsold twelve other salespeople at the dealership. That means lots of cars per month. On a primal level, it means lots of positive encounters, or victories, per month. We must recognize that *this* is what drives Robert—frequent victories.

When Robert was hired away by one particular (very impressed) customer to be a sales executive for a software company, no one could understand why Robert floundered. He was back at the dealership before six months had gone by. Why? Because the daily pace at the software job was deathly slow compared to selling cars. Robert told me he only had to make "a couple" of sales per quarter. There was still a full-time amount of work to do—preparing information for prospects, having many meetings to discuss specific needs, and so on, but the number of victories per period was miniscule compared to selling cars.

Understand, the money was better at the new job, and the perks were better. There was more room for advancement. Some people would say there was nothing that was better about the car sales job. But the issue of quality versus quantity is a fundamental one. Robert told me that he was never able to "get going"; he never got into "that groove" that he would get into when handling many car deals at once.

On the flip side, I have seen many top salespeople flounder after coming to a sales job that has them doing far more work than they thought was required. After all, it is not very common to address these types of things during an interview. The interviewer is usually busy enough trying to decipher whether the candidate "can sell." How much work they are used to doing is rarely addressed, and even when it is, your candidate will usually provide whatever answer you're looking for.

Respecting this daily work ethic talent when hiring is critical, as a quality salesperson simply *cannot* perform the daily routine of a quantity salesperson, or vice versa.

2. Tolerance: High Versus Low

Tolerance refers to your candidate's pain threshold, how "thick skinned" they are. Every job contains multiple tasks; some are enjoyable, others far less so. But there is a big difference between tasks you don't like very much and those that paralyze you. Sales-people with high tolerance are those who embrace something they don't like—without any hesitation—in order to get to the end goal. Someone with low tolerance will completely avoid those tasks they hate or fear, and when we talk about fear, there is no sales activity that invokes more fear than prospecting.

The ability to embrace prospecting is the most elusive talent to identify in candidates. I have seen more owners and managers reduced to tears of frustration over terrific salespeople who can't seem to prospect—salespeople who were hired with an under-standing that a certain level of prospecting was a requirement who then disappoint in that area. It is not the only representation of the **Tolerance** talent, but if there was ever a perfect illustration of the philosophy that talent cannot be taught but must be hired, prospecting is it. A great many managers try to get their nonpros-pectors to prospect more, and the vast majority of the time all their efforts to that end are in vain.

It took a long time to identify this fact, and people still love to debate it. Many managers continue to train prospecting skills with the belief that their trainees' performance will rise signifi-cantly. But remember, when I say that something is a "natural talent," I'm referring to the way people are hardwired, and there is no changing that. When it comes to activities that we consider primal, true colors always shine through. Primal activities always reveal a person's hardwiring, and prospecting is comprised of sev-eral primal activities. They are watered down compared to our cave-dwelling days, but the triggered human response is no dif-ferent. Prospecting in its primal sense involves hunting, fighting, venturing into the unknown and not knowing what to expect when you get there, and meeting new people (who you know will not always welcome your presence). What's fascinating is that this exact combination of activities thrills certain people (those who actually get a charge from confronting and overcoming their reluctance) and simultaneously terrifies others.

Understand that just because a candidate hates to prospect does not mean they are a bad salesperson; it just means they will not perform well at the prospecting stage of the sale. As we discuss in the next chapter, a salesperson can be a very high performer at one stage of your sale and quite poor at another, and we will cover how to structure accordingly. But if indeed you require prospectors you must learn to hire them rather than hope to create them through training.

Finally, appreciate that some prospecting sales jobs have a very low conversion rate, which means salespeople must endure twenty or thirty "no, thank-you's" to get to one relevant, interested party. That's a lot of doors slammed just to get a few interested parties to first base. As you can imagine, this requires very thick skin. Then there are the sales jobs that have a higher prospecting conversion rate, which have salespeople off and running with new prospects one out of two times.

Until you have actually worked these two jobs for a week, you cannot appreciate how completely different they are from each other—and yet as I pointed out above, most recruiters would not differentiate beyond, "Did you prospect in your last job?" You must be sure to uncover a candidate's true tolerance level to properly match your sale.

3. Persuasion: Adviser Versus Pleaser

Another ideal example of where training fails to produce top levels of performance (in the absence of the required talents) is closing. The persuasion talent states that there are born advisers (which is my word for "closers"), and there are born pleasers. Unfortunately, the line between the two can be very faint—particularly during a job interview, which explains why so many of you have hired awesome salespeople who, to your surprise and disappointment, just couldn't close.

I like to call closers advisers because clients actually prefer to be *told* what they need. There are sales courses going on in every major city today teaching salespeople to "ask for the business." But as long as the required rapport is in place, clients don't want to be asked; they want to be told. They want to be advised by an expert—by what I like to call a trusted adviser.

Salespeople with the adviser talent have no problem at all moving things forward when it is time. All that training and practicing and role playing is unnecessary. All those silly closing techniques— forget it. They just do it; no thinking, no wondering if this is the right time, no hesitation. They just wrap up the business. They take the next logical step. They simply lead and clients follow, and they do so without any trace of pushiness or aggressiveness.

If you are lucky enough to have seen such a natural adviser, you know that this level of ability cannot be taught. That said, there is another group of very talented salespeople who perform every stage of the sale brilliantly, until they get to the close. And then they're done. They can't do it. Ultimately, they are too empathetic and don't know how to respond to, "I'll think about it" or, "We'll let you know." They feel that all those closing techniques they were taught, even the very benign ones, are manipulative and pushy. They feel if the client wants to think about it, then he should be allowed to think about it!

Luckily this empathy makes them very good at other sale types. They are great listeners. They open people up and gain deep levels of rapport very easily. Clients like them and trust them, and it is these folks who make the best customer service reps. They handle complaints well. They service territories well. They are what I call pleasers.

This is a good opportunity to point out how important it is to have a trustworthy interview methodology, a methodology where you feel confident that you are seeing the candidate's true talents—not just the talents he is telling you he has. It is very rare for sales candidates to tell you they have trouble with closing, and moreover, quite often they don't even realize it.

4. Executive Rapport: High Versus Low

It is not my intention to insult anyone's position or to sound snobby about different job classes or any such thing, so please accept that as my disclaimer as I point out that some salespeople bond instantly with the "common man," and others gravitate to rubbing noses with top brass. It's a fact of human nature.

I have watched salespeople cold-call plant managers and shop foremen and within minutes secure a loyal, long-term client. But I have also watched these same, gifted salespeople strike out when addressing a Fortune 500 CEO. And those who command the room and impact the CEO group do not always bond well with the average guys, as they can unwittingly intimidate them.

It is, once again, a primal thing with people. We still very much use our sixth sense, that sense that warned us of danger when we were a much younger species. We now use it in very different situations of course but it is still quite alive. It is a primal trigger, helping us to identify threats, leaders, and peers. All you need to know is that some salespeople will naturally impact a higher rank in a company, and others a lower rank.

In 1998 I broke my own rule for the last time and hired someone who did not score high with this talent. (As I have said, you want your candidates to possess *all* of the first six talents.) Our prospects were top officers—typically a VP Finance, a CEO, often a principal—of very large companies. Gary had more drive and determination than anyone I had ever met. I happened to know something of the personal reasons behind his drive and I knew no one would ever work harder—at the job itself and at whatever self-improvement might be required to succeed. He was mature and intelligent, and he was capable of creating need and elaborating our service (the **Need** and **Explanation** selling talents). And while I knew he could influence a lower-ranking executive level, I had serious doubts about his ability to sell to our target prospects. Nonetheless, I gave in to his persistence and offered him the job. And he failed. Or rather, *I* failed.

Many people will tell you that drive and determination are all you need to succeed, that if you work hard enough, you can overcome anything. While I love the passion behind such an ideal, it is not true where this selling talent is concerned. While it is true that Gary can find a way to succeed, this sale was not the vehicle to that end. No matter how hard he tried, and despite all our training together, he could not capture the attention of those top officers. He could use the very same words as my other salespeople, and he could show all the same data and support material, but nothing could change the fact that he lacked a primal trait that tells certain other humans you are someone to be listened to.

Don't make the mistake I made, no matter how much you might like someone. Always match the executive level of your clients and prospects with a salesperson who naturally impacts that level.

5. Need: Created Versus Established

A client of ours is a partner in a construction company specializing in commercial ventilation systems. They have a good reputation and they bid on, and win, many commercial installation jobs.

A few years ago this company took on a new "product." They felt that annual maintenance contracts for commercial building ventilation systems (not unlike an annual maintenance contract for a home furnace or central air conditioning) would be a relevant addition to their offerings. And they were right. But from a **Need** point of view, these two sales jobs are completely different.

When the salesperson tries to illustrate why her company is the best choice for the construction side of the business, the need is known. That is, we already know that there is a building project going on. Without having to ask, we know there is the need for a ventilation system. The prospect does not have to use my client's company necessarily, but they *do* have to have a ventilation system. The need has already been established before the sale even begins. But this is not true for the maintenance side of the business. Although there may be tremendous value to purchasing a maintenance contract, it is not essential. The need must first be created.

It is of course very common to have related product lines like this; it's just good business. But in this example, the two sale types are very different for the salespeople, and certain things must be structured accordingly. This is why you have heard me say that you may well have several different sale types in one company—requiring different talents—and many of you may have had experiences where your salespeople just don't do well with certain products or services that you feel are such "natural companions" to your core products.

Some salespeople do very poorly when it comes to creating the need but excel when the need is already established. Others thrive on the challenge of *creating* need. We must appreciate that when the need has not yet been established, the sale has a whole extra step. You can't even begin the "selling process" until there is need. Now, if leads come in to your company through marketing efforts, understand that need has been established. Prospects would not, after all, make an inquiry if there wasn't some sort of need. Even if only for preliminary information, need has been declared.

6. Explanation: Obvious Versus Concept

Selling a product or service whose benefits are obvious requires different communication talents than explaining a more complicated concept.

Concept sales require on-the-spot adaptation; they require salespeople to take the solution's usual benefits and tailor them to each prospect's unique situation and probable usage, so that prospects can better visualize their own benefits of owning the product or service. Mental pictures must be painted in lieu of obvious, unchanging features and benefits. Unique benefits must often be conceived by the salesperson in the moment.

This is not the same as tangible versus intangible sales. Despite what many people might believe, I have found no instances to date where a good product salesperson cannot sell an intangible or vice versa, provided the other selling talents are respected. The **Explanation** talent has more to do with the amount and the type of explanation involved.

A good example would be a courier service. It's not a product that we can hold and demonstrate—it is a service and it's intangible. But it is not an abstract concept that requires a prospect to use his or her imagination as to its application. Explaining what a courier service does, and what the benefits are, is as straightforward as explaining the benefits of a tangible product.

An example of a concept sale can be found in a company I worked for that provided an auditing service for industrial and commercial utility expenses (electricity, natural gas, oil, telecommunications). When I say "auditing service for industrial and commercial utility expenses," you do not instantly think, "Oh, we need that right now."

But as I explain a little further, telling you of the tens of thousands of pages of tariff classifications that no one in your company knows about or really has access to, in whose pages are quite possibly contained some sort of reduced rate on your electricity consumption from this day forward, the benefits of owning such a program start to become more visible (this sale is also a classic example of having to "create the need").

I could then explain that my company is the world leader in this field and that even the utility companies themselves buy our proprietary information. Again your interest deepens. Or I could explain that we have thirty thousand clients and I know what everyone pays for their gas and electricity and long distance—your neighbors and competitors included. With these utility costs representing your second largest expense (typically second only to payroll), do you see your interest deepening every time I impart more information?

The fact is, the salespeople of this company have a vast compilation of information at their disposal—accumulated from more than sixty years in business in eighty countries—to educate their prospects. With an information library this vast, knowing what exact information to pull out at what point in which meeting and with which person is a talent that some salespeople have and others simply do not. I used to watch uneducated, new-to-the-industry sales reps impact top officers of Fortune 500 companies—simply because of their instinctive talent of knowing how to carry out a concept sale—while experienced, polished salespeople who did not understand this type of sale failed miserably.

THESE NEXT FOUR talents are not necessarily deal breakers. With the first six, you *must* match all six to your sale type because, as I have said, your candidates will either possess or not possess these abilities. There are no gray areas.

But these last four are more preferences than talents, and you have some flexibility. A good analogy would be hiring a guitar player for your jazz quartet. A talent for music (what some people call an ear for music) would be a must—it would be one of our first six talents. Asking this guitar player to play on a cruise ship from 11:00 P.M. to 4:00 A.M., compared with doing the 8:00 P.M. to midnight gig at a swanky restaurant, is a good example of a *preference*. While this musician will certainly have a variety of job preferences, they will not necessarily affect performance.

Your salespeople have job preferences and it is definitely in your best interest to try to match as many as you can, but they will not necessarily affect performance.

7. Sale Cycle: Short Versus Long

Strange as it may seem, some salespeople excel at either a short or a long sale cycle. Once they have successfully engaged a new prospect in discussing possible solutions, some salespeople have, for lack of a better expression, no patience. They must bring the situation to fruition soon. These salespeople do not do as well in a much longer sale.

I have found that the other side of the coin—those salespeople who have no problem with a long sale cycle—can usually do *both* equally well. In other words, if you have a relatively short sale cycle you can ignore this factor, as either candidate will do. But if you have a long sale cycle, you would do well to find someone who understands the nuances of such a job.

8. The Solution: Unique Versus Commodity

Some salespeople very much prefer to represent a solution that is unique to their company; they do not like to represent a solution that the prospect perceives can be "bought anywhere."

If your prospect's hotel laundry machines can use your company's soap or anyone else's, it's a commodity, and the final supplier will almost always be chosen based on price. Less experienced salespeople will claim that the difference with *their* soap is the outstanding service that comes with it, but I'm sorry to say that to a large degree, the word service has lost its meaning today. Everyone says that they have the best service, and like it or not, if there is nothing to distinguish uniqueness, clients will buy on price.

It's very tough today if you're selling a commodity, and there are books and experts that can help with breaking out of the commodity trap. For our purposes, understand that some salespeople prefer to sell a unique solution while others actually do much better with a commodity sale; they use nothing more than their own relationship-building abilities to woo clients from their current suppliers.

9. Products: Many Versus Few

"Account penetration" refers to selling as many of your company's relevant products as possible to clients. Assuming for the moment that your many products are all the same sale type, and will therefore be handled by the same salesperson, we want that salesperson to develop the account as much as possible. The hard part is done—getting a new client. Now let's supply him with eleven things instead of only two.

You will find that certain salespeople love this sale; they excel at account penetration. They cannot rest until their clients have had every product in the line demonstrated and explained.

This same sale type, however, frustrates certain others. They find it too meticulous—almost like a paperwork kind of task: keeping track of who buys what and what new product has been demonstrated once or twice to whom and when so and so might actually try product number 8624. . . . Some salespeople are in the game just to win a new client and then move on to the next challenge. So whether your company has a vast product line or just one solution, be mindful to match the right candidate to your sale.

10. Decision Makers: Many Versus Few

Some salespeople have a great deal of trouble orchestrating the whole decision-making process when many people are involved. They are fine with one or two decision makers but when it comes to selling a solution that requires them to work the whole multi-person, multidepartment dynamic, they get a little lost. A multi-layered decision requires a certain combination of talents, from diplomacy to strong leadership to rapport with many personalities; it requires a person who naturally leads the whole group involved, and who addresses the issue of "final" decision making without any trepidation and without insulting anyone else. I know a lot of great salespeople who are not as comfortable with this multilayered dynamic, and I know many who are born to do it.

Always

Note at the bottom of the 10 selling talents chart there are two additional talents: **Speaker** and **Listener**. They are under the heading "Always" because I cannot imagine any sales job (and I've tried) where you would not want a good speaker and a good listener. And as obvious as this is, I have fallen under a candidate's spell in more than one interview, and then offered a job to someone who has all the talents I was looking for, but is also a pretty boring speaker. Or a bad listener. Or both.

When you are listening for your candidate's answers to be spoken a certain way, and you are consciously separating your own emotions out of the interview, and you are adapting the interview questions in this direction or that—and a host of other interview duties that you will be learning—you sometimes forget to pay attention to the speaker/listener factor. It is for this reason that I include these two important talents on the chart, as well as on the interview sheet you will be taught to use in chapter 5.

It's a sad truth that some candidates will impress you with their background and their accomplishments, and they may indeed possess the talents you seek—but they're boring speakers. You must be sensitive to this. They do not have to be brilliant orators capable of rallying troops to battle, but if you find your mind wandering when they speak, or you find they go on and on and on, remember that this person will behave exactly the same way with your prospects. The same goes for the bad listener. I'm always a little amazed when a brilliant candidate keeps interrupting me, or worse—they appear to be listening but they're not really *hearing* what I'm saying.

THERE YOU HAVE the 10 selling talents. Right now, you're either relieved to have greater insight into the corporate selling psyche, or you might be thinking something along the lines of, "This is way too complicated. I'll never manage to hire someone with all these talent combinations!"

Don't worry! Chapter 5 gives a very usable process for identifying these talents during an interview, and the good news is there isn't the infinite number of combinations you might be thinking there are. It turns out that many of these talents are "related" and grouped. I would also point out that those of you who work with salespeople are *already* living and interacting with these talents— you just didn't have their names before now.

I hope this chapter has given you a sense of how different one sale can be from another from a talent perspective. You may have come to the realization that some of your salespeople do not perfectly match your sale type, or perhaps you have multiple sale types being performed by the same people. If this is the case, you should consider rearranging certain things—but not just yet. We have one more level to examine: the number of selling tasks— better known as *sales stages*—that you ask your salespeople to perform. If you're like most companies, and you ask your salespeople to scout prospects, make appointments, sell these prospects, and perhaps even service them ongoing—you're about to see that you're probably asking too much.

BEST PRACTICE #2: SORTING SALES STAGES FOR TALENT

N ow that you better appreciate the impact of matching exact selling talents to your specific sale type, we take the process one level deeper to examine the different stages of your sale.

Did you ever have an outstanding salesperson who was a poor prospector? Did you ever have a powerhouse prospector who, unfortunately, was not a great seller? Have you noticed that your best salespeople seem to very much dislike paperwork and re-porting, and those who do report on time are not usually top producers? If your sale is the type that requires both the servicing of existing clients *and* ongoing hunting for new clients, have you noticed that some of your salespeople service well but don't hunt much, while others hunt but don't service well?

Most sales jobs have salespeople performing too many stages. The problem is from a standpoint of the talents required, many of these stages end up being totally unrelated. Asking a salesperson to be a top communicator, influencer, leader, diplomat, closer, lead researcher, *and* prospector is a pretty tall order. One cannot expect this individual to perform at top levels in *every* activity—the fact is you will find such a person only once in a blue moon. You will have much more success finding people who are top performers at one or two sales stages only. Top sales teams isolate selling tasks and assign them to different groups, so as to match talent with pinpoint accuracy.

I know that many of you have experimented with assigning different salespeople to different stages of the sale, but most companies approach this topic only from an efficiency point of view, and not a talent point of view. I have seen many companies, for example, experiment with one group of people that makes appointments for another group that sells and, while this is a good idea, it will raise overall performance if, and only if, the required talents for each stage have been properly cast.

I worked with a very large company in 1994. With offices in eighty countries, it is a world leader in its field and a well-respected organization. It also has one of the most difficult sales processes I have ever worked with.

It was a concept sale (the **Explanation** talent). The concept must be explained to a president, CEO, or other top officer—typically of very large companies (the **Executive Rapport** talent). Salespeople must diplomatically but authoritatively illustrate to this executive that his own top people are not at all in control of certain costs that, prior to the meeting, he thought they were. This means, of course, need must be created (the **Need** talent), which generally takes a bit of time, and presidents don't usually grant a lot of time for a first meeting of this nature.

We definitely needed to be advisers (the **Persuasion** talent)— impacting and assertive—and oftentimes had to lead a conference room full of very skeptical executives. We were selling a cost control program that required a significant upfront investment, with no guarantee of any future savings, to executives who honestly didn't really care that much. The sale typically spanned several months and had a pretty low closing ratio. It was also 100 percent commission.

As challenging as it was, the sale itself was not the hardest part of the job. The really difficult part was that we had to make our own appointments with these top officers—an extremely time-consuming and difficult job in itself. On top of all that, we had to find our own relevant candidates and submit them for approval before even making the first call.

I would watch polished, experienced sales professionals come and go—a terribly small number lasted more than a few months. This company needed a revolving door to handle the turnover of its salespeople. It was a clear (and all too common) case of a formidable product being sold through a disastrous arrangement of our 6 best practices. I sold fairly well for about eighteen months before being enticed away to another company (I would later be invited to return, in a management capacity).

The ensuing experience with my new employer helps to illustrate this chapter's best practice. The new sale was virtually identical—top officer, create need, concept, adviser—but this new company had *different* groups of people working *different* stages of the sale. They had one group sourcing and managing leads. That's all they did. These leads went to a second group, the "business coordinators," who called company owners and made appointments on behalf of the salespeople. That's all *they* did. Finally, the salespeople sold—they did nothing else. So instead of my day being filled with activities like finding leads and endless telephone appointment work, which is not my particular forte, I was in front of no fewer than three new prospects every single day, doing what my talent set does best: *selling.* By the end of my first year, I estimated that I had visited *three times* more prospects than when I was performing all the sales stages myself.

As always in sales, the results tell us which approach is more effective. For ten years I have watched the first company go through salespeople. As far as I know they still struggle with this issue, which has seriously affected their growth. The second company went from being a privately owned start-up to a $100 million multinational in about eight years. In its fifth and sixth years of business, it landed on *Inc. Magazine*'s list of fastest growing companies, and today it is among the largest management consulting firms in the world. I can also tell you that the employees of this company are infinitely happier than those at the first company.

Many professions have come to appreciate the impact of this "specializing" mentality. When a movie is being made, a great many talents are needed. The two that have always interested me are the writer and the director. Great directors of course possess talents that make them excellent at adapting a story to a movie. Once a story sufficiently moves them, they immediately begin to visualize how this scene will flow into that scene, and what camera angle will best achieve the desired emotion. But I have learned that many of these talented directors are *not* excellent at conceiving and writing a story. They are not terrible, mind you, but they do not write at the necessary "top performance" level. Likewise, many top writers have all the talents to make them great writers but they are not at all excellent at transposing the story to film—they need the director for that stage. The two of them together create a far better end result than one of them performing both stages would. This is why we have these talent specialties—so as to *isolate the outcomes that each person's talents best generate.*

It seems obvious when I use an example where specializing is not new to us, but this idea is not well understood in the sales department. When an employee is being asked to perform tasks that actually require different talent sets, you will always find weaker performance in the overall job. Yet it is likely that that same employee is performing very well at one or maybe two stages of the job—just not at all of them.

A salesperson's life would be grand if they could spend their whole day just talking with sincerely interested prospects. No trying to create interest and create need and build engagement and qualify buying ability—just *selling* to people who have already acknowledged an interest in exploring a solution like the one you happen to represent. The point is to appreciate how many sales stages come under the grand heading of "sales" that are actually not yet "selling" at all. Knowing this you must recognize the importance of assigning your different sales stages to the talents that perfectly correspond.

Before I explain the process to do this, we must define some sales stages. Although it would be most handy, it is difficult to come up with one and only one set of sales stages that fit every company. (Certainly every company has a "selling" stage, where a prospect and a salesperson interact, but not every company has, for instance, a "prospecting" stage.) Nonetheless, let me quickly define the most common stages so we're all using the same terminology.

Engagement

As we discuss the various marketing and sales stages, it is important to recognize that every stage for every company can be divided into two very different categories: everything that happens *before* client engagement and everything that happens *after*.

"Client engagement" is our term for that moment when the prospect starts to care, starts to take interest. If you called a prospect out of the blue to try to interest him in meeting a representative from your company to discuss, let's say, your consulting services, please realize, he is *not* engaged. He is thinking, "Oh no, another salesperson." You would be trying to get from the coldest stage there is to the "don't-hang-up-on-me" stage. From there, you might be lucky enough to make it to "mild interest" or "curiosity." But there is no engagement.

The selling stage cannot even begin until there is engagement.

The prospect must begin to visualize owning your product or service, what it would be like, what it would do for him. He will then start to ask questions, and a dialogue will begin.

Recall a situation from your own past where someone was trying to interest you in something—perhaps even a spouse. Remember how you went from nonengaged to engaged as you learned more and more about the offering.

If you were fortunate enough (or good enough) to have secured an appointment with the prospect that you cold-called for your consulting services three paragraphs above, chances are he is *still* not engaged. I have made several careers out of calling and making executive appointments in this way and, let's face it, there is some arm twisting involved at this stage. Professional appointment makers do just that—they make appointments. They do not create engagement. They get a salesperson in the door who then tries to *build* engagement, so that the selling stage can begin.

Preengagement Stages or "Marketing Channels"

There is an endless menu from which to assemble engagement-building stages. Cold-calling, prospecting, Web sites, Webinars, trade shows, sales meetings, free seminars, free samples or product trials, advertising of all kinds, publicity of all kinds, referrals, and myriad other marketing activities. The goal of every one of these stages, and combinations of these stages, is the same: to create prospect engagement and get to the selling stage. I call the various combinations of these preengagement stages "marketing channels."

Most companies have many such marketing channels to generate leads for salespeople. As an example, one client of ours develops and sells specialty software to large organizations. As you would expect, they have salespeople who explain the software's benefits and intended use to prospects, but the number of different sources that bring these prospects to the table—the marketing channels—are many. For instance, our client has been building its prospect database for many years by asking Web site visitors to register for the usual e-newsletter, free white papers, free product demos, and so on. This results in names of prospects who are then called by salespeople. The client also attends several trade shows each year—more leads. They partner with companies that sell related products. They do publicity and speak as experts in many publications, which brings more Web site traffic. They even have salespeople cold-call relevant-looking prospects. Note that these are all different marketing channels, the importance of which will be explained shortly.

Postengagement Stages

Selling

Once your prospect is engaged, selling can begin. You can now begin the stage of understanding your prospect's situation and needs, and building value in the notion of your (and your product or service) being the best way to address this situation and these needs.

For our purposes, the stage we call "selling" goes from the moment of engagement right up to a successful sale. Some people performing this stage may well get involved earlier in the sale—*before* there is engagement; many sales have the same salespeople creating engagement and then taking the sale to its end. In some cases it *should* be the same person, in others cases not—you will determine this in the upcoming process.

Technical Support

Technical support (where applicable) refers to the participation of those with more technical or specialized expertise than the salesperson, which may become necessary during the selling process. Technical support also refers to any such assistance immediately *after* the purchase (i.e., "We will help you install this, following the purchase").

Servicing

The servicing stage begins of course when a new client comes on board, and lasts for as long as you serve this client. While some products and services are purchased once in a while, like, say, computer equipment, others are repurchased every month, like ink and paper supplies for those computers.

The important question when assigning people to this stage is "Will there be selling involved?" Some servicing positions require nothing more than keeping the client happy. But others require "account penetration"—selling more of your goods and services in addition to servicing. As we learned in the previous chapter, this will require different talents (i.e., **Work Ethic, Tolerance**), and since many sales jobs have salespeople selling *and* servicing, overall productivity will drop if the salesperson possesses the talents for only one of these two functions.

SORTING SALES STAGES

Here is the three-step process to determine which talents are needed for each sales stage:

Step 1: Identify the sales stages in each *marketing channel*.
Step 2: Determine the ideal *result* needed from each stage.
Step 3: Determine which of the *10 selling talents* are needed to achieve each of these results.

The following work sheet will assist you and is available to download at www.theperfectsalesforce.com/tools:

Sales Stage Work Sheet for:

Product _____

Marketing Channel _____

Step 1 ⟶ Step 2 ⟶ Step 3 ⟶ **Talents**

Sales Stages	*Desired Result*	*The 10 Selling Talents*	*Talents Needed*	
1		**1 Work Ethic** Quality vs. Quantity	1	6
			2	7
		2 Tolerance High vs. Low	3	8
			4	9
			5	10
		3 Persuasion Adviser vs. Pleaser	1	6
2			2	7
		4 Executive Rapport High vs. Low	3	8
			4	9
		5 Need Create vs. Established	5	10
ENGAGEMENT			**ENGAGEMENT**	
3		**6 Explanation** Obvious vs. Concept	1	6
			2	7
		7 Sale Cycle Short vs. Long	3	8
			4	9
		8 The Solution Unique vs. Commodity	5	10
4			1	6
		9 Products Many vs. Few	2	7
			3	8
		10 Decision Makers Many vs. Few	4	9
			5	10

Chart by John Del Gaizo

In step 1 you list the different stages of the sale. In step 2 you assign the primary result that is desired from each stage. Step 3 is to run each desired result through the 10 selling talents to determine which talents you need to achieve such a result.

As you can see, the exercise is carried out for each marketing channel. Perhaps you have salespeople calling to make appointments from a list of leads. This would be one marketing channel and, therefore, one work sheet. Another marketing channel might be inbound leads generated by your e-newsletter that are followed up to try to make an appointment or to send a sample. This would be another work sheet. The purpose of the exercise is to fill in a work sheet for each marketing channel, for it is in this great mix of very different daily activities that *productivity falls victim to the absence of well-defined sales stage results and, moreover, bad talent casting.* If you have even one sales stage cast to the wrong talent, productivity bottlenecks at that stage, and the whole machine slows down.

The best way to illustrate how to use this work sheet is with a case history example. Earlier I referred to a software client of mine. By going through the work sheet exercise with them, we identified numerous obstructions that were significantly affecting sales performance. I will describe what we found, and then show you a sample work sheet that revealed these obstructions.

The software company's main marketing channels are:

1. Building their prospect database by asking Web site visitors to register for their e-newsletter, free white papers, free product demos, etc.
2. Attending several trade shows each year.
3. Partnering with companies that sell related products.

4. Doing publicity and speaking as topic experts in many publications.

5. Cold-calling relevant-looking prospects.

Certainly employing more marketing channels to generate leads is better than employing few. But this company was giving its leads—which came from any and every marketing channel—to any salesperson who was available. This is little more than a "hit or miss" approach to matching selling talents to different sales stages. First, this company sells several different software products. We pointed how one product—their most popular—required no abstract or conceptual explanation (the **Explanation** talent) as to its application or its benefits. But other products *did* require the explanation of a concept and, furthermore, they also required a need to be created (the **Need** talent). Certain salespeople in the company were selling more of one product, while other salespeople gravitated to other products—something that baffled and frustrated our client until they came to understand the 10 selling talents.

The second problem was with different marketing channels that were designed to reach different executive levels in prospect companies. The decision maker for one product was a C-level officer, while the decision maker for another product was almost anyone in the IT department. Marketing to these specific decision makers is indeed the right idea, but the resulting leads were then given to the next available salesperson—without considering what executive level that salesperson impacts (the **Executive Rapport** talent).

The company's third sales stage obstruction lay with the salesperson it chosen to host the Webinars (their most popular marketing channel). His talent set was not a good match for this sales stage. The company spent time and money attracting prospects to the Webinars, and then dropped the ball by assigning the wrong person as host. This individual was from the marketing department and was responsible for attracting as many people as possible to the Webinars. It was "his baby" so the company just let him go ahead and host, but he did not possess the talents to lead people and impact them in the Webinar. His job was largely the technical side of Internet marketing—*not sales*. This is a perfect example of a company assigning tasks and sales stages that may well be logical from some internal perspective, but not at all functional from the most important perspective—talent casting. The job actually contained contradicting talent tasks. With the right person hosting the Webinars, far more participants would be converted to the next sales stage—the selling stage. Instead, productivity bottlenecked right here.

The fourth sales stage problem was asking salespeople to make outbound cold calls to relevant-looking prospects when they "weren't busy with inbound leads" (those generated from the various marketing channels mentioned). As I have said throughout the book, most salespeople hate cold-calling and avoid it at all costs, and very little outbound cold-calling was getting done. Everyone was always "busy" with other leads and other tasks. By using the sales stage work sheet, our client was able to see that a very different talent set was needed for cold-calling. Furthermore, upon completing the work sheet it was obvious that this marketing channel should not be mixed with any other—that calling prospects should in fact be a sales job all its own.

Here is the work sheet we did for the first marketing channel, where leads are gathered from various Internet marketing activities.

Sales Stage Work Sheet for:

Product   Antivirus software

Marketing Channel   Web site leads

Step 1 ⟶ Step 2 ⟶ Step 3 ⟶ **Talents**

Sales Stages	Desired Result	The 10 Selling Talents	Talents Needed			

1 Call prospects; try to arrange product demo — Minimum 3 product demos scheduled/ day

1 **Work Ethic** Quality vs. Quantity

2 **Tolerance** High vs. Low

3 **Persuasion** Adviser vs. Pleaser

1	Quantity	6	Obvious
2	High Tolerance	7	Short
3	Adviser	8	Unique Solution
4	IT Manager	9	Few
5	Established	10	Few

2 Do product demo with prospect — Create need & develop interest in product (obtain engagement)

4 **Executive Rapport** High vs. Low

5 **Need** Create vs. Established

1	Quality	6	Obvious
2	Low Tolerance	7	Short-Medium
3	Adviser	8	Unique Solution
4	IT Manager	9	Few
5	Established	10	Few

ENGAGEMENT

3 Selling stage (to close) — Minumum 4 new clients/week

6 **Explanation** Obvious vs. Concept

7 **Sale Cycle** Short vs. Long

8 **The Solution** Unique vs. Commodity

ENGAGEMENT

1	Quality	6	Obvious
2	Low Tolerance	7	Short-Medium
3	Adviser	8	Unique Solution
4	IT Manager	9	Few
5	Established	10	Few

4 Develop account, interest client in additional relevant products — Grow each account by average 25% per year

9 **Products** Many vs. Few

10 **Decision Makers** Many vs. Few

1	Quality	6	Both
2	Low Tolerance	7	Medium-Long
3	Adviser	8	Unique Solution
4	IT Mgr./Execs	9	Many
5	Create	10	Many

As you can see, the first sales stage of this marketing channel is to call these leads to try to arrange a product demo. Note that these are "warm" leads—a prospect has voluntarily registered their name at some point—as opposed to a cold call. Once the product demo is successfully scheduled, the second stage of the sale is to actually do the demo with the prospect—which will hopefully lead to client engagement. Next comes the selling stage and, finally, ongoing account development.

Look at the *Desired Result* columns for these four sales stages. Thinking in terms of the *results* we desire from each stage can be helpful in identifying the stages themselves. If you are uncertain just how many stages you should boil your sale down to, you will have your answer after you complete a couple of practice work sheets.

Notice we assign a number and time frame in the *Desired Result* column. Instead of saying "make product demos" for the first stage, we want to say "minimum 3 product demos scheduled per day." Numbers and time frames assure that there will always be enough leads, enough appointments—enough of *every* stage, so that growth is never slowed by one stage waiting for another. (You will soon see that these results ultimately become *quota* for the salespeople. They also set up the pay plan and establish exactly what the sales manager will actually be "managing.")

As we now beginning to work with results, I must caution you once more on the difference between defining *results* and defining *activities*. An example of defining activities would be naming how many calls must be made in the first sales stage. You could easily write, "Make a minimum of 75 calls per day" in the *Desired Result* column but this would be wrong. The truth is, we don't care how many calls it takes—we want three *demos* scheduled per day. That's a *result*.

Some salespeople might take all day to accomplish this while others will have it done in three hours but that doesn't matter. If we speak in terms of activities, an employee could do exactly what is asked of her—make 75 calls—and get no appointments at all.

What would you say to such an employee? She actually did what was asked of her! It is a simpler, clearer management practice to name *results*. (As for that employee who gets to quota in three hours, don't worry—we will be "incentivizing" much higher results than these minimums.)

The final step of the work sheet is to list which of the 10 selling talents will be required to attain each of the results you have listed. This is the whole point of the work sheet exercise. Notice that all the talents required for stages 2 and 3 are the same—they can be done by the same salesperson, but they differ from those needed for the first sales stage. Selling Talents 1, 2, and 7 are different in the first sales stage. The first stage of this sale is a very different job from the second and third stages. It is repetitive; some might say mundane—calling from a list, getting many noes before you get a yes, scheduling demos but going no further in the sale. Some salespeople want this repetitive kind of job—and excel at it—while others need the diversity of stages 2 and 3, where each sale would be a little different from the last.

It will be easier to find top performers if we turn the first stage of this sale into its own job, and make stages 2 and 3 another job—and that's just what we did with our software client. They used to have their salespeople performing *all* of these stages. By isolating sales stages we identified not only that different talent sets were needed for different sales stages, but the exercise also identified the specific results (quota) that each stage should regularly generate. Not only did productivity go up, the need to micromanage went down.

Notice in the fourth sales stage, which involves developing the account further, we again see a different talent set is needed. Remember that certain products are sold to IT managers but others are sold to CEOs (the **Executive Rapport** talent). Also, the need is known when it comes to the antivirus product (everyone has an antivirus product today; creating need is not necessary), but other products in our client's catalog require creating need (the **Need** talent). The fourth sales stage also differed in Selling Talents 6, 7, 9, and 10.

Does this mean we *have* to have a different salesperson for this stage? This seems a good opportunity to remind you—it's all up to you. It is easier to find top performers when you require them to perform fewer sales stages. It is also easier to manage and to grow such a structure. It is what we recommended to this client, and productivity increased significantly, but ultimately it's your choice. You may have exceptional situations or extenuating circumstances that I know nothing about (a typical example of which—the long-sales-stage factor—is upcoming). You might choose to make the first stage its own job, but let another salesperson do all three remaining stages, in which case you simply need to look a little harder for people who possess the talents for *all* these stages. My responsibility is to report why certain salespeople are such high producers and why some companies are able to grow so fast. My job is to arm you with the human performance equation. As long as your setup respects that, you can structure things however you deem necessary for your company's situation.

BE OBJECTIVE AND START OVER

The most difficult part of the work sheet process is *being objective*. When we work with companies to create better team arrangements and shuffle tasks according to talent and such, we are constantly met with, "Well, Alan can't do that. . . . He's already taking incoming calls" or, "If Mary does that, who will take her clients?" Some people find it quite difficult to be objective when it comes to the place they go to work at every day, and so I recommend you recruit others to brainstorm with you.

I tell my clients to pretend they're starting over. Pretend you are redesigning things right from scratch. Your current sales department does not exist. Your current employees do not exist—take them out of the equation. The only way you will create the perfect arrangement of sales stages according to talent is by starting from zero, with a blank page. Yes, you will have to bring reality back into the equation but reality will always restrict the creativity needed for brainstorming. You must first imagine the ideal arrangement. Only once you have imagined it can you begin to move toward it, and that means leaving the current arrangement completely outside. We will discuss integrating any new arrangement of sales stages later in the chapter.

THE LONG-SALES-STAGE FACTOR

Despite the serious improvement in overall performance when talent is assigned to isolated sales stages, I must caution you about a situation where the alteration of your sales stage structure may affect your clients or prospects.

If your sale type contains any sales stages that take a very long time, it can be disruptive to the prospect to insert a "new player" midway. For instance, if your sale averages one year to close, and there is ongoing client servicing following the sale, the 10 selling talents have taught us that servicing requires a different talent set than closing. This chapter suggests you should consider *two* salespeople for the job—one to close the business and one to service afterward. However, we must acknowledge that after an entire year of sales meetings and technical discussions and lunches and general rapport building, your client may not want to be "handed over" to someone else.

Another typical example can be found where one team of

salespeople makes appointments for the "road salespeople." If the appointment setting is a fairly quick process, there is no harm. But if *many* calls are required before a prospect will grant the appointment—perhaps information needs to be e-mailed and follow-ups made—then by default the appointment setter has begun to develop a relationship with this prospect, and the prospect may not be open to "starting over" with someone new.

I have a commercial insurance client. Its salespeople build relationships over a long period—often many years—before the prospect even becomes a client. The top seller at this company, Gene, told me his clients would never stand for him leaving the picture. They have come to trust him and him alone with what is a very expensive and important business expenditure. Gene does, however, make extensive use of his company's customer service representatives and inside account managers, and will often direct his clients to this support staff. But his clients always know that Gene is their primary contact, and that *he* is accountable.

So what do you do if you indeed decide that two groups of salespeople will be disruptive to the client? What do you do about the fact that I keep telling you to assign specific sales stages to specific talents? Don't worry. I said it is *easier* to find top performers when you can narrow the number of sales stages they must perform. It's preferable. But it does not mean that it is impossible to find salespeople who are top performers at more than one stage—it's just less common. You'll have to look a little harder, and remember that after you read chapter 5 you will have a superior tool to that end. You can also make use of support staff, the way my insurance client does, as long as your clients understand their primary contact is still accountable.

In general, if you have a sales stage that lasts long enough for a significant relationship to develop, then switching salespeople may do more harm than good. If your sales stages do not take too long, you would do well to consider this chapter's best practice—a practice I would like to reinforce with one more reference to Gene. It would not seem unreasonable at this point to ask, "Why even bother? Why should we monkey with assigning different stages to different salespeople if there's a chance clients won't appreciate it?" The answer is because Gene's talent set makes him a top producer at getting new business. He told me he does not enjoy the ongoing servicing stage nearly as much as the hunt and victory of bringing in new business. Gene's book of business is twice that of the second best salesperson. Of the 45 salespeople in the company, Gene's sales represent *one sixth* of the company's total revenue.

It is in your best interest to keep a Gene happy, to capitalize on his strengths, and to avoid time being spent on his nonstrengths. By working exactly where he thrives, and staying away from sales stages that he told me "put him to sleep," he produces far more for the company. He's also much happier. As I said earlier, top sales forces have learned to structure their sales stages so as to *isolate specific talent sets*. It's easier to hire "specialists."

TESTING AND INTEGRATING

By now some of you know you have misalignment of talent and task. Some of you are less certain. My recommendation is to do a contained test of any new sales stage arrangement. If you feel that productivity will jump, for instance, if you assign lead generation to one (lower-paid) group, appointment setting to another, and the entire "selling" stage to yet another group, it is always advisable to test and tweak the process on one team of people before rolling out a new structure companywide. You must be sensitive to how your employees perceive such changes. You want to avoid making frequent structural changes like this, as it can affect your salespeople's confidence that management knows what it is doing. Depending entirely on how you handle it, changes to an employee's daily job can be a positive experience or a negative one. Always test and tweak to be sure, before you announce a companywide change.

This type of testing is a valuable tool. Needed changes are often clear, but not always. The whole point of this book is to become aware of the talent law, to come to understand once and for all what types of (and how many) selling tasks your salespeople should be performing. If you are less than 100 percent certain whether a proposed change will raise productivity, test it. If you take on a new product or service and, thanks to your new understanding of selling talents you suspect that a different group of salespeople should sell it instead of the existing salespeople, test it. Test and measure. As you will now be approaching these "structural" questions from a talent perspective, before long you will be finding more and more productive arrangements.

Remember to include some of your employees in the testing of new ideas and sales stage structures. Too many executives are in the habit of dictating the details of proposed changes. Instead, discuss the reasons for these changes *with* your salespeople. Listen to their feedback. You may choose to include certain salespeople in the brainstorming process. Remember that every day, they are the ones in front of the most important person in your company—your client. When your reasons for making changes are intelligent business reasons, they will not only understand, they will likely have very helpful ideas. Salespeople are the most entrepreneurial employees in your company. Most think like business owners. They will understand. If you include them in your thought process—and invite their feedback and participation—you will not only design better sales stage arrangements and practices; you will also have their support during integration, instead of their resentment.

★   ★   ★

MAKE SURE YOU think through all your different marketing channels, and prepare as many work sheets as you can. Don't cut corners. When you use this exercise as intended, you will see patterns emerging. You will notice the same recurring sets of talents in that right-hand column, despite different products or marketing channels. (After all, the talents needed to make appointments or schedule demos all day will, with very little exception, be the same regardless of product.) Certain product lines or services will strike you as needing to be sold by a different group of salespeople. You will begin to envision people who collect leads from *all* channels and then distribute them to the appropriate sales group. You will see cross-selling in a new light.

With all of the different marketing channels and lead-generating activities available to you today, and all of the combinations and arrangements of selling activities that you could delegate an infinite number of ways, you must employ some sort of logical discipline that will dictate the "right" arrangement of it all, and the only definition of "right" is *talent*. This simple work sheet exercise should be brainstormed regularly and by as many participants as you would like to recruit to help you.

Now that you can isolate the specific talents that excel at the specific stages of your sale type, you have a foundation in place for a sales force of top performers. Turn the page and let's look at the interview process you will use to identify whether your interviewees truly possess the talents you seek.

BEST PRACTICE #3:
THE TALENT-BASED
HIRING PROCESS

alent-based hiring has two steps. The good news for you is you're already halfway there.

Most hiring interviews do almost nothing to uncover a candidate's talents. Interviewing is a colossal weak spot in corporate America. But the interview itself is actually the second step in the talent-based hiring process. The first step is to understand, very specifically, which talents you are actually out to hire. And, as we have just spent two chapters learning about those talents, this chapter covers step 2: the talent interview.

Every executive will tell you that hiring top talent makes all the difference, yet almost no one understands how to interview for talent. There are four things to look for when hiring a salesperson (I will not be discussing criminal records or equal rights or anything other than *job fit*):

1. Skills that may be required to do the job
2. Specific knowledge that may be required to do the job
3. Experience, if necessary
4. Natural talent

Of these four things, talent is the only reliable predictor of future performance. Equally critical to understand is that talent is the only one that cannot be *acquired*. Skills can be trained, new knowledge can be acquired, and so can experience. You may need to hire people who already have the first three, or they may get these from you once they're on board—but they will *not* be getting that fourth thing from you or from anyone else. If a candidate were to score higher than anyone in the world in the first three categories, but the talents needed for the job were not revealed during the talent interview, *I would not hire them*. Talent is the only trustworthy indicator of future performance.

There is a plethora of clever interview questions to choose from, questions that are designed to see how well candidates do under pressure, how well they present themselves, how well they know their subject matter. Unfortunately, the only thing this really reveals about a candidate is how well they *interview,* and the peculiar thing is, many of the top salespeople I have worked with do not interview particularly well! I'm sure many of you have hired someone who interviewed fabulously but went on to disappoint in the actual job. This is most common—especially in the world of sales.

How about the flip side—have you ever hired someone who *didn't* interview well but went on to perform very well? I certainly have and that alone should tell us to put those clever-sounding and intimidating interview questions away once and for all.

So what do we ask? How do we identify the presence (or the absence) of the talents we want to hire? By knowing just what to listen for. You want to have conversations with your candidates and listen for certain clues in the *way* they say things. You're going to be a little bit sneaky; you're not going to let on about what you are looking for specifically. You're just going to chat and listen for patterns that develop—repeated patterns in the way the candidate answers that reveal whether this is an *actual* recurring behavior for them, or one that they are just telling you is a behavior. It is the recurring behaviors that we all keep coming back to—without even realizing it—that reveal the presence of natural talent. There are two steps to this interview process.

Step 1. Know what you're looking for, but don't reveal it.
Step 2. Structure your questions—and the entire interview— around the talents needed and then listen for patterns of behavior.

Step 1. Know what you're looking for, but don't reveal it.

Most job ads give far too much detail about the behaviors being sought. They tell applicants whether there is prospecting involved, often exactly how much prospecting. They declare whether the job requires territory building or account management or cross-selling; whether strong closing skills are needed, or leadership skills or an ability to assess need and articulate detailed solutions.

This level of detail then continues right into the interview process, as the interviewer describes to the candidate every required behavior of the job. The reasoning behind all this detail is by no means illogical, but it is wrong nonetheless. The interviewers who go into the greatest detail are those who have had the most disappointing hiring experiences. They feel that if they are extremely clear about which behaviors the job requires (i.e., lots of prospecting, strong closing ability) there can be no misunderstanding. The reason this backfires is your candidates now know exactly what you're looking for and, therefore, exactly what to say during the interview. Unfortunately candidates rarely read these ads and say to themselves, "Oh, I'm not the strongest closer . . . good thing the company listed that requirement. I won't apply." They *will* apply, and then they will play to all the behaviors that were mentioned in the ad.

If for example you need an adviser for the job—someone who naturally and easily leads prospects to the close—you must appreciate that if the candidate knows this ahead of time you will have a harder time getting to the truth during the interview. It is better to be vague about the exact type of sale you are hiring for, so the candidate has no game plan coming in; he doesn't know what profile to play to. I do not mean to make these candidates sound scheming or devious. Most do not see this as manipulative, certainly not dishonest. As I cited earlier, a shocking number of candidates do not know which specific selling behaviors are their strong or weak ones. Because they have been "in sales" for a time, and because they are good with people, they feel quite qualified to apply for almost any sales job.

You need to be more generic with your job ad. Describe your company. Sell yourself as a great company to work for. State that you are looking for a sales representative or an account executive or whatever the case may be, but don't get too detailed. While you may think this might generate résumés from candidates who are not relevant, isn't that what's already happening now? With the automated services available today from all the job Web sites, most of my clients get a tremendous number of résumés that are quite irrelevant to the job. More and more I am seeing résumés come in that are obviously being sent to anyone with a job opening. Unfortunately, writing a very specific job ad does *not* reduce this irrelevant volume.

Actually, a higher volume of résumés is what you want anyway. Since your candidates do not understand selling talents to the degree you now do, you really don't want to trust them to self-assess and to tell you what sale type they are best at. *You* need to make that assessment. Very often candidates are surprised when we offer them the job! They tell us they never saw themselves in "this kind of sale" or in "this industry," but they go on to become top producers. So the more résumés you have to work with, the better. You're being more selective now. Your interview process may well take a little longer than it used to, but the time and money saved by getting the right person into the right place more than makes up for it. Especially when you snag a top producer.

Continue your vagueness during the interview. You do not want to appear to be elusive or avoiding certain issues, and you can do so while still avoiding specific answers. When a candidate asks if the job entails servicing clients for the long term, or just hunting for new ones, you can answer, "Well, I think most sales jobs kind of need a little of both—and that's a great question. . . . Tell me, what have you done more of in your past sales jobs?" This answer does not appear evasive; candidates do not think you are trying to skirt the question. They think you answered them. But you don't want the candidate to know the job requires, for instance, hunting new business *exclusively*, as their answers could be tailored to hunting from that point on. Give a watery answer and then end it by asking your own question about the same topic. If a candidate is asking about hunting, as in the example above, I want to know *why* he's asking. And when you do ask a direct question, and there certainly are times when you will—like "How do you feel about hunting new business?"—remember not to blindly believe the answer. We will be examining "good answers" and "bad answers" shortly.

Step 2. Structure your questions—and the entire interview—around the talents needed and then listen for patterns of behavior.

Here are the talents needed for one of the selling positions we identified in last chapter's work sheet.

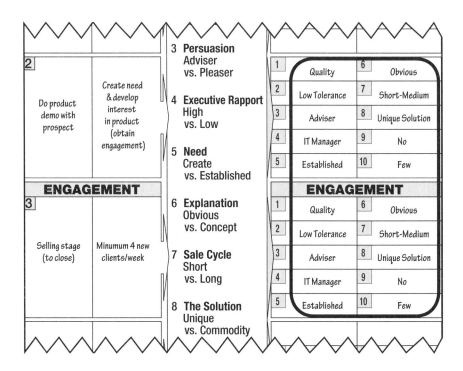

Let me synopsize the first six required talents into a couple of paragraphs. (You will remember the last four are more job preference than talent. They are less critical and are pretty straightforward to find in an interview.)

In short we are looking for someone with a quality over quantity **Work Ethic,** someone who gravitates toward jobs in which impacting, leading, and convincing others represent a typical day rather than jobs that require a greater volume of the more repetitive, mundane type of activity. This is someone who excels at making presentations, going on a few sales calls per day, having conversations about the ideal application of your product or service—rather than sitting at a desk making many client calls, one after the other. Because the job calls for low tolerance (the **Tolerance** talent), we do not need to look for behavior patterns where this candidate regularly forces himself to embrace tasks that he does not like.

The candidate definitely needs to be an adviser (the **Persuasion** talent). She needs to illustrate patterns of leading, of taking the reins, of not always agreeing with everything you say (you will soon see that we sometimes *deliberately* make a statement that we know the candidate will disagree with). She will offer her own opinions—without necessarily having been asked about a topic— and illustrate a pattern of past leadership, of immediately taking the bull by the horns when things aren't going exactly the way they are supposed to. Because we need an adviser, not a pleaser, the candidate will not necessarily be overly flowery or attentive or complimentary or empathetic. She will have a strong will.

Because the job sells to a middle management level (the **Executive Rapport** talent), the candidate will not need to convince you that he impacts a board-level top officer.

As for Selling Talents 5 and 6 (**Need** and **Explanation**), the need is already established for this product, and it does not require explaining a concept; the benefits of the product are fairly obvious. We will not therefore need to look for these abilities in this example (we *will* be looking for these in upcoming examples).

In preparation for this interview, list the talents you're looking for on a sheet of paper, keep it in front of you, look at it often, and always take a lot of notes during the interview. Unless you have a photographic memory, it's just too difficult to remember all that you're interviewing for, and how the answers are being worded and delivered. I keep two pieces of paper in front of me; the first has the list of talents I need and a few questions that I may want to be sure to ask, and the second is a pad for all my notes. Remember to always include speaker and listener on your interview sheet. You're looking for a particular talent set but remember you're also looking for a good speaker and listener at the same time.

Give yourself at least an hour for the talent interview—an hour and a half is better and I often go longer. (The exception of course is if you know in very short order that the candidate does *not* fit.) Because you are looking for repeating patterns, you need a certain amount of time before they are revealed (*if* they are to be revealed). Do not try to accomplish any other typical hiring business at the same time (i.e., skills testing, any written tests that you might do); just interview for talent. You can conduct your other job interview business following the talent interview, and only if you have decided the candidate passes the talent stage. You may even need to have certain candidates back for a second talent interview if you are unsure. If so, choose a different setting the second time— perhaps lunch at a restaurant or in an employee lounge.

Since the goal is to reveal "who the candidate really is," do everything you can to put him at ease. I see some interviewers being quite intimidating during an interview, whether intentionally or otherwise, and this will inhibit the process. When a candidate relaxes, you will see their true colors more easily. If they joke a little, laugh. If they talk about something you're not interested in, pretend you are. Wherever the early part of the conversation goes, go there willingly. Mirror your candidates. If they are a little more reserved, you be the same. If they are outgoing, you are too. We all gravitate to those who are like us, and mirroring (covered in chapter 7) is one of the most powerful tools for gaining instant rapport with other people.

We are going to examine how to control the direction of the interview by using questions, and how to use the candidates' answers to reveal their talents. There's no perfect series of interview questions that you could use every time, simply because all people interpret what they think you want from each question quite differently—*and this is the whole point*. Each of their interpretations will offer a peek into your candidates' habitual behaviors; their answers help disclose how they are wired. Some of the most varied answers I get from candidates are to the question, "Tell me what an 'accomplished day' is for you." Some answer with all the many things they got done while others will cite one large accomplishment, and as you will see shortly, this is exactly what we want. Once you are a little more practiced you will find yourself identifying peoples' talents during idle conversations, without consciously constructing questions at all. As long as you know how to guide the conversation once it has begun, your candidates will be talking about the things you need them to talk about.

Talk show hosts illustrate an important lesson in interviewing. Good hosts may have a list of prepared questions, but they know how to listen to answers and improvise. If something interesting is developing, they will continue down that story line to its very end, even at the expense of all those other questions they had prepared. Jay Leno certainly has questions prepared about his guests' current projects, but if they are telling a hilarious and compelling story, he will allot all the time necessary to hear it out—even if it wasn't on the question list. I used to watch Arsenio Hall ask one question and then, after the guest had finished answering, ask the next question on the list—even if that guest's last answer absolutely begged a follow-up question. I would be thinking, "Arsenio . . . ask her *why* she felt that way! Ask her *why* that happened. Ask her what happened *after* her dress came undone at that party!" But Arsenio would obediently march on to the next question on the list, partly because he was only half listening and partly because he's simply not a good interviewer.

So be a good interviewer. Tell your candidate that your company's interview style is informal and you're just going to chat, that you will certainly talk some business and ask some past job questions, but there is no formal protocol. Encourage her to ask questions anytime along the way. Your goal is to create a setting akin to listening in on a conversation between your candidate and her close friend, where there would be no pretense at all.

All of the following dialogue examples are pulled from actual interviews, and they illustrate how a talent interview goes.

After some easy small talk, I generally slip in one of the standard open questions you will learn to work with: "Tell me about———" (and then insert anything you want into the blank). I usually start with, "Tell me about your last job." Many candidates will ask for clarification—"Which part of the job? What exactly would you like to know?"—but maintain your "vague" rule. Tell them, "Whatever part you'd like to talk about." If they begin with something like, "Well, it was (is) a good company to work for . . . ," ask why. What did they like particularly? What didn't they like? Before long an opportunity will present itself where you can guide the conversation toward the talents you're looking for.

Let's look for that first talent, **Work Ethic**. We will be looking for as many instances of gravitating to quality sales jobs over quantity sales jobs, as well as instances in other nonsales jobs if applicable. So if during the chat your candidate offers, "It was a lot of work," you want to probe that. Never assume they are referring to what you think they are probably referring to. "It was a lot of work" might simply mean there was a lot of reporting or paperwork attached to the job. Get used to saying, "Tell me about that" and, "How do you mean?" Eventually you will get to something like, "Well, I love to sell, but this turned out to be a lot of *dialing* and not much *selling*." Now the conversation is heading where we want—to a quality versus quantity chat.

Throughout the conversation you will likely bump square into other talents you eventually need to know about, even though you weren't intending to just yet. Take whatever comes along! If your candidate says, "It was a lot of work" as you're probing for quality/quantity and you casually respond, "Oh, yeah? Tell me about that," she may say, "Well, it was *very* technical." Ah! Let's follow that road then.

"Is that right? How technical?"

"Well, we almost had to be engineers! Clients seemed to want to understand every detail of *how* the packaging machine worked. I enjoyed explaining what it would do for their business—you know, the benefits, the cost savings, and all that. But everyone wanted to know *how* the machine worked."

This statement points us toward a few things we can work with. It illustrates that she may not be very technical, and remember, the job entails selling software to IT managers! But don't jump to any conclusions just yet. You need to probe more. Remember that we are looking for *repeating* patterns, not just something that was said one time.

The statement certainly also illustrates that our candidate likes to talk about cost-saving benefits and such. As you know, many salespeople get hung up on features and never talk about the benefits of those features. If our candidate is itching to talk benefits, it's a glimpse into her selling style. If she's frustrated talking about features and how the machine works, it might be an indication that she's a strong closer. Let's find out.

"Technical stuff aside, it sounds like it kind of frustrated you that everyone wanted to know how the machines worked."

"Yes, I guess it did."

"Why do you think that is?"

Notice how we continue to probe but remain vague enough that many things can be revealed. Notice too how many balls you may need to juggle at the same time! This is why you need to keep that talent list in front of you. It will keep you on course. When you feel certain that the prospect has or does not have a particular talent, scratch it right off your list and continue. If you become certain that the candidate does not possess a talent that is critical to the job, then your interview is over. You don't hire them.

Let's continue. We asked our candidate, "Why do you think that is?"

"Because *how* the machine does what it does doesn't matter! What really matters is, does it save money . . . is it an intelligent purchase for the company? That's what matters."

As a skilled talent interviewer you see another opportunity to guide the direction of the conversation. If you picture this candidate in one of the selling situations that she is obviously visualizing, what you'd ultimately want to know is, what does she do about her frustration? How did she respond? Did she begrudgingly describe all those features to the client, or does she perhaps tell them *what she feels* they should be focusing on? If the latter, it would certainly suggest the presence of the adviser talent we're hoping for. A pleaser would instantly do whatever the client wants, would jump at the chance to fill the client's needs. A pleaser would not question the client, but an adviser sure would. An adviser would advise.

This is a good segue into the topic of *how* the candidates answer our questions. While I'm certainly hoping that she tells me she takes the reins and tells the clients what they should do—and ultimately closes a lot of sales—how can I believe it's true? How do I know if it really happened or if she's just *saying* that it happened? I have made reference to the way your candidate answers questions. There are two indicators that suggest the behavior your candidate is talking about is in fact a habitual behavior and not a fabricated answer.

First, the answer is quite spontaneous; the candidate did not visibly take a moment to think about it. And second, the answer contains specific details. When there are specific details—that didn't require a bit of time to think about—the story is more likely true. Let's continue. The last exchange was "Because *how* the machine does what it does doesn't matter! What really matters is, does it save money . . . is it an intelligent purchase for the company? That's what matters."

"Hmm, you're right about that." (Agreeing regularly and often—whether you really agree or not—will prompt your candidates to continue to be honest with you. They come to feel that you two are on the same page about things.) "So tell me, what do you do? How do you handle it?"

This is a telltale moment. Whatever the candidate says next will offer real insight into her adviser talent (or lack thereof), so it's very important that I believe whatever she says to be true, not fabricated (or exaggerated).

"I tell them!"

Hmm, no detail but, of course, not everyone will launch into all the details. We need to discuss this a lot more to have enough to make a judgment.

"Wow! Tell me about that." Note that I am acting impressed with the candidate. If I were to say, "No . . . you don't tell them, do you?" the candidate might think that I feel this is wrong and again, she might close up. I want her comfortable. I want to see the real person.

"I recently told this one prospect that I would be happy to explain all the specs but that the real reason to make this purchase was the cost saving."

No hesitation. . . . She certainly looked like she was remembering an actual event. But anyone could say this. As I continue to let the story unfold, she will either be recounting the story as it happened or making things up—these are the only two possibilities. And the further we go the more she'll have to make up if it is indeed fabricated. My next question is pretty obvious.

"So what did he say?"

"He said he already knew about the cost-saving part and that was the main reason he was speaking to me right now. I didn't realize he knew about us already from a colleague."

Okay, we're getting some meat now. Understand that if you wanted to make up a story that would impress your interviewer, you would answer with something more like, "He thanked me for explaining that. He also made the purchase." But our candidate's answer was kind of neutral; it didn't boost her or hurt her. It sounds like something that quite likely actually happened. The level of detail was good, and the answer was *immediate*—the two clues that indicate the presence of a true behavior, or talent. I am, of course, going to probe more. I can't put a checkmark on my interview sheet beside "adviser" just yet.

"Do you usually tell your prospects what you think they need to know about?"

"Yes."

"Is that what your past employers recommended or just something you do on your own?"

"I guess I just do it."

"Can you tell me about another instance where you felt you really needed to lead a prospect?"

"What would you like to hear about?"

Once again, be vague. Whenever you ask a question that you feel is probably pretty straightforward, and the candidate asks for clarification, it is an opportunity to see how they interpret and what kind of answer she gravitates toward. After several such instances, you will see a pattern developing.

I once interviewed a very pleasant and polished gentleman for a higher-level sales position. He was articulate, intelligent, and great to be around. I knew he would impact a C-level executive, he was definitely an adviser, he possessed a quality **Work Ethic**, and his **Tolerance** level was irrelevant in this case. I was looking particularly for the ability to create **Need** and explain a conceptual application of the product (Talents 5 and 6), but for the life of me I couldn't get any specifics. I would say, "Can you tell me about an instance where you needed to explain your solution to a prospect?" He would always answer with something like, "I think being able to explain things well is critical in sales. You must be able to get your message across."

An untrained interviewer might think this is a good answer—it sounds like this fellow knows what's important in selling! But notice the glaring absence of *specifics* in the answer. I asked for a specific instance! So I obediently followed with, "Yes, very good. . . . Can you give me an example of what you mean?" He would always answer, "What kind of example would you like?" My response: "Any example at all will be perfect. I am more interested in what *you* choose." Steer your candidates toward the examples you are interested in but if they ask for clarification, tell them any answer is fine, that their interpretation is what you want. It is their interpretation of what they think you probably mean that will begin to reveal how they behave. As for my distinguished candidate, he kept asking for clarification; I kept saying, "Any instance you choose" and he kept answering without specifics. He kept telling me that this thing and that thing are very important in sales, but I never got any real life instances of his past experience—so I did not hire him. As far as talent interviewing goes, I had nothing to go on. The things I *did* know about him had more to do with personality than the talents I needed and, remember, *talent is the only indicator of future job performance.* When you're not sure, it's just too costly to hire incorrectly. Wait until you interview someone who obviously has the talents you need. Even if their personality does not happen to impress you as much, their performance will.

Back to our candidate who likes to tell her prospects what *she feels* they should be focusing on. I had asked for "another instance where you felt you really needed to lead a prospect." She asked what I'd like to hear about and I answered, "Anything you'd like to share."

"Well, there was this one guy." A good start—immediate and with "case history" type details. "He wouldn't stop asking about specs, how this works and why that does what it does. I kept telling him that those were easy to explain and I would do that for him, but that to me it made sense to first run the numbers to even see if this made monetary sense for his company. If it didn't, and the purchase wasn't a smart one for him, all those specs would be irrelevant."

"Makes sense to me. What did he say?"

"He wouldn't let go. He just kept going back to the details of it. So I realized he was one of these guys who just need to know this stuff before he can move on. We wouldn't have gotten *any* further if I hadn't explained all the tech stuff to him."

"So you gave in and did it his way?"

"Well, I'm there to make a sale. I find it time saving to point out the logic of looking at the financials first. Most people bite but some just can't. I've learned that with that type of personality, you have to give them the minutiae. Over and over. So even though it kind of frustrates me, it's needed for the sale."

"And did you get the sale?"

"I did."

We learned a lot in that exchange. Did you notice that I asked for another instance where she led someone to her way of thinking and, when I told her to pick anything she wanted, the instance she chose *wasn't* in fact an illustration of her leading? It was the opposite really; it was an example of her giving in! But this is why we give a wide berth and then watch where the candidate goes—we learn more.

We learned that she will try to lead but that she has the ability to back down if she deems it necessary. I was becoming worried that she didn't *ever* do what the prospect wanted. Now that worry is gone. We got a glimpse into another talent too. Did you catch it? We know that this woman does not enjoy that part of her job that has her explaining the technical side of the products. That has become quite clear. But without hesitation she *will* do all the explaining needed the moment she believes it is necessary to close the sale. This illustrates the presence of the **Tolerance** talent, jumping right in to something you don't like simply because it's necessary to get to the end goal. Even though high tolerance was *not* required for this job, I continued to probe that, looking for examples where she forced herself to confront unpleasant tasks for the greater gain.

Remember that I didn't get another example supporting the adviser talent, so I would continue to probe there as well. One note regarding that adviser line of questioning: at this stage I am not going to judge whether or not I feel this candidate *should* be leading her prospects the way she does, whether I think that's the right way to handle the sale. My job at this point is to identify behavior patterns, which is the strongest indicator of the presence of natural talent. If she *does* have the adviser talent, I can always discuss whatever selling suggestions I may have after she is hired.

SAMPLE QUESTIONS

Now that you're getting the gist of the talent interview, some sample questions will be helpful. Remember that these are only suggestions—each candidate will interpret what he or she thinks you mean quite differently. As such, these questions will get some of your candidates talking about the things you want them to talk about, but perhaps not others. As I said before there are no questions that, once asked, will immediately get every candidate to go where you want. The talent interview is about where *you* direct them after each thing they say.

That said, the following samples will start you off. While they are listed under our selling talent headings, many will in fact identify several talents, and they should be mixed and matched. You may download these questions (as a Word document) from www.theperfectsalesforce.com/tools.

General

These start things off in the right direction:

- What was your favorite job ever? Why?
- What was your favorite part of the job? Why?
- What was your least favorite job/part of that job? Why?
- Tell me about something you're really proud of.
- Tell me about a real victory.
- Take me through a typical day (of any past job, or perhaps of a particular past job). Describe the various tasks or how the day was divided.

1. Work Ethic: Quality Versus Quantity

- Tell me about a time you had to work much harder than you wanted to.
- Describe an "accomplished day."
- Do you like being busy? What's "busy" for you?

- Which of these two jobs would you prefer:
  1. Sitting at a comfortable desk telling about fifty people a day on the phone about a new product, or
  2. Sitting at a conference table twice a day to explain to six executives the way we do things (which is slightly different from the way they're *hoping* we do things).

2. Tolerance: High Versus Low

Using questions that refer to past jobs—like those in the "General" heading above—probe to see *what the candidate did* about those parts of the job he disliked. Did he avoid or embrace? Remember to listen for *immediate* responses with *specific* details of events.

3. Persuasion: Adviser Versus Pleaser

- Tell me what you think it is to "properly serve" your clients. (Some will answer, "Get them whatever they need"; others will say, "Give them what I *know* they need.")
- Tell me about a time you overcame a lot of resistance to your ideas or to your proposed solution.
- Tell me about a client who was really happy with your service. (Then find out what your candidate did for them—was the candidate filling a client's request or telling the client something they needed to know but didn't necessarily request?)
- What do you do when a client or prospect doesn't agree with you?

One tactic I like to use to test for adviser/pleaser is to *disagree* with the candidate at some point. Once you have come to know them a little bit, make a statement that you know they will not agree with and see what they do. They will agree with you, disagree with you, or just keep quiet. I will sometimes tell a candidate that I don't think they are right for this job—again, to see how they react.

I once did this with a female candidate whose answers throughout the interview suggested she was a pretty strong adviser, but who really didn't *act* the part. Erika's answers contained many specific examples of past leadership, but she was being proper and polite for the interview. When you want to be more certain, disagreeing or challenging the candidate can help. After about an hour I told Erika flat out that I didn't think she was right for the job. She asked why not, so I listed a couple of criteria where I told her I felt she was weak. The key is to make sure they are criteria where she is *not* in fact weak, and also to not mention the actual talent you're looking for—that would be telling her exactly how to behave.

Well! Off came the gloves! She was still proper and professional but she absolutely straightened me out where my supposed doubts were concerned. She even got a "receipt" from me; she said, "Does that clear things up on that point? Are we clear?" I hired her and she went on to become a top producer.

4. Executive Rapport: High Versus Low

I do not use any particular questions for this talent. I ask the typical past job questions—about both good and bad past jobs—and look for the executive level the candidate seems to gravitate to selling to. Look also at which jobs the candidate was most successful at. After an hour and a half with a candidate you should have a sense for whether this individual will impact a C-level executive or the "common man." Remember to mirror your candidates to make them comfortable and bring out their true colors.

5. Need: Create Versus Established and
6. Explanation: Obvious Versus Concept

The presence or absence of Selling Talents 5 and 6 is pretty straightforward to identify. If your sale type does not require need to be created or a talent for explaining concepts, then this section is moot. But if your sale *does* require one or both of these talents, ask about past jobs. Have your candidate explain as many of their past products or services as you need. Ask how the products do what they do. Ask why it was a good purchase, or who it would be a good purchase for. Play dumb if need be and ask as many questions as you need to. Play the part of the prospect. Before long you will see your candidate's true communication talents. These cannot be faked.

INTERVIEW TIPS

Divide Your Mind

One of the biggest hindrances in hiring is how we *feel* about a candidate. It is a fact of human nature that we all gravitate to those who are like us. When meeting new people we very quickly form opinions about whom we do and do not like. How many times have you heard yourself say something like, "I don't know. . . . I can't put my finger on it. I just really liked that candidate." Or, "He just rubbed me the wrong way."

There is no place for this in the hiring process. Let the science behind the talent interview be your guide, not your gut. You need to divide your mind into two (sometimes conflicting) halves. Half of you must pay attention to mirroring the candidate and making him feel as comfortable as possible, while the other half must remain quite objective and emotionless. I often find myself falling for a candidate. If they are particularly clever or personable it is easy to be affected. Remember to look for needed talents as objectively as you can. I have learned to say no when the data tells me that no is the right answer. I have also learned how to hire someone who I don't particularly like—someone I wouldn't ever go for coffee with—because they possess the perfect talent set for the sale.

Guide the Interview, but Not Too Much!

Another caution: while you are guiding candidates toward needed topics and discussions, be careful not to put the words you want to hear right into their mouths.

I have interviewed some pretty terrific candidates who have possessed the perfect arrangement of the first four selling talents. In addition, they were great speakers and listeners. And so, if the remaining talents (5 and 6) now need to line up, I have caught myself (and many trainees) "guiding" the conversation to the point where *almost anything we ask* will produce the answer we're so hoping to hear.

Remember that you're listening for as many specific, case history details that launch out of a person without a lot of thinking. Yes, you often have to guide them toward specific topics, but if they are not giving the detailed answers you need to hear after a few opportunities, they may not possess those talents no matter how much you want them to. Again, remain objective and emotionless.

Keep an Answer File

For those candidates who you choose to hire, I recommend you keep a file of the answers they gave to your most common questions. Mark your agenda six months from their hiring date and pull out their answer sheet. Add notes to the file regarding how well or how poorly they are performing, and in which stages of your sale (if relevant). After a time you should be able to identify patterns in how top performers in your specific sale type answer questions and behave during the interview. This will help with future hires.

Note: For those who would care to, I would appreciate you sending me any answers that you compile—good or bad. I am building a database of these answers myself. You may send them to interviewanswers@theperfectsalesforce.com. Thank you!

BEST PRACTICE #4: THE
PAY PLAN AND QUOTAS

We are now into the performance conditions half of *The Perfect SalesForce*. Once again, a top performer is *natural talent operating under specific conditions*. Now that you've had three chapters of talent, chapters 6 through 8 will describe the ideal performance conditions.

Make no mistake. The conditions are as important as natural talent. I have personally witnessed a shocking number of companies that lose top salespeople to an intolerable arrangement of these conditions and, quitting aside, I have witnessed an equal number of top talents who end up performing at only mediocre levels because of them. And I am not talking about whips being cracked over the heads of overworked salespeople hunched over a rotary phone in poor light under leaky ceilings, being screamed at by an abusive, cigar-smoking tyrant. The large majority of these "intolerable conditions" completely elude executives, and certainly baffled *my* clients. Most of them felt the job, the pay, and the perks were very good. And they probably were.

There is almost no excuse for this misunderstanding. If you have managed to find and hire a top performer into the specific selling role for his or her talent set, you have accomplished something significant. Losing this person due to a lack of understanding of their needs and wants is inexcusable.

What your salespeople really need and really want will likely surprise you. As I was writing this chapter, I took a break and thumbed through a copy of *Fortune* magazine, the "100 Best Companies to Work For" issue. The article confirmed what some of us have always known. Employees perform much better when they love coming to work. They spread the word about how great their job is, and then other talented people want to come work there too. Turnover is of course much lower, which is a huge cost savings. But the main benefit to the company is *getting an employee's best.*

Workplace performance expert Dr. Dean Spitzer quotes a variety of disturbing surveys in his book *Supermotivation* (Amacom, 1995), including the fact that 84 percent of workers could perform significantly better if they wanted to, and a full 50 percent said they are exerting only enough energy to hang on to their jobs. So few employees today go anywhere near "above and beyond," and most executives do not appreciate the financial impact this has. If you could stick a productivity barometer into any employee at a Best to Work For company, the reading would be at least double that of other companies. What would a group of these employees do to *your* numbers?

The conditions we will be discussing are performance influencers, those that affect one's ability to consistently perform at the pinnacle of their talent, and they all serve to answer that big question: what conditions do your employees need and want? What is it that Google and these others are doing so differently? What do I need to do to have employees so fiercely loyal and ultraproductive?

The answer is only these two things. You have to:

1. Provide clear parameters
2. Treat them right

Some of you are thinking it's not these two things—it's the swimming pool or the gourmet chef who Google has. Not true. I have worked with companies whose employee productivity rivals Google's and they had none of those things. The flip side of that statement is, Google could be offering all those perks but if they didn't treat their employees right, no one would stick around to use the gym or the rock climbing wall—they would clock out at five o'clock sharp.

The human behavior formula has never changed. You don't necessarily have to pay more (most Best to Work For companies pay well but not a lot above the average). You don't need Google-size perks. All you need to do is *provide clear parameters* and *treat them right*. Sadly, most companies have no idea what "right" is. Many try quite sincerely to treat their people right but badly miss the mark. We will discuss more what is meant by "right" in chapter 8. Here we look at the very misunderstood topic of *clear parameters*.

Do you realize just how few salespeople know precisely what is expected of them? I have asked hundreds of salespeople how things are going only to hear answers like, "Okay I guess" or, "Good I think" or flat out, "I don't know." The answers that reveal well-defined and well-communicated expectations are, "I am at sixty percent of quota and we're not even halfway through the month!" or, "Not so good this quarter—I'm behind where I should be right now." In other words, *they know*.

In March 2005, Microsoft published the results of a survey they conducted on employee productivity. The results did not surprise me and echo the results of most studies done on this topic. The "Microsoft Office Personal Productivity Challenge," which drew responses from more than thirty-eight thousand people in two hundred countries, rated workers' individual productivity based on their responses to eighteen statements about work-related practices. Cited among the top reasons for lost productivity were unclear objectives and lack of team communication.

There is really no excuse for vaguely communicated deliverables, given the huge cost of the resulting loss of productivity. While some jobs are admittedly more difficult to define in terms of one or two concise results, sales is not difficult at all. This chapter will describe exactly how to establish and communicate job parameters that are fair to all without being limiting, contain strong motivational elements, stimulate performance growth without overpressuring, and leave no doubts as to exactly what must be accomplished in what period of time. These parameters are set by your pay plan and quota system. Before jumping into the specifics, we need a quick lesson in behavior analysis.

BEHAVIOR ANALYSIS AND PERFORMANCE INFLUENCERS

Shaping, association, Pavlov, operant conditioning, consequence, reinforcement, stimulators, antecedents, motivators, triggers . . .

Why do people behave the way they do? What external influences and conditions alter that behavior? Today we have these answers. It has all been studied and formulated and yet it is so rarely applied in the workplace. If you work with other humans, you are subject to the laws of human behavior. Shouldn't we all have at least a crash course in what *really* influences human behavior?

The tool used most by managers to get people to perform as desired is *telling*. Most managers *tell* their people what they want and need them to do. "I need four sales from each of you this week!" "I need that extra effort from you guys." They tell them in meetings. They tell them in e-mails. It's mentioned in passing in the hallway. It's written into contracts. Sometimes it's said in a positive, encouraging way, and other times in a negative, threatening way.

How often have you participated in meetings where some salespeople are "on track" and others are not? What does the manager do in such cases to increase the performance of those who are lagging? He *discusses* it. Either privately or publicly, he discusses it. "You seem to be a little behind." "You'd better get going!" "What can I do to help?" While this may appear supportive, it's really just more *telling*.

Behavior analyst and nationally known performance expert Dr. Aubrey Daniels did a survey that suggested that 85 percent of the average manager's job is spent either *telling* his people what to do, figuring out what to *tell* them to do, or deciding what to do about employees who weren't doing what they were *told*. Many managers believe that's the job description of a manager: to "keep after" their people. But it doesn't work. If it did, performance would at some point raise to the desired level and the manager would no longer be spending 85 percent of the day chasing and *telling*.

While telling your salespeople what is required of them is certainly a necessary step, it actually only needs to be said once. With the right management conditions in place, once is enough.

ABC

The following formula is used in behavior analysis:

Antecedent→Behavior→Consequence

There are only two ways to generate a desired behavior. An *antecedent* is something that comes before the behavior and is intended to generate a particular behavior. A *consequence* is what happens to the person after the behavior, as a result of the behavior.

The big difference between the two is an antecedent will only generate the behavior *once*. How you handle consequences, however, allows you to control behavior over the long term.

Consider a young child who is told by her friend that sticking her tongue on a frozen railing is a wonderful and fun experience. In behavior analysis terms, this is the antecedent—the promise of a wonderful and fun experience. It will likely generate the desired behavior *once*. But it is the consequence that will determine whether the behavior is repeated. If it is indeed fun, the behavior will likely reoccur. But when the child's tongue freezes to the railing and won't come off, she will not likely repeat this behavior.

If you promise a salesperson a huge bonus for opening a record number of accounts this month, this antecedent has a good chance of generating the desired behavior from the salesperson. If he opens those accounts and you *don't* pay the bonus, will he believe you next time you promise the same thing? Of course not. Antecedents generate a behavior *once*.

Consequences, however, are *ongoing* as far as behavior goes and, as such, they are very powerful in stimulating desired behavior. Because if you do pay that bonus you will likely stimulate the same behavior again. And if you were to pay the bonus *and* publicly congratulate the salesperson *and* give her an unexpected dinner for two with your sincere thanks (three consequences), what do you think the behavior might be next time? Furthermore, appreciate the impact this has on the behavior of the other salespeople who witnessed this event. Consequences have been shown to be the most powerful tool for shaping behavior. If you think about a company that you know fairly well, you will agree that most companies use only antecedents—which are considerably less powerful—and don't really understand how to exploit consequences. Let's look at the three dimensions of consequence in ABC analysis, so that you can generate the exact behaviors you need.

1. *Positive* or *negative.* The consequence can be either a positive or a negative one.
2. *Immediate* or *future.* Will the consequence occur immediately after (or during) the behavior, or will it happen some time in the future?
3. *Certain* or *uncertain.* The degree of certainty in the employee's mind that the consequence will in fact occur.

These three dimensions of consequence will be referred to throughout the rest of the book. They are the secret ingredients in your quota, your pay plan, training, and most impacting of all, in the daily relationship between employees and managers. Let's look at some examples many of you are likely experiencing right now.

Many companies pay their salespeople with a base salary plus bonus at year end. All too often the criteria of that bonus are not at all well defined (e.g., exactly when it will be paid, how much it will be, how the amount is calculated, etc.). Sometimes the bonus is dependent on how well *other* people do by year end. This bonus is of course intended to motivate higher sales from the salespeople. Let's see how it measures up as a motivator.

1. *Positive* or *negative?* This consequence will be a positive one.
2. *Immediate* or *future?* End of the year. Definitely future.
3. *Certain* or *uncertain?* Uncertain.

As you're starting to gather, the most impacting arrangement of these three dimensions of consequence is: *positive, immediate,* and *certain*. To that end you can see that this example scored only one out of a possible three. In more human terms, try to put yourself in the salesperson's shoes and imagine the antecedent you're being offered: a bonus that may or may not materialize, whose amount you do not know and is affected by other people's performance (which you have no control over), and all of this will be decided "some time in the future." Not a very big motivator.

Knowing this, let's tweak numbers two and three. A monthly or even weekly bonus, rather than only once per year, would solve number two. So would smaller *short-term* incentives, which we discuss later in the chapter. As for number three, all details of the bonus must be clear, and you must pay the exact amount at the exact time you said you would if you hope to generate the desired behavior repeatedly.

Those of us who have children have the absolute best lessons in behavior analysis right in front of us every day. Now that mine are grown and, I'm proud to say, two very terrific gentlemen, I can attest to how well behavior analysis works. Have you ever watched a parent tell a child that if they don't eat a particular thing on their plate, they won't get dessert? How many times does the child actually eat everything up? Not very often. And are they denied dessert? No, usually they still get the dessert.

This is a psychological mistake for many reasons, but to stay on point, here are the three dimensions of consequence for this example:

1. *Positive* or *negative*? No dessert? It's a negative consequence.
2. *Immediate* or *future*? Immediate.
3. *Certain* or *uncertain*? After this instance, the child now knows it's uncertain.

I said that *positive, immediate,* and *certain* (often referred to as "PIC") is the strongest arrangement. The second strongest—a close runner-up and one that has a specific use—is *negative, immediate,* and *certain* ("NIC"). This is what the parent was going for and, had he stuck to his guns—in this instance as well as those in the future—this consequence *would* have generated the desired behavior. Unfortunately, another effect would have been a screaming child, which is the very reason most parents give in. The lesson for parents is, don't use the antecedent if you don't intend to enforce the consequence. Find a different antecedent.

A worthy side note: this same dessert antecedent could have been made into a *positive, immediate,* and *certain* one (the strongest motivator) just by changing the wording. Instead of "If you don't finish the broccoli, you won't get dessert" try, "If you eat that broccoli all up, I have a nice dessert for you!" Sticking to your guns with consequences is called *reinforcement*—as you are reinforcing certain behaviors repeatedly—and in the workplace positive reinforcement is stronger than negative reinforcement.

One more sales team example—from the most impacting influencer of all: the sales manager. Let's say our sales manager has a promising young salesperson new to his team who, for whatever reason, has had a slow start. If you know what it's like to work among other sales producers, you know the pressure that goes with the job. Nothing feels better than when you're having a great month, and nothing feels worse than when you're behind the eight ball.

Our sales manager wants to get this new salesperson going. Furthermore, the company execs have put some pressure on this sales manager to get everyone up to speed. This is a very realistic, everyday situation. How do the managers you know handle this situation? What do they choose to do to get this new salesperson going?

Remember, the most powerful influence on future behavior is how we handle the consequences of today's behavior. We also know we want to use PIC (*positive, immediate, certain*). So all the sales manager needs to do is find a behavior (almost any behavior will do) to be positive about—perhaps an appointment the salesperson just made. It doesn't matter if the other salespeople have made *three* appointments in the same time frame; this behavior must be reinforced. It need not be over the top; a simple, "Nice job, Jim. I heard you on the phone—that was nicely done" will do perfectly. Soon after, the manager needs to find another behavior to positively reinforce. "That was a good morning, Jim. I can feel your momentum building!"

Prior to these two very simple reinforcements, all of our new salesperson's consequences were negative. He is behind, he feels the pressure, he feels like everyone is watching him. Our sales manager has very quickly created a pattern of positivity. From an ABC perspective, the new salesperson's subconscious has created a cause and effect association—I make a little forward progress, I get praise. Picture how other managers might handle this situation. Some will say, "You'd better get going there, Jim." This is NIC. Every time Jim behaves in this way (lack of productivity) he knows he will be met with a similar remark—a remark that leaves him feeling very negatively. The cause and effect that is created in Jim's subconscious—after only a few instances—is: I'm trying my best and I'm getting scolded.

Another manager might say, "What can I do to help, Jim?" While this is a far more diplomatic and sensitive approach, understand that the message is the same! The message is, "You're behind." The manager has chosen to comment—albeit carefully—on the *negative* side of the situation. The manager above who was versed in behavior analysis waited to comment on a *positive* event—no matter how small. The point is to wait for a positive and then reinforce it. And then do it again. Immediately, consistently, and often (PIC). This approach, known in behavior analysis as "shaping," very quickly builds subconscious cause and effect associations and shapes future behavior.

Do not think this recommends a touchy-feely, "all positive" management style. There are times when reprimands and other negative reinforcements are absolutely necessary to the performance equation. For now, understand that positive reinforcement has long been known to be *the most powerful tool* for programming the desired behaviors in the workplace. PIC and NIC are all you need to understand to create perfect antecedents and consequences—to create the perfect *conditions* for all those top talents to thrive in.

I watched a behavior experiment involving a box full of mice. The goal was to get these mice to exit the box through a little door in the corner. I watched them all scurrying around, apparently quite busy, though I can't imagine with what. It made me think of certain micromanagers I know (those who manage by "telling") who would probably stick their hands into the box to guide all the mice, one by one, through the little door. The mice would likely scurry all around, the manager would then chase them with his hands, and do his best to force all the mice to behave the way he'd like them to.

As many of you may have guessed, the behavioral psychologist leading the experiment put some cheese outside of that little door. The cheese of course is the *positive motivator*. I sat and watched many of the mice scurry through the door but to my surprise, not all of them. Some of the mice—for reasons we can only speculate upon—ignored the positive motivator (the narrator suggested that some of the mice had recently eaten).

The behavioral psychologist then introduced the *negative motivator*—a mini cattle prod that zapped the mice in the behind with a low charge of electricity. Each time a mouse was zapped, it ran for the door. Interestingly, the last remaining mice ran out the door before they ever got zapped. They seemed to understand what was happening; they watched the others and *learned*. In any case, all the mice left through the door. If you alter conditions, you alter behavior.

There you have it—Behavior Analysis 101. Let's return to the program now and apply behavior analysis to this chapter's two performance influencers—pay plan and quota—so we can establish those clear parameters. These parameters form the foundation of the salesperson's world. The reason we cover pay and quota together is because they are the yin and yang of parameters. They are the positive and negative motivators—the PIC and NIC.

PAY AND QUOTA ARE YOUR POSITIVE AND NEGATIVE MOTIVATORS

Most owners and executives focus on all of the *positive* motivators: a strong commission plan, bonuses, perks, and incentives. This is certainly not wrong, but it *is* incomplete (think of those mice). It turns out that a full half of the world's best salespeople are actually more motivated by *negative* motivators—by the ramifications of what will happen if they do *not* accomplish something—than they are by all the rewards of the positive motivators. In spite of the nasty connotation of the word "negative," negative motivators do just that—they *motivate*.

I realize many of you forward-thinking executives will recoil at the phrase *negative motivator*. We have all become so conditioned to the importance of treating our employees well that we

walk on eggshells in the face of anything that might seem negative. While this is understandable, and while I am probably the
world's number one advocate for treating your people like kings
and queens, I must tell you that a negative motivator is not
negative at all. As a matter of fact, you are doing your valued
employees a *disservice* if your program lacks negative motivators.

The explanation is certainly a primal one. You must realize
that there is positive motivation and negative motivation in every task we undertake in our lives. We don't eat just for pleasure
or to become full; we also eat to avoid the very negative feeling
of being hungry. We seek companionship not only for the positive feelings of love, trust, fun, and so on, but also to avoid the
negative feelings that come from being alone. We so often hear
of rich people whose primary reason behind their tremendous
drive to make a lot of money does not come from the list of obvious positives; it is fear of poverty—a negative motivator if I
ever heard one.

Negative motivators are not a negative thing. They are a positive thing with a negative-sounding name, and if you are going to
succeed in creating a top-performing sales force, you must incor-
porate both positive *and* negative motivators in your communal
conditions. The positive motivator is your pay plan. We will start
with the negative motivator: your quota.

PART I: QUOTA

Top sales teams follow this definition of quota:

> The results that a properly cast individual can regularly
> accomplish with reasonable effort.

When quota is structured and used correctly, it is supposed to serve two purposes. First, and as discussed in the previous section, it is a negative motivator. Second, quota becomes the yardstick for assessing properly cast, or miscast, talent. If eighteen of your salespeople consistently exceed quota and two salespeople consistently fall short—despite all the training and support you have provided—then these two are likely miscast in the position and belong elsewhere. When we observe the vast majority of the group happy, thriving, and surpassing quota, while a couple of others seem to work harder but achieve less, it is a clear indication that their talent set has been miscast, despite our best efforts to the contrary.

Quota clarifies everything. The process of choosing specific results that you feel are right for a job—which you do with the sales stage work sheet we went through in chapter 4—will leave you wondering how you ever managed without. It will let you and everyone on your team know precisely what is expected from the position, what they must accomplish as baseline performance, and who is well cast and who is not. It will eliminate the gray areas that inevitably end up creating a model of only *average* performance, and that keep miscast individuals in the wrong position for far too long. A good quota does not necessarily "raise the bar" of expected performance, it merely clarifies it. It also expedites the inevitable. If someone is indeed miscast, then a change in his position is inevitable. And if the employee will perform better and be happier in another position, why prolong the change?

Do not be concerned when you read phrases like *"what they must accomplish as baseline performance"* and *"minimum acceptable performance."* You will not be asking your salespeople to achieve only the minimums. You will be motivating them to levels that are much higher than quota with your pay plan—the positive motivator. But without quota as a reasonable and common base-line, you are not being fair to your salespeople. And without quota as a negative motivator, you are only half motivating.

Let's look at the four components to the definition of quota; they're all important to understand. Once again, quota is:

> The results that a properly cast individual can regularly
> accomplish with reasonable effort.

Results

Results can be defined as monetary values or nonmonetary accomplishments, but they must be results, not activities. As I have stated throughout the book, top performers reach the top via combinations of activities that often differ from performer to performer. If your quota is ten new clients per quarter and Mary achieves this by seeing forty new prospects and closing 25 percent, and John sees sixty-five new prospects and closes only 15 percent of them, the result is the same: ten new clients each.

Picking the perfect results, or quotas, for each job is a critical step, and I absolutely caution you against doing it alone. Enlist the assistance of trusted colleagues. I have often requested input from the salespeople themselves—whatever it takes to get the right number. You very much want to avoid changing quotas once they are in place. The following exercise will help you pick ideal results.

The tasks of every job can be divided into three categories: primary tasks, secondary tasks, and tertiary tasks. Primary tasks are those tasks that make money, and there are usually only two or three in this category, often only one. Secondary tasks are important and support the primary ones, but do not directly produce revenue. Tertiary tasks are everything else: paperwork, reporting, administrative tasks—those things we typically procrastinate about but that are a part of the job.

As an example, suppose your salesperson's job is to visit prospects who were identified, and appointments set, by the appointment-setting team. This salesperson explains your company's product or service and tries to sign up a new client. There will be no ongoing servicing—that's handled by another, internal team.

The various tasks of this job would include:

- Staying current with the industry norms and the market
- Knowing your competition
- Sitting with your prospects (the actual "selling")
- Completing postsale paperwork for the service department
- Making one postsale follow-up call (by phone) to assure client satisfaction
- Attending weekly planning meetings
- Calling to reset appointments for those prospects who had to cancel your appointment at the last minute
- Writing weekly reports
- Attending monthly sales training sessions
- Meeting with your appointment setter regularly to brainstorm ways to lower cancellation rates and improve meeting quality

Of all these job tasks, which would you put into the primary task category? Think of it this way. If the definition is that primary tasks *make you money*, and if you only had time to do one or two of the above tasks, which of them will directly make you money? I see only one: "Sitting with your prospects (the actual 'selling')"—definitely a primary task. I would not argue, however, if you insisted on adding: "Phone calls to reset appointments for those prospects who had to cancel your appointment at the last minute," because this task is directly attached to "sitting with your prospects," but the point is not to debate it. The point is there are only one or two primary tasks.

Secondary tasks include most of the others, with the exception of weekly reports and the like, which are tertiary tasks. The reason these distinctions are important is that *we only attach quotas to primary tasks*. We will not be attaching expected results to, for instance, how current your salespeople remain with industry norms, or how well they know their products, or how fast they get reports to you. The fact is, I have worked with too many superstar, record-breaking salespeople who are *not* the most up to date on product knowledge, know very little about their competitors, and are notoriously late with reports. But they sell four times more than their average counterparts. Would you rather your sales manager manage *this* salesperson's "deficiencies" or those of a fully informed, very report-punctual average seller? I'm not saying we ignore things like tardy reports and poorly informed salespeople; we just don't attach quotas to anything but primary tasks.

Let's take the two primary tasks we identified and turn them into quotas (I'm including that second one, for the illustration). I would say, "Bring in fifteen new clients per quarter and reschedule at least 80 percent of all cancelled appointments." Notice that quotas, or outcomes, always have an amount that defines performance, and a time frame in which to do it. "Fifteen new clients per quarter," "$10,000 revenue per month," and so on. That's it. That's quota. That's what you plug into your sales stage work sheet in the *Desired Result* column.

One more example—this time let's pick the appointment-setting sales stage. Of all the tasks of this job, from compiling lists to regular training and role playing to schedule coordination to actually talking on the phone, we determine that calling new "cold" prospects (as opposed to those you've spoken to before who endlessly tell you, "Not now, call back another time") is the only primary task that should have a quota. How about, "Make no fewer than ten appointments per week for each of your salespeople." That's it! We have the number and the time frame, and it's a result rather than a list of activities (we didn't make quota a number of phone calls. We made it appointments—the *result*). Plug this *Desired Result* into your work sheet.

If the sale is more of an ongoing servicing type, your two primary tasks might be discussing new products with existing clients and maintaining client satisfaction. Your quota therefore could be, "Increase territory revenue by 3 percent per quarter, and maintain CSR (customer satisfaction rate) at no less than 95 percent."

I am often asked about attaching quota to a number of new clients per period versus making quota only a revenue number or a combination of both. In certain sale types, salespeople can grow their territory either by getting more new clients or by selling "deeper" to existing clients. Each of you will have your own internal reasons for wanting either more new clients or more depth—or perhaps a combination of both—so it's really up to you. Just make certain that whatever results you choose to fix with a quota are primary tasks.

Here is a brutally concise tool I have seen used if you are uncertain which results to make into quota. Ask yourself, "If a salesperson does *not* achieve this, will I fire them?" Now, I would ask you to finish the chapter before you e-mail me to tell me off for making such a heartless statement. You will see that this is the perfect tool to cut through the sea of tasks and find exactly what you really want most from your salespeople. Asking yourself this question will save you from having to make a change to your newly created quota—something you very much want to avoid doing.

For instance, if you are considering making quota, "four new clients per month and $10,000 in sales," then test this by asking yourself if you would fire the salesperson who brings five new clients but only $8,000 in sales. If your answer is no, then you need to rethink the wording of this quota. Salespeople must know without any doubt that quota must be attained; you're sending a mixed message if they did *not* attain what you named as quota, but they still had what you all would consider a good month. You might rewrite it to be, "$8,000 per month in sales from new *or* existing clients." You can even make a graduated mix of the two, whereby the more new clients you bring each month, the less revenue you need from existing clients. It depends on your own needs. Just make sure the results you pick are primary tasks only, and that they pass the "brutal" test above. Keep the wording of this test to yourself; it is a tool for creating your quotas, not enforcing them. We do not rule by fear.

Notice how concise the quotas are. They are direct and simple, not verbose. The impact of this step—of simply imparting and imposing these concise deliverables—is staggering. While you will be incentivizing much higher results than these with the pay plan, everyone must be clear on what the acceptable baseline performance is for each job.

Properly Cast Individual

"Properly cast individual" is pretty straightforward. Just remember this is a method that helps you determine whether your recruits are indeed the right talents for the sale type. Quota should be fairly easy for properly cast individuals. It will *not* be easy for those you have unwittingly miscast talentwise.

Regularly

If properly cast, your people should reach quota every period. This is the whole point. It is not a quota if the majority of the salespeople do not attain it regularly. It is also not a quota without ramifications, which we cover shortly.

The correct length of time for a quota *period* is dictated by the sale cycle and by which stage of the sale you are dealing with. If your sale cycle is many months, your quota period might be a calendar quarter, or even a half-year. If your sale is a shorter one, your period might be monthly, or even weekly. When it comes to each sales *stage* (i.e., appointment setting), you might choose "number of appointments per week." If your sale is a one-call-close, and your salespeople see several prospects per day, you might even make quota *daily*.

The rule of thumb is, the shorter the better. Your crash course in behavior analysis taught you *positive, immediate,* and *certain* is the best positive motivator, so we want to reward people *immediately* and *frequently* when they go over quota. The same goes for the negative motivator; if someone misses quota, we want to address it immediately, not once a year. If your sale cycle averages two months, then make your quota four sales (for example) per quarter, rather than sixteen sales per year. Rewarding four times per year is better than once.

With Reasonable Effort

The definition of quota ends with "with reasonable effort" for growth reasons. Quota should define—*very reliably*—what each selling position will produce on a regular basis. If the quotas are reliable for each position you can forecast better and plan a better hiring and growth strategy. Many executives do not currently trust their sales forecasts, particularly when there are many newly hired salespeople, and as a result they spend conservatively. The thinking is, let's see how this new group is doing before we hire any more. But how can you assess the new group's performance if you don't first define what results are correct for the position?

With a hiring process that more reliably casts needed selling talents, and a quota system that clearly and quickly identifies those who may not make it, growth through an aggressive hiring campaign is less risky. And so "with reasonable effort" is in the definition to remind you to define results that can be achieved regularly. We know that with extra effort the salespeople will surpass this number—and they often will, but they cannot be relied upon to do so all the time, which hinders forecasting.

What Quota Isn't

Quota should not to be used to attempt to increase salespeople's performance. A tremendous number of companies increase their salespeople's quota every year in the hope of increasing performance. They sit with each salesperson annually, look at last year's numbers, and then "mutually" agree upon the next year's quota. They are unwittingly employing a negative motivator to do the job of a positive motivator. (It is true that certain territory-building sale types require salespeople to sell *more* each year. We will cover the correct way to structure quota for this sale type.)

The first problem with this approach is, as a motivator—which is the intention—it fails. Test it with PIC.

1. *Positive* or *negative*? Managers believe this to be positive, and sometimes it is. But it is more often negative, as the story in the next paragraph will illustrate.
2. *Immediate* or *future*? Future. One year. Far too long.
3. *Certain* or *uncertain*? Uncertain. If there is a bonus attached to reaching the new annual quota (often there isn't, which instantly renders quota dead as a motivator), reaching it becomes increasingly uncertain, since quota is raised higher—becoming less attainable—each year.

We only want to work with three out of three (PIC or NIC). The above approach to quota scored between zero and one out of three. The following example illustrates the human side of the score above.

I did some work with the sales force of a newspaper. The salespeople had to prospect potential advertisers and then sell them ad space, hopefully week after week.

Of the more than twenty salespeople, the top producer was a woman named Susan. What Susan said to me one afternoon—through teeth clenched tight from stress—should be repeated to all managers who believe in endlessly raising quota year after year. Susan said, "God forbid I make quota this year." When I asked her why she had said that, she looked at me with eyes that I can only describe as *sad* and said, "Because they'll raise it next year."

Think about that. Susan is the newspaper's top salesperson. Are they *trying* to stress her out? Do they *want* her to leave? Of course not. They just don't realize what they're doing. The sad part is, stressing Susan out is the only thing that raising quota each year will accomplish—there isn't even an upside. At least if Susan's performance went up each year there would be something positive (for the company) coming from this situation. But when I asked Susan if she had ever missed quota, she said, "Sure." And when I asked what the ramifications were when quota was not attained, she said that her quota was simply lowered for the next year! At least if there were ramifications enforced we could call this a negative motivator. But you're certainly not going to dismiss or demote your best salesperson.

This is not only a dysfunctional approach to quota, this actually *sabotages* performance. It delivers the exact opposite of what managers are hoping it will. You need to let your pay plan be the positive motivator, not quota.

Earlier I referred to the top salesperson at an insurance client of mine. Gene's book of business is more than *twenty times* the company average and yet year after year, the sales manager imposes an expected increase. Most salespeople in this company will not reach one quarter of Gene's numbers in their entire career. Gene has no time to prospect new business; he takes care of the business he has already built, and rightly so. But every year management asks for more. When I interviewed Gene, he was, to put it mildly, frustrated with management. This man should be treated like gold; instead his company is unknowingly pushing him away.

The second problem with increasing quota each year is that each salesperson can end up with a different quota. I have never met a sales team that agrees with different quotas for different people, and neither do I. If everyone is selling the same things, has the same opportunities with commission and bonus earnings, has the same access to company resources (whatever they may be), and faces the same challenges every day in territories that are more or less equal, then why would one salesperson be expected to sell one amount each year while another salesperson is asked to sell more? Or less?

The Territory-Building Quota

I have said it is wrong to raise a salesperson's quota year after year with no real end in sight. But a great many sale types involve "building a territory" and, therefore, *must* raise quota each year. However, the very same quota definition and rules are applied to this sale.

If your salespeople prospect and close new clients, and then continue to service (and hopefully upsell) these clients into the future, the proper way to structure quota is to identify just what results are the right results for different career levels (i.e., year one, year two, etc.) and these quotas will apply to everyone.

With this sale type, you must also decide on a quota "cap," whereby the career quota levels no longer get higher. You will identify a maximum that you feel is correct for the job, a point where asking the salesperson to hunt for more would be too much. This always makes executives nervous. There's no such thing as too much! For your *company*, perhaps. But for *people*, there is always a point that truly is "enough."

You will not be telling your salespeople to stop. You will simply no longer make "more" an enforced requirement. The pay plan will still do its job and motivate salespeople to higher levels, but the pressure of always having to do more will be removed. In these types of sales, when the various levels are reached (i.e., *Elite Level* or *Presidents Club Level* or *Gold Level*), expected results change. The very job status changes, complete with different pay plans and perks at each new level, as recognition of accomplishment certainly, but moreover because in this type of sale the actual daily job in year one compared to year five is very different. The job changes so the conditions must change as well.

When salespeople of this sale type reach the company's identified "peak"—the highest level—they can just "maintain" if they like. For example, when salespeople reach the million-dollar mark, further growth is no longer mandatory, it's optional. This peak number must be identified carefully of course, but it *must* be identified; otherwise you're working with undefined deliverables. And do not dismiss the importance of taking good care of that million dollars' worth of clientele. I am amazed how many companies lose those clients they spent so much time and money to obtain, because their salespeople are under so much pressure to get new ones that they don't take proper care of the ones they have. We've all heard some variation of the adage that it costs four times more to acquire a new customer than to retain an existing one. In the territory-building sale, every salesperson will reach a point where their primary focus should be service their existing client base; just don't make the mistake of leaving that point ambiguous. You will be hiring new salespeople, into new territories, in order to grow.

There are three additional benefits to working with identified career levels. First, when new salespeople see the higher-level salespeople enjoying the "easier" life, they build their territories faster. They too want that higher-level job. This of course benefits the company.

Second, when you remove the mandatory growth requirement, we tend to see the higher-level people *getting more business.* Definitely a study in psychology! If you continue to force prospecting beyond a point that the salesperson feels is reasonable, they resist. When instead you reward them for their achievements, and then remove further *mandatory* prospecting, they prospect more!

The third benefit is employee retention. Salespeople move around more than other employees do. They are a more entrepreneurial and more confident employee than many others, so leaving one company for another is less scary for them, and we see salespeople moving to new opportunities often—with their clients in tow. But many of these good salespeople will stay if the job and its challenges change and if they know they are working for a company that will gladly discuss their changing career needs. It not only costs less to keep a good client than to find a new one, it also costs less to keep a good salesperson than to find a new one. Remember Susan, the top newspaper ad salesperson, and Gene, the top insurance salesperson? Both were burned out and ready to quit, just because management kept asking for more. Well, there will always come a point where more is simply no longer possible. The funny thing about sales is, it seems to be a profession where admitting this is seen as a weakness. But the smart executives plan for their top salespeople's career high points. They change the job status, pay, duties, and quotas. If a salesperson has several million dollars worth of your clients eating out of the palm of his hand, I recommend you understand his needs and keep him happy. I would also suggest to you that he or she has earned it.

And so our definition of quota still applies, even for the territory-building sale; it's just tailored to this sale type: *"The results that a properly cast individual can accomplish with reasonable effort* **in period one, period two, period three, etc."** These career levels will be addressed again in the pay plan section.

The Salesperson's Contract

Once you have your quotas for every sales stage plugged into the *Desired Result* column of the sales stage work sheet, this becomes the agreement between management and the salesperson and, as such, should be put into the salesperson's contract. If you don't get quite as formal as a contract, write it into the job description that you have for each sales position, but *put it in writing.* We do not do this for the legal reasons usually associated with contracts. We do this because it reinforces quota's intended message: that this is the level of productivity associated with this job, in return for the salary paid.

Put quota in the same section of the contract as the pay plan— right on the same page if you can—again, to emphasize that last sentence. Remember that the quotas you will write into a contract are *only those results that you are enforcing,* not all the details of the job description. Keep your quotas as brief as we did throughout this chapter. If you want to have a list of duties (secondary and tertiary) that are associated with the job, fine. Just don't put them with the quota in the contract; make a separate job description sheet.

Ramp Up

See that you give new hires ample time to learn and adjust and generally acclimatize to their new post, before imposing a quota. This will be written into the salesperson's contract right along with the other details of quota. Example: "After three months of training and field sales coaching, the quota detailed below will commence. No specific quota is imposed during the first three months."

What to Do When They *Don't* Make Quota

Understand: for a ramification to be a ramification it must be enforced. People must *believe* that it will be enforced.

Remember that quota is supposed to describe the job; it quantifies the acceptable level of productivity in return for the salary paid. If the job is not being done, the employees should understand that their position will be given to someone who *can* do the job. This is true in any job, but sales jobs so rarely have clear lines drawn as to what is okay and what is not enough. As I have said before, if eighteen people regularly surpass quota and two rarely even make it to quota, they are simply miscast in this sale and need to be let go. This is why picking the "right" quota is so important; why you need to stick to the definition and guidelines we have just covered.

Please understand that you will not be sitting waiting to pounce on those who miss quota. Turnover is costly. You want to do everything possible to get each and every salesperson to beat quota every period. Chapter 8 gives a sense of how it feels to work for the right manager in a result-managed culture, which is an extremely positive experience. You will be working hard to create a workplace that salespeople love to come to every day, so please do not think this discussion of ramifications harsh. Unfortunately, without clear parameters the picture is incomplete, and parameters are not parameters unless they are respected. These parameters, however, do not need to be broadcast over and over. We don't want a threatening atmosphere of, "You know what happens if you don't make it. . . ." Quota fulfills its intended function perfectly as long as it is *known* and *enforced*.

And so despite your best efforts to hire perfectly every time, despite all the training, coaching, and support you are providing, you will from time to time end up casting someone in a selling role that they are simply not talent equipped for. You will know that this has happened when the salesperson falls short of quota regularly. If they have passed your initial ramp-up period and regularly miss quota—while the majority of the other salespeople meet or surpass quota—you will know. Remember, one of the principal benefits of this quota system is to know with complete certainty, and to know sooner than later.

What do we do with this salesperson now? Ideally, along the way you have come to better understand the person's talent set and see that it fits a different sales stage, so you recast them. This will not be the case every time, however, and this is where *The Perfect SalesForce* is possibly the most reassuring. Releasing someone from his or her job is never an easy thing, and it shouldn't be taken lightly. But the majority of the negativity associated with releasing someone comes from the uncertainty that generally accompanies the decision. Most managers wonder what more they could have done, or if a little more training

THE PAY PLAN AND QUOTAS

might have helped, or if they should wait a little longer. With *The Perfect SalesForce*'s quota system—together with your intimate understanding of selling talents and your knowledge that talent *cannot* be trained—you always know you are making the right decision.

Every salesperson I have managed since the early nineties has understood natural talent and the idea behind quota, because I explained it to them. The people you manage need to know just how you make these hiring and firing decisions. This way, when the unfortunate time comes, everyone knows that it was a case of bad casting, that the person in question is not a "bad" person. This system removes any trace of judging a *person*. It's about the talents we all possess, and finding everyone's perfect job match. It's not about how we feel about someone; it's about whether they delivered the results that everyone knows are the right results for that job. Whenever I have had to release someone, I make sure they understand this, and I coach them on the type of job I feel they are better suited for. And you should know that a great many of them have contacted me down the road and told me how well they're doing now that they're better cast.

One last thing about missing quota. If a salesperson who usually reaches and surpasses quota suddenly starts to fall short, there's no need to instantly pounce on him. You're not looking to reprimand, you are looking to praise. It's all about catching people when they do things well, not when they err. You are looking to celebrate victories every single period. If personal issues begin to affect an employee's performance, the sales manager needs to step in immediately, but not to scold or to wave quota in someone's face. One of the sales manager's primary jobs is to care for those in her charge. If a valued employee is having trouble, he deserves help, guidance, and support.

Now that we have established the performance baselines for

each selling role and established the negative motivators, let's get positive. It's time to create pay plans that *really* motivate.

PART II: PAY PLAN

Let's balance those parameters now and create the positive motivators. Let's tell salespeople what happens when they blow quota out of the water every period.

In the behavior analysis discussion at the beginning of the chapter, I explained how an annual bonus does *not* create PIC motivation (*positive, immediate,* and *certain*). In this section I will impart and dissect pay plans that *do*. I'll also share some stories of the companies that pay in these ways.

Every sales pay plan must address three components:

1. Base salary
2. Commission
3. Short-term incentives

For those of you asking where the "perk" category is, you will remember that perks may help in attracting new employees to come work for your company, but they are rarely performance influencers. We do need to touch on them, though, and they are discussed with the base salary.

1. Base Salary

Interestingly, the base salary is not a performance influencer either, at least not the way we see base salary typically being used. If I tell you that I will pay you more if you sell more, then I am incentivizing performance. The base salary, however, is paid no matter how much or how little you produce and is therefore not usually a performance influencer. The exception to this would be to offer a salesperson a $300,000 base salary with no commission component at all, but with a required productivity level (i.e., $1 million in quarterly sales) that he *must* meet each period or be fired, no questions asked. By definition this would turn the base salary into a performance influencer.

Of course, this is not an affordable approach, since salespeople need a training period, a ramp-up period, and a time period for filling the pipeline once they start. You would be out of pocket a lot of money by the time you found out which salespeople are going to make it and which aren't. And so performance-based remuneration was born.

In past decades, paying a salesperson 100 percent commission was the norm. In a time we now refer to as the industrial era of selling, base salaries and perks were not used in sales. "Perks" wasn't even in the vocabulary. Those were the days when people were thankful to have a job at all, a contrast to today's mind-set of entitlement.

I will leave it to you to debate whether it is better or worse today, but I'll say one thing for certain. Pay plans were easier, quotas were easier, hiring was easier, and managing was easier. If you were to turn the clock back thirty years, there would be no need for this book or for my consulting company, and this is why an understanding of the "100 percent commission culture" is a valuable lesson.

While it does not go over very well today, a terrific argument can be made for a 100 percent commission culture. Management doesn't have to pay a base salary. No special hiring methodology or talent-identification process is necessary since the salespeople who end up selling well obviously possess the correct talents for the sale—whatever they might be. You hire almost constantly and whoever makes it makes it. The pay plan couldn't be easier to conceive and manage.

Most companies that pay 100 percent commission pay a very good commission rate, so those who sell well make an exceptional income, are quite happy, and stay. (To this day, the highest-paid salespeople I have seen—across all industries—are paid with a "no ceiling" straight commission. I know quite a number who make over $1 million annually.) With no salaries, those who don't sell well cost you nothing to try out. Quotas aren't even necessary because there is no salary to offset. Although turnover is higher, those salespeople who do "make it" tend to be superior producers. Managing is far more straightforward.

I cite this older sales model because it demonstrates the simplicity and clarity of purpose of a sales-centric culture. *Get sales.* The simple fact that I have to remind companies how to clearly communicate and enforce deliverables is testimony to how recent generations have strayed from that clarity.

So why not simply make your pay plan 100 percent commission? Why not return to the simple clarity of "You sell, I pay. . . . You don't, I don't"? Because times have changed. Over the last thirty years the 100 percent commission sales job has by and large disappeared, forced out by a generation that wants to know what the employer is going to do for them before they even consider working there. This mind-set is due in large part to the massive increase of people who now have university degrees compared to thirty years ago. The employees who you hire today are far more "qualified" and you have to pay for that with a fairly substantial base salary and perks. This has become the norm and if you don't offer this, you aren't current. Right or wrong, the mind-set has changed and a 100 percent commission job is perceived to be not as good. Most salespeople will walk away from the interview as soon as they learn the job is commission only.

There are still industries that pay 100 percent commission today and do very well. Insurance, financial planners, real estate, and time share salespeople are just a few. It is interesting to note that these sales jobs do *not* require a university degree (though some require certification), yet their salespeople are among the highest paid. These industries do well because they have made adjustments to address the downside of straight commission—the perceived lack of security for salespeople. They have addressed this by properly managing and budgeting for the higher turnover that accompanies these jobs, and by introducing a base salary component and perks—which brings us back to the topic at hand.

Your base salary and perks are more of a hiring tool than a motivator. The 100 percent commission industries mentioned above have begun to offer a base salary (they might call it a draw or a guaranteed minimum) during the initial training and ramp-up period, to address the money you won't be making while you're new at the job. But after a specified amount of time, you're flying solo at 100 percent commission.

I am always being asked how much should be base and how much should be commission. The answer is this: the ideal pay plan is the one that pays just enough of a base to attract the person you need for your sale type, and enough commission that high performers make a lot of money. *That's* the right balance.

My expertise lies in human productivity and I am a real advocate for performance-based remuneration. Straight commission— long term and short term (we will discuss short-term incentives shortly)—is simply the best way to motivate performance but, as we have noted, it is no longer realistic today. You need to offer a base salary just to get the caliber of candidate you want to come to interview with your company. But there are many ways to blend the base salary into the commission plan, to in fact offer the security of that base salary and yet still make use of a very performance-driven remuneration—the best of both worlds. I will give examples of this when we put all the pieces together later in the chapter.

2. The Commission Component

I think every position in every company should be remunerated based on performance. If you are a better cashier than the one beside you (you're faster, you make fewer mistakes, et cetera), then you should make more money than she does. If you are a shipping and receiving clerk who picks up and ships orders faster than the other shippers, you deserve to make more than they do. If you program faster than the other programmers do, your paycheck should reflect that. The more you think about this idea the more sense it makes. Performance-based remuneration should not be limited to sales positions.

That said, this book deals with sales positions only and I hope you have guessed what our gauge is when creating pay plans. *Positive, immediate,* and *certain.* And where pay plans are concerned, the *positive* component means that you pay top performers very well.

There are books and courses on the supposed myriad of ways to remunerate the sales force. Too many of the pay plans in such books are conceived with management foremost in mind—simple to administrate, straightforward to calculate and measure. Contrary to this approach, I urge you to first create the most motivating pay plan possible for your *salespeople,* and *then* make it fit with management. When you filter out those plans that do not respect PIC, that myriad of pay plans is reduced to only a handful. Paying salespeople a percentage of the sale is a pretty straightforward concept; there are only so many variations. I will share with you the practices that I have learned from the best out there.

We will go through the three-step process to create the perfect pay plan in the next section. First, I'll discuss some commission concepts that we will be using there.

Complacency and the Sliding-Scale Commission I'm sorry to say that every salesperson has a "complacency point"—we all do, actually. There is a point where we will work no harder, despite the knowledge that we would make more money if we did. Everyone's complacency point is a different number, but everyone has one.

Most managers and executives I know want endlessly *more* from their salespeople, and most get quite frustrated when their salespeople reach that complacency point. As I have said, decide what amount you'll be happy with and call it quota, and then *incentivize* much more. A complacency point exists in all humans; it's as human as getting hungry. We grow companies by identifying these "correct" levels of productivity for each sales position and then hiring aggressively to plug more people into the model—not by constantly exploring ways to get more and more from existing people.

This of course does not mean that we don't keep trying to incentivize higher performance and find conditions that will push the complacency point ever higher. That is allowed. Why? Because if a manager is pushing *conditions* rather than pushing each salesperson, it will be the *salesperson's choice* whether or not to reach higher. There can be no resentment, because no one is continually asking for more. The conditions simply provide new opportunities for the salespeople to pursue, if they so choose.

That said, the following commission practice is the only one I have ever found that addresses complacency. I have watched it push people right out of their comfort zone into new levels of productivity, changing behavior by changing the conditions. It's called "sliding-scale commissions" and it's simple and customizable. In a nutshell, the more you sell, the higher *rate* of commission you will receive on your total sales. If you are currently paid a commission of 15 percent, then certainly it is true that the more you sell, the more you make. But this model does not address complacency very well.

If I tend to sell around the million-dollar range, then I make $150,000 a year. Let's say it's late Friday afternoon and my son has a baseball game at 7:00 P.M.—something I look forward to all week. A prospect I have been working on is ready to go ahead very soon, and he's on my way home. The sale would be about $2,000, putting $300 in my pocket. Do I go see him now or do I catch up with him early next week? That prospect will still be there Monday, and I don't want be late for the baseball game. What's $300 today versus next week, right? Welcome to the complacency zone.

It is hard to argue with this situation. You cannot tell this salesperson what his values should be—they are what they are. What you *can* do is use a sliding-scale commission plan. Instead of paying that 15 percent across the board, pay 11 percent, 14 percent, 17 percent, and 20 percent depending on the volume that is sold in a period. When you introduce different revenue levels, and attach higher commission rates at each level, salespeople immediately begin to do the math in their heads.

EXAMPLE OF A SLIDING-SCALE COMMISSION PLAN

Quarterly Sales	Commission	
$125,000	11%	←(Quota)
$175,000	14%	
$225,000	17%	
$275,000	20%	

The first level, $125,000 in sales, is the quota. As stated in the quota section, keep your quota periods as short as they can be. If your sale cycle averages two to three months, make your periods quarterly.

For reaching only the quota level in this example, salespeople will make a commission of 11 percent on that quarter's sales (the equivalent of $55,000 annually). Remember, we're defining quota as *the results that a properly cast individual can regularly accomplish with reasonable effort,* which means this level is supposed to be pretty easily achieved.

If by quarter's end salespeople have surpassed quota and made it to the $175,000 level, then the commission jumps to 14 percent on the total sales for that quarter; $225,000 in sales will raise the payout to 17 percent; and $275,000 pays 20 percent.

As a salesman, my brain is suddenly telling me, "Hmm . . . if you stop by that prospect on the way home and close him, that $2,000 sale brings this quarter's numbers into the $225,000 category—which means everything jumps to 17 percent. Seventeen percent of $225,000 is $38,250 for the quarter. If I *don't* make the sale this quarter, I'm still at 14 percent of $223,000, which pays me $31,220." On the old pay plan that little $2,000 sale I was reluctant to go to on a Friday afternoon was only worth $300 to me. On the sliding-scale pay plan it's worth over $7,000 to me! I think my son will forgive me if I miss the first inning.

Whenever I design these sliding-scale plans with a company, and we are identifying the different revenue levels, there always comes a point where management says, "We can stop there. . . . No one has ever reached those numbers." I encourage them to continue, just in case. And salespeople go ahead and break these records every time! When you identify a target, human nature says, "Oh look, a target. A target with a bigger prize than the one down here." And when someone reaches that target others are compelled to follow, and then that *other* human trait, competition, kicks in: "Who will be the first to break the *next* level?"

Hoarding Sales The sliding-scale mentality addresses another sales department nuisance: *hoarding* sales. If you have been a salesperson you know how it feels to be behind the pack. And you also know how great it feels to be ahead of where you need to be in the period. An interesting side effect of this sales life is hoarding when you are ahead of the game. Like a squirrel packing nuts away for a less abundant season, our nature tells us to store. If the sales manager wants $125,000 per quarter, and I'm already ahead of that with three weeks left in this quarter, I'm going to stall those sales that I know are imminent in order to have them go to next quarter's numbers. I'll be starting ahead of the game next quarter! This applies in certain sale types only, but it happens often.

You can see how sliding-scale payouts address hoarding when crossing each new level means thousands in income. You can see why we want shorter periods wherever possible. Payouts are very *positive,* they are *immediate,* and they are *certain* (PIC). If payouts only occur annually—even if the total amount earned is the same— you lose your *immediate* component, and the *certain* component becomes far less so.

3. Short-Term Incentives

I worked with a management consulting firm in the mid-nineties that was, in short, a sales machine. I learned a lot there.

In their fifth year they began to experiment with short-term incentives, in addition to an already compelling pay plan. Their periods were weekly—nice and short—so victories were celebrated often. There was a very positive atmosphere, with a dynamic and caring owner, and they were growing at record-breaking speed. A result-based management system had created autonomous, ultra-productive employees. I don't mind admitting I was skeptical that the introduction of short-term incentives would actually raise productivity—particularly because they were *small* incentives (i.e., two extra sales today gets you a dinner-for-two certificate) and salespeople were already making very good money.

But I was wrong. After a very successful test and some tweaking, short-term incentives became part of the budget. They now have several every single day. The deeper understanding of behavior analysis I acquired a short time later taught me why it works.

Short-term incentives have many benefits. They keep things fresh and fun. They definitely fit PIC. They also fit a behavior analysis technique known as "shaping." Shaping tells us to reward smaller (hence very achievable) victories often, which quickly forms cause and effect associations in our salespeople's minds. Shaping allows you to program, or *shape,* behavior.

Another benefit of short-term incentives is control. If you have a surplus of a particular product that you want reduced, attach today's incentive to the sale of that product. If you have a huge surplus of frequent flyer points, make today's incentive free airline passes. If you need that new product market tested quickly, incentivize it over the other products for a week or two.

Short-term incentives should be part of any sales-centric culture. They complete your dedication to PIC. Now let's assemble these three pay plan components.

Putting It All Together

With these components explained, let's construct some pay plans. First, forget about your current pay plan. Just as you did when you brainstormed new arrangements of sales stages in chapter 5, you must put aside your current reality and pretend you are writing the perfect pay plan from scratch, and for a whole new group of salespeople. We'll deal with how to introduce a new pay plan to your current people later.

Let me answer the very popular question, "How much should they make?" Your top producers should make a "whole lot," your really good producers should do "really well," those who only make quota should only make the base, and those who never make quota (after sufficient ramp-up of course) should be replaced.

Each of you has a different profit margin on your products and services and this is certainly relevant to how much of the pie can be shared. My advice is, do not be greedy. If you are lucky enough to enjoy decent margins, and you implement the practices in this book to cast top producers, it will not serve you to be stingy on pay day. The best sales teams are stingy with their stingy producers. They pay their top performers well.

You want to keep your pay plans as simple as possible (just like in the old days). Use this three-step process to build your perfect pay plan:

1. Calculate exactly *how much* pay you have to share with the sales department.
2. Decide exactly *who* you'll share the pay with.
3. Divide the pay among the three pay plan components: *base, commission,* and *short-term incentives.*

Before I explain these three steps, let's be clear on *what* you are rewarding. Just as the quotas are attached to the *Desired Results* you entered on your work sheet, so are the pay plans. By deciding which results you wanted from each stage of your sale, you simultaneously decided exactly what it is that you will be paying for. If the *Desired Result* of the first sales stage is "not less than three product demos scheduled per salesperson per day," then product demos are what you're paying for—it's the very thing you're now incentivizing for this sales position. The next sales stage (and

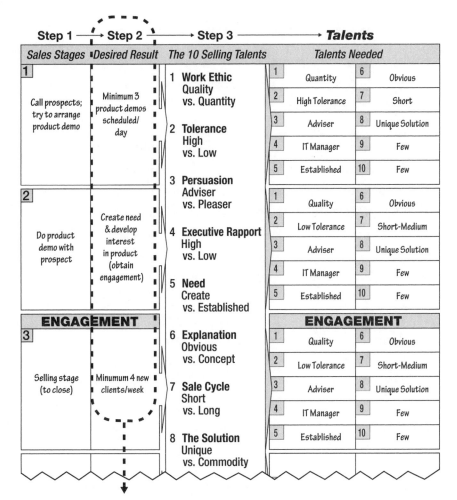

Step 1 →	Step 2	→ Step 3			Talents		
Sales Stages	Desired Result	The 10 Selling Talents			Talents Needed		

Sales Stage 1 — Call prospects; try to arrange product demo
Desired Result: Minimum 3 product demos scheduled/day

The 10 Selling Talents:
1 **Work Ethic** Quality vs. Quantity
2 **Tolerance** High vs. Low
3 **Persuasion** Adviser vs. Pleaser

1	Quantity	6	Obvious
2	High Tolerance	7	Short
3	Adviser	8	Unique Solution
4	IT Manager	9	Few
5	Established	10	Few

Sales Stage 2 — Do product demo with prospect
Desired Result: Create need & develop interest in product (obtain engagement)

4 **Executive Rapport** High vs. Low
5 **Need** Create vs. Established

1	Quality	6	Obvious
2	Low Tolerance	7	Short-Medium
3	Adviser	8	Unique Solution
4	IT Manager	9	Few
5	Established	10	Few

ENGAGEMENT

Sales Stage 3 — Selling stage (to close)
Desired Result: Minimum 4 new clients/week

6 **Explanation** Obvious vs. Concept
7 **Sale Cycle** Short vs. Long
8 **The Solution** Unique vs. Commodity

ENGAGEMENT

1	Quality	6	Obvious
2	Low Tolerance	7	Short-Medium
3	Adviser	8	Unique Solution
4	IT Manager	9	Few
5	Established	10	Few

*Establishes the quota for each sales stage
*Establishes what the pay plans will be based on

salesperson) in our example is accountable for "minimum four new clients per week." Per our formula, that means they will be paid the base remuneration for those four, and we will seriously incentivize reaching *beyond* four new clients per week in the pay plan.

Step 1: Calculate exactly how much pay you have
to share with the sales department.

For many of you this is a straightforward calculation. If, however, your company has different profit margins on different product lines or services, you may choose to factor that in. If you pay 20 percent commission on *everything* you may well make money on some products but lose money on others. If a salesperson gravitates to selling only those low-margin products, you're in a pickle. I have witnessed this many times and management usually addresses the situation by telling the salesperson to sell the other products more, or they even make alterations to the commission. This is wrong. The salesperson did what was asked of him; it is management's duty to structure a pay plan that is profitable to the company as well as the salesperson. We know how it goes when managers tell the salesperson to sell those other products more. . . . Telling doesn't work, conditions do. The conditions of your pay plan will help to create the behaviors you seek. If you do in fact want certain products to be sold more than others, you know by now that you need to attach more attractive conditions to those products. You may even choose to write this into your quotas. The point is to address these details *before* the behavior, not after. That's the thing about behavior analysis—whatever behavior your salespeople are engaging in, you can be sure *you* created it. Set your antecedents correctly.

I participated in creating a pay plan for a manufacturer that had thousands of products. Some were manufactured on premises, others purchased and distributed—so they all had different margins. The old pay plan paid the same commission rate, regardless of the product. This meant if one salesperson sold $500,000 worth of a manufactured product, and another sold $500,000 worth of a distributed product, they would both receive the same commission payout. And yet, the profit on manufactured goods was 30 percent, where it was only 5 percent on distributed items! Obviously, management wanted more high-profit sales, but the salespeople gravitated to all the lower-profit, distributed products because they tended to be much higher priced! Salespeople made more money with less effort selling these products.

Behind closed doors my client would tell me how disappointed he was in his salespeople, that they didn't see the bigger picture, but the fact is the salespeople were behaving perfectly in accordance with the conditions my client had created. We scrapped the old pay plan and implemented one based on *profit*, not sales, which solved the problem.

The profit-based pay plan addresses a second, very common issue—*pricing*. Salespeople will most often do whatever it takes to get the sale, including dropping the price more often than management agrees with—particularly in the commodity sale where, unfortunately, it is all too often necessary. Management responds by insisting that any price change request be approved, which has salespeople on the phone to a manager for almost every sale. Once again, these are dysfunctional conditions. You would be removing some of the control the salesperson has over getting the sale, control over his very income. In PIC language, you must appreciate that you would affect the *certain* element, and perhaps even the *positive*.

The salesperson *should* have control over pricing—to a preset point. In the first chapter I noted that companies seem to have lost trust in their salespeople's in-the-moment judgment. Assuming you implement these six practices as intended, you will have cast top talents into their perfect selling roles, you will have trained them well (including training on how to handle price reductions), and each salesperson will bring you the desired amount each period. You now have to trust this behavior system, and trust that each salesperson will do everything they possibly can in the moment to avoid a price drop, particularly when they are paid based on profit! The more they drop the price, the less they make. By paying this way, you have set the correct conditions for the behaviors you seek; you cannot then go and micromanage it by insisting on manager involvement for every price talk.

I am not suggesting that every pay plan should be based on profit, but if you have varying profit margins or in-the-moment pricing, you may want to consider it. However you do it, calculate how much of every sale you have available to pay out in commission. Pretend there is no base salary involved. Pretend it's the old days of 100 percent commission. What is the total percent of the sale (or the profit) that you can give to those who participated? We're trying to keep this as simple as "If a salesperson sells $50,000 worth of my product each quarter, I can give a total of 15 percent of it away. I could give less, but I cannot give any more than 15 percent."

Step 2: Decide exactly who you'll share the pay with.

We want to incentivize every selling position. If, following the sales stage work sheet brainstorming, you do in fact have more than one selling position contributing to a final sale, then you have to divide up the pie. Go back to your work sheet and look at the flow of sales stages. If you have for instance telephone "openers" setting appointments for your salespeople to demo your software, then they need to get a piece of that commission you calculated in step 1. If there is the need for a technical specialist to help the salesperson with some of the more specialized aspects of the sale, then they too get a piece. And you will incentivize the *Desired Result* that you need from them.

Caution! As you create your sales stages and their corresponding pay plans, *do not* have Peter pay Paul. If our technical specialist Paul is needed on a sale, and you have structured your pay plan in such a way that Tech Paul's piece of the pie is taken from salesman

Peter, realize that Peter will never call upon Paul for assistance. I know a car dealership that encourages its salespeople to call upon the sales manager to help close deals. The sales manager is a valuable resource—bringing him into the sale at a strategic point is *known* to raise the closing ratio. However, on these manager-assisted sales, the dealership decided the sales manager's commission would come from the salesperson. The salesperson's commission is split with the manager. As you can imagine, the salespeople at this dealership do not often ask their manager for help.

This dysfunctional arrangement of conditions costs the dealer significant revenue, since they know they close more when the manager gets involved. The manager should obviously be paid out of the available total commission you calculated in step 1, not out of the salesperson's pocket. If the manager is not used on a particular sale, that extra commission doesn't need to be paid out, but you should always budget for it.

List every participant who is, or can be, involved in the sale, right back to lead generation. Think of the bottlenecking we have referred to. If leads don't come in at a rate that satisfactorily supplies twenty-five appointment setters, who must then supply appointments to eighteen salespeople, productivity will bottleneck. This is why we quota and incentivize the *Desired Result* of *every* sales stage. If a manager is needed only sometimes (as in the car dealership above), or perhaps a technical person from time to time, factor them in. Make sure you list everyone.

Step 3: Divide the pay among the three pay plan components: base, commission, and short-term incentives.

Now that you've decided exactly how much you have to share, and everyone you will possibly be sharing it with, you can break it into the three pay plan components for each selling role.

We want the performance-based components (commissions and short-term incentives) to make up as much of the total remuneration as possible. Remember, there is no pay plan more motivating to performance than 100 percent commission. We have acknowledged, however, that we need that base and those perks today to attract the right people to your company. So remember the rule of thumb cited earlier: *The ideal pay plan is the one that pays just enough of a base to attract the person you need for your sale type, and enough commission that high performers make a lot of money.*

Let's start with that first sales stage in the example we have been using. In the *Desired Results* column on the work sheet we wrote: "minimum 3 product demos scheduled per day." As you know it is this result that we attach quota *and* incentives to. Three product demos is the quota, and the base salary should cover this level of productivity. The salesperson who performs at this level only should not make a fortune. The base salary you choose should be only as high as is needed to attract the education and experience needed for this job.

Next, apply the sliding-scale commission philosophy. Create different commission percentages for four product demos per day, five demos, six demos, and so on. Remember that for this to work, the extra earning potential at each new level must be significant. If I consistently give four demos per day and earn $900 a week, and reaching the six demos per day level earns me a total of $950 a week, this is *not* enough extra money to motivate me to give the extra effort required. I'll settle for the $900.

Another caution: don't make your levels unreachable. Don't create a plan that promises huge earnings at levels that no one can ever reach. The mind-set is you *want* to pay this money out; you *want* to motivate everyone to give the effort required to earn the big money.

You may be wondering how to attach a monetary value to the

demo scheduler's sliding-scale payout. After all, salespeople sell: they generate revenue that we can pay a percentage of. But the only thing a demo scheduler "sells" is an appointment for the salespeople—no monetary value to attach a commission rate to. There are only two choices. You can decide on a flat value per demo appointment, or a percentage of the final sale if and when it happens. Note that if you choose the first one, it should be a flat value that increases as the employee reaches those different levels. Don't just pay $30 for every appointment over and above those three per day that are required. Instead, make it $25 each for the fourth and fifth, and if they make it to six the $25 changes to $30, but not just for that sixth appointment—pay $30 for *each of the fourth, fifth, and sixth*! And if they get to seven or eight per day, they *all* change from $30 to $35. *This* is how we use a sliding-scale commission plan. If you do the math, payouts change significantly at each level, which is the motivating factor. With this plan, it is common to have salespeople sitting in the same area, doing the same job all day (although at different levels of productivity), and earning *very* different livings! There is no animosity because there is no favoritism—everyone has the *same* earning opportunity. Instead, people are *motivated* by the high earners they see around them.

The second way to pay out the different levels in this position is to give a percentage of the final sale. Let me share my experience with these two different payouts and save you learning a lesson the hard way. *You must be mindful of the behavior you will be creating.* Remember I said that whatever the salespeople are doing, *you* created those behaviors with the conditions you chose. If you incentivize the *quantity* of demo appointments (which we did above), you may find that the *quality* of the appointments suffers. I have structured these selling positions and corresponding pay plans many times, and people "react" the same way every time. Human behavior is actually quite predictable.

You may try to control the quality of the appointment for instance by insisting that appointments are to be made only with a decision maker. Well, if you are incentivizing *quantity* of appointments, and a demo-scheduling salesperson has someone on the line who is very interested, she won't be as respectful of that decision-maker criteria. She is thinking, "Another appointment, another $35!" (Which is what she is *supposed* to be thinking—it's the behavior you created.) What I have done to address this in the past is to pay the commission only if and when the *sale closes*. This way the demo scheduler will try to make the quality of the appointment as high as possible, so that her chances of another commission go up. This has usually worked well but brings up another pay issue: the idea of remunerating team performance. I will discuss teams shortly. Let's finish this pay plan.

The only component left to create is the short-term incentives, which are pretty straightforward. Some examples: "Everyone who writes at least six appointments today gets $50 today." Or, "Your sixth appointment gets you $25; your seventh gets you another $50!" Pay out the incentives the same day; don't add them to the bimonthly paychecks. Remember PIC. *Immediate* should mean immediate, especially since we're talking short-term incentives that you offer several times per week, if not daily. It also contributes to the *certain* aspect of PIC motivation when employees watch a manager walk around handing out checks. You can also use gift certificates; just make sure they are for products or stores that people really want. Another short-term incentive idea is "[your company name] Dollars," which can buy various prepurchased items. Have the items *there* (in the lunch room, for instance), not in a catalog. It needs to be *immediate* and *certain*.

Beware of contests in your short-term incentives, like "Whoever writes the *most* appointments today gets a $100 dinner gift certificate." This will only pay *one* person whereas "Everyone who writes at least six appointments today gets a $50 bill" will likely pay *many* people. There is nothing wrong with contests as long as you make sure to include enough of the other incentives as well. Mix it up. Play with it and measure the performance results.

Let's look at the pay plan for the next sales position. The next sales position that our work sheet produced consisted of sales stages 2 and 3 (because the talents needed were identical for both), and the ultimate *Desired Result* of the job was "minimum 4 new clients per week."

The structure of this pay plan will be very similar to the last one. You may need a higher base salary, as the salesperson will likely need to be of a higher caliber (more experienced, perhaps a little older, possibly having a university degree). This salesperson must after all bring the sale to a close and get someone to spend money, where the demo scheduler just writes appointments, which is an easier "sale."

Aside from the higher base, the sliding-scale commission plan and the short-term incentives would be used in exactly the same manner for this pay plan.

The Territory-Building Pay Plan

In the quota section we discussed the territory-building sale, where salespeople must close new clients *and* continue to service those clients ongoing. We talked about the need for identifying different "career levels" for this sale, and this of course fits very nicely with the sliding-scale levels we have been talking about.

There is an extra layer to consider in the pay plan of this sale type. When your sale only involves selling something and then moving on to the next prospect—with no future servicing—then your salesperson is simply paid their commission for that sale. But if the salesperson will continue to service the account, she should be compensated for that ongoing effort. You must reward her for getting the new client, and you must reward again for keeping, servicing, or upselling the account. While execs know this, most battle with the correct balance; that is, they want to reward well enough that their people are motivated to sell a lot, but not so well that salespeople stop working after a point because they're making so much money (the complacency point).

In the territory-building sale, different industries will all have different levels of effort required to service and retain clients. Some sales require nothing more than popping in from time to time to make sure everything's still okay—the insurance business, for instance, where clients only renew annually. Others require nearly full-time effort, like the transport and shipping business, where salespeople compete daily for the many shipments each month that the client can buy from almost anyone. Office supplies, industrial cleaning products, and packaging materials—to name just a few more—will all require different amounts of time and effort to retain and service the client. Many purchasers are instructed to shop such services regularly, regardless of how many years they may have been buying from your company.

Remember that in the territory-building sale type we want to set quotas for year one, year two, and so on that represent acceptable performance levels as the career evolves. (In the first year only, you can break it down even further—into quarters or months.) Well, you want to do the exact same thing with the pay plan. And knowing that the structure of your pay plan has the power to produce whatever behaviors you want, what exactly do you want to incentivize? New business? Selling more to existing clients? Both? The fact of the matter is, it's a different answer at different points in the salesperson's career!

Always start with your work sheet. This will determine the *Desired Results*, which you then incentivize. Ask yourself which one or two primary results you want from this job, recognizing that in the territory-building sale the answer to that question changes throughout the salesperson's career. In the early years they will prospect more and service less (they have fewer clients to serve). As time goes on, that balance will flip the other way as they get more and more clients. This is why top sales teams designate "career levels," with different conditions at each level.

Most companies have not considered this. Their pay plans are simply "15 percent commission on everything you sell" or "base plus 10 percent." This is not *wrong* but if you hope to capitalize on behavior analysis and PIC, it's not nearly as effective as it could be.

The following chart offers an example of evolving career levels.

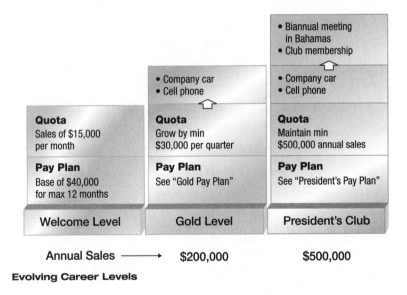

Evolving Career Levels

For simplicity I have identified three levels but, of course, this is up to you. Note that the perks increase with each level, as does the pay plan (we will look at a sample pay plan shortly). *The more appealing each level is, the more motivated your salespeople will be to reach it.* The pay plan at the first level is that guaranteed base that we need to offer in order to attract good salespeople. This base lasts a maximum of twelve months—the negative motivator that will motivate salespeople to reach $200,000 in sales more quickly. After twelve months of base salary, 100 percent commission kicks in.

Notice that the quota does not distinguish between new and existing clients, it's just a revenue amount. This means that the company has chosen not to designate; all they want is growth, whether that growth comes from new clients or account penetration. You will see that the *rate* of growth (in the quota) decreases in the Gold Level, to acknowledge that salespeople will be able to spend *less* time prospecting new business now that they have more existing clients to maintain.

Everything is simple and clear. Revenue levels clearly state *when* you will jump up. The pay, perks, quotas, and resources are clear at each level. If you imagine what it is like to work with career levels like this, compared to the contrasting and more typical "base plus 10 percent," it is easy to see why growth rates are faster with career levels. Now let's dissect a little further and look at a sample pay plan taken from the Gold Level.

The first step in creating a pay plan is determining how much you have to "give away." This amount is then split between commissions, short-term incentives, and so on. For this example let us assume we have a total of 30 percent (of sales) to give to the salesperson. Our goal with this pay plan is to get salespeople from $200,000 in sales to $500,000 as quickly as possible. Yes, the changes in conditions at the President's Club level are a motivator, but you must always think PIC—*positive, immediate,* and *certain.* It could take two years to get from one level to the next and remember, we want to reward *frequently* and we want to capitalize on the motivating properties of the sliding-scale commission.

You could simply pay 30 percent of sales at the Gold Level. If you do the math at that level you can see the earnings would be quite good. But remember my Friday-afternoon-going-to-my-son's-baseball-game story. If we can break up the $300,000 that it takes to get to President's Club level into smaller pieces, and have the commission percentage jump as salespeople reach each one, they *will* reach President's Club sooner.

SLIDING-SCALE PAY PLAN: *GOLD LEVEL*

Sales	Commission
$200,000	22%
$275,000	24%
$350,000	26%
$500,000	28%

Here we have broken that $300,000 into four "jump points." Each time a salesperson reaches the new sales level, their commission increases by 2 percent *on their total sales*. When you're selling around the $300,000 mark, a 2 percent jump represents a $6,000 raise!

We said we had 30 percent available to pay in total commission. The reason the chart stops at 28 percent is because you want to keep some money in the budget for short-term incentives. You want to take that maximum available payout and spread it among different incentive levels, *and* make good use of PIC in your short-term incentives. In addition to the commission rate jumping up, you might also want to throw in an additional bonus (i.e., $1,000) as salespeople reach each new jump point. As long as you are respecting *positive, immediate,* and *certain*, there is no limit to how creatively you can motivate with your pay plan.

One suggestion before you finalize any new pay plan. Gather a few salespeople who you have come to know and trust and run it by them. You'll get good feedback from the most relevant party. You want to tweak everything *before* you launch so as to avoid changing things around all the time.

A Few Pay Plan Details I'm Always Asked About

Team Remunerating and Bonuses

Remunerating teams is sticky. I know there are times when working in teams is unavoidable. But it does not necessarily mean you have to remunerate in a team way. If one salesperson on the team performs at a significantly higher level but earns the same money as everyone else, it would be counterproductive to everything we are trying to build. At all costs you want to avoid a situation where one person's performance affects another person's pay.

Many managers tell me they pay this way so that the stronger team members will raise the performance of weaker members, but raising performance is not the salesperson's job—it's the manager's. You can work in groups but still pay people for their individual productivity. If for example you have lead-generation people, appointment schedulers, and salespeople (separated sales stages because of different talent needs), you do not *have* to assign one lead-generation person to work with one appointment scheduler and one salesperson (a typical team example). You can have a manager who gathers *all* leads from the lead-generating department and distributes them appropriately, and who gathers *all* appointments from your appointment schedulers and assigns them. This way, you can give better leads to better schedulers, and better appointments to better salespeople. And if you think that sounds like favoritism, you will read in chapter 8 why this is one of the practices of the world's best managers.

Should a Salesperson Ever Earn More Than the Sales Manager?

If the salesperson in question is a top producer, absolutely. If the sales manager is doing their job well, they should make a good living. But it is not uncommon, or wrong, for a sales manager to earn less than top salespeople. If the sales manager is doing their job well and the *majority* of the salespeople are making more than the manager, then things are skewed.

The primary responsibility of the sales manager is to assure that the output of the sales team is all it can possibly be. Furthermore, the manager's pay plan is structured like that of the salespeople—heavily performance based. Therefore if the manager is doing their job well it will mean the salespeople are doing well, and the manager should be making good money right along with the salespeople. He should be making more than the average salespeople but not necessarily as much as top producers.

Transitioning to a New Pay Plan

Imagine that your day begins with your boss announcing that your pay plan is going to change. It is an understandably nerve-racking announcement.

We need to be sensitive to how any change will be perceived, but particularly when it comes to pay changes. And so, whenever you make a change to your pay plan, I recommend the following.

1. Tell Them Why

As I have said before, communication with your salespeople should be regular, frequent, and two way. Whenever I begin a consulting project with a new client, I learn more from the salespeople than any other source, and you can too. It's amazing how many important sales department decisions get made without including the salespeople.

Tell them why you're making changes: that you have just learned about behavior analysis and your current plan isn't what it could be; that you're doing what any forward-thinking company does—you're keeping up with best practices. Get their feedback on the pay plan's proposed structure.

2. Tell Them It's Not to Save Money

Let them know you're not doing this to try to *reduce* payout—quite the opposite.

3. Tell Them It's Optional

Yes, optional. Once you have discussed and possibly tweaked the new plan with your trusted group of salespeople, it's time to announce the change to everyone. Wherever possible do this in person, not in writing. The pay plan will need to be put in writing, of course, but that's not the way to announce it. People will have questions. And one of them will likely be "What if I want to stay on the old plan?"

Almost every time I have altered a pay plan, there were those who continued to resist. We explained that they would actually be making *more* money; we plugged real numbers into the new formula, from existing salespeople, in order to illustrate what the same performance would earn on the new plan, but still there were the skeptical. My position on this has always been to tell them, "As you wish." You want a culture of trust, a culture where the employees truly believe you have their best interests at heart. If that's true, I can't think of any good reason *not* to allow someone to remain on the old pay plan. It is a very powerful gesture to say, "Okay then. As you wish."

Of course, when "old pay plan people" see what "new pay plan people" are earning, they usually end up, at some point, asking if they can cross over. And the answer is, of course you can. These types of changes iron themselves out in time; it's very important that the salespeople catch you as often as possible doing the right thing. If you were to say no to the old pay plan request, you may reason that it's only one or two people out of many. But don't kid yourself—everyone else was watching exactly how you handled the situation. Their attitude is affected, and your very culture is created, by all the daily things they catch you doing.

BEST PRACTICE #5: SALES BEHAVIOR TRAINING

et us now examine how sales training fits into the plan. I have spent a good portion of this book explaining why sales training alone will not produce a sustained increase in performance. You have come to understand the roles and the necessity of the other practices. Assuming these are in place, training *will* augment performance—as long as it too is implemented correctly—but I must be honest with you. Of the 6 best practices that this book elaborates, sales training has proven to have the *least* impact on overall performance. The greatest impact on performance is understanding how to cast top talents into their ideal selling roles, supported by ideal performance conditions for that group.

That said, training *is* a performance enhancer under the right conditions, and it is an expected company practice today. New hires must be trained. Best practices in all stages of selling must be discussed and shared. In this chapter I will reveal what I have learned from some of the best sales teams—and some of the worst—about the two equally important sides of sales training: the *curriculum* and the *delivery*. I will not be going into great detail regarding curriculum—sales training is not the focus of this book. I will tell you *what* to teach your people, *how* you should teach it, *how often*, and to *which* salespeople. In other words—and as with every other element discussed to this point—I will tell you how training fits with everything else, so that it can actually augment performance rather than sabotage it.

SALES TRAINING CURRICULUM

Every sale is about influencing someone and then leading them to make a decision. This is consistent for all the sale types we have discussed. The only exceptions that I will note are those sales that are far more "customer service" than "sales," requiring salespeople to keep clients happy so they'll keep buying from your company. There is no advising, only pleasing (the **Persuasion** talent). We call these employees CSRs (customer service reps) and they are the exception to the upcoming training details. CSRs need *customer service* training. If at any point, however, that rep needs to try to sell something *new* to the client they've been pleasing for years, or perhaps ask the client to buy *more*, or maybe even simply get a referral, understand that that CSR is now asking the client to make a decision about something. And the better they are at influencing and leading, the better chance that decision will be a favorable one. They're now *selling*.

The training we discuss here relates to influencing and leading someone to make a decision. After scouring the four corners of the sales training world and experiencing every program—from the extremely impacting to complete nonsense—and after working closely with some of the best salespeople on the planet, I have found that the most successful and highest-producing salespeople seem to have mastered three different dimensions of influence. With very few exceptions, all successful sales have had these three dimensions in place. I will share with you the best practices I have gleaned from each dimension. They are:

1. The attaining of **rapport**
2. The discussion of the **solution**
3. The **advising** process

1. The Attaining of Rapport

With the exception of a quick, over-the-counter-type sale—like when you buy a pack of gum—influencing someone to make a decision requires that you first establish some level of rapport with him or her. (Buying gum is not really a "sale" anyway; the client was already "sold" when he came in for the gum.)

You have come to learn that this book is very much about human behavior, about why people do the things they do, and I don't think most people appreciate just how much of an impact rapport has on a potential customer's final decision. For those of you who have a lot of sales experience, how many successful sales can you think back on where there *wasn't* good rapport between you and your prospect? Not too many. And how many situations can you recall where the sale went to the *wrong* person? That is, you *know* that your solution was truly better for the prospect but they chose someone else? And you know perfectly (frustratingly) well that your prospect made their decision based on criteria other than each company's solution.

Although buyers will rarely admit it, largely because they don't even realize it, how they "feel" about you very much impacts their final decision. I'm sure you've heard all the talk about left brain and right brain—logic and emotion. Well, prospects will always justify their purchase with logic. But make no mistake;

their final buying decision is very influenced by emotion. Sales-people need to be left-brain selling and right-brain closing.

I have taught a lot of salespeople how to do this. I have also learned and used many of those personality systems that teach us the four main personality groups—which are further divided into four subgroups—leaving a salesperson to assess exactly which of *sixteen* personality types he is sitting with, so that he can then tailor the whole selling process to an "extrovert intuitive" or an "amiable" or worse, an "INTJ." Unfortunately, while these systems surely have their place, they are too hard to use when you're in the hot seat.

So what can be done about this? We acknowledge how impor-tant rapport is but also how difficult it can be to wear two hats simultaneously: the psychologist hat and the salesperson hat. So how can your salespeople more easily exploit the right brain?

There are two ways. The first you're already doing—you are casting selling roles based on talent now, and many top salespeo-ple know instinctively how to bond with different personality groups. But not all of them. Which brings me to the second way: *mirroring*.

When I learned mirroring in 1992 I don't know which impacted me more: the increased rapport I enjoyed with all the different per-sonality groups or how *fun* it is to play with. You see, even the most "personable" person has certain personality groups that will con-flict with her own—we all do. Every top salesperson I ever met had trouble connecting with certain personalities. Sometimes an ultra-empathetic, over-the-top service-oriented salesperson has trouble with very arrogant people. The nicer she is the more arrogant they are, and she doesn't know what to do about it. More often it's the opposite, where a very confident and assertive salesperson uninten-tionally clashes with a timid, introverted buyer. Whatever the case, one thing's for sure—these opposites will not have rapport and, hence, not even get to stage one of the sale.

Mirroring not only addresses this but is also the simplest thing to do. Mirroring (as well as leading, pacing, matching, and a few other related practices) is part of a discipline called neuro-linguistic programming. Many of you have heard of NLP and perhaps read that it is controversial, so let me clear that up right now. The only controversy is whether or not NLP should be considered an official discipline of psychology. Frankly, I don't care how it gets classified. This book is about what works and, as I said, not only do I find mirroring to be more effective, but it is also easier to learn and immediately apply than any other rapport practice.

NLP has a tremendous following, many thought leaders, and countless books and Web sites. Anthony Robbins has been talking about it for years, and includes NLP practices in *Unlimited Power* and *Awaken the Giant Within*. There's even a *Neuro-Linguistic Programming for Dummies* book.

Again, I cannot train the process in this book but I will give you the gist of it (I'll also give you some further reading). In short, we all gravitate to those who are "like us." This is a subconscious thing and, while most people appreciate this fact, most don't really know what is meant by "those who are like us." Like us *how?* In social status? In religion or color or beliefs? In industry or vocation? No—nothing so deep.

All you have to do to mirror someone is to mimic their physiology. Ninety-three percent of the meaning derived from any communication is derived nonverbally. The actual words you choose account for only 7 percent of the perceived meaning of any communication. Fifty-five percent comes from your physiology and 38 percent from tone of voice. To illustrate this in front of a group, I often ask a female to join me at the front, sitting on the edge of the stage. I tell her that we are coworkers who have just completed a long project together with a few others. I look at her and say in a very sincere, professional—almost humble—voice, "Hey Mary, I really enjoyed working on that project with you. I thought we worked well together and I'm looking forward to our next project." At this point Mary and the whole audience are thinking, so what? You paid a nice compliment.

But then, using exactly the same words, I change my facial expression to sly and creepy. I lick my lips as I slide over closer to Mary. Half of my mouth—now moist—is curled up in a smirk. My eyes are burning into a deeper part of her than she wants to allow. And I speak to her slowly, "Hey, Mary . . . I ree-aaally enjoyed working on that project with you. . . ." I look left and right, as if to make sure we're alone. Mary is leaning away. I lean in closer and my voice gets even more throaty, "I thought we worked well together and I'm looking forward to our next project."

Obviously this makes everyone in the room uncomfortable, especially Mary, but think about *why*. The words I used were identical both times! Only my physiology and my intonation changed. Once you experiment with this a bit you realize the words almost aren't necessary; the meaning would still be clearly received. Picture a nice, professional, likable coworker paying a sincere compliment, but totally fumbling with the actual words, or completely butchering the grammar. Mary would still receive the exact intended message, even if the words were barely comprehensible! The physiology, the inflection, and the intonation are responsible for 93 percent of communication.

Mirroring a person's physiology takes a little practice but it is *not* difficult. If they slouch, you slouch (I'll never forget when I *slouched* my first sale!). If they are fast talkers, so are you. If they're loud and confident, you're loud and confident. And if they are quiet, calculating, and reserved, then so are you. Read that last one again. . . . It doesn't sound like too many salespeople you know, does it? Most salespeople are a little more outgoing, demonstrative—certainly confident. But you must appreciate that *that* recipe, when sitting with "quiet, calculating, and reserved," will clash. There will be no rapport. Like oil and water, they won't mix.

I once had a prospect who was a rich, arrogant, rude, insulting business owner. I had definitely interested him in my company's services but for the life of me I couldn't ever get him to say yes. I was very professional. Over the months I would bring samples of how other businesses like his had benefited financially from our services. I got him a free trial period that would save him money. I bent over backwards *but* I always did so professionally and politely. I had not yet learned about mirroring.

My manager would come to town from time to time and, among other duties, he would ride along to visit whatever prospects I might want his involvement with, so I brought him to see my arrogant prospect. My manager was a senior, in-your-face, straight-shooting, not-terribly-polished sales veteran. One might even call him—you guessed it—arrogant.

Well, the deal was done about ten minutes after we sat down. This amazed me. My manager showed no documentation, no stats, no financials. He simply asked what point we were at, and then listened while my prospect listed all the benefits that I had taught him over the months. After the prospect had finished, my manager leaned forward and barked at him, "So what the hell are you waiting for?" I was shocked. He was nearly yelling. It was his *tone* that I remember most—like he was *angry,* angry that his time was being wasted by all this procrastination. My prospect answered, "Nothing, how do I get started?"

Mirroring is easy and it will "connect" two people who would not otherwise connect. So the first dimension of influence in sales is rapport. Get ahold of one of the books mentioned at the end of this chapter and have everyone practice.

2. The Discussion of the Solution

The solution dimension of influence refers to the entire selling process: *how* you sell, and the best way to do it. From the time you begin speaking with a prospect right up until the close, what should you be doing? Making presentations? Explaining features and benefits? Asking questions? Talking about your kids? Talking about your company's reputation? This is the dimension addressed by all the sales training courses out there and the *one and only* curriculum I recommend to this day is *SPIN Selling*.

Neil Rackham's twelve-year study of ten thousand salespeople in thirty-five thousand sales calls clearly illustrated what the world's best salespeople do differently. They ask questions. They know how to *interview* their prospects—very much like the talent interviewing you have learned. Rackham's team at Huthwaite found that there were four types of questions that need to be asked in certain ways and at certain points in the selling process. Their research and resulting book ushered in the "consultative" selling style that countless others have now copied. It is a far more natural way to communicate with others and a welcome departure from the overly contrived (and sadly, still very common) approach we were all taught: make a presentation, probe for need, trial close, handle objections, and then close, close, close.

So for those of you who have always wondered which of the many sales training programs is best, I recommend *SPIN Selling*. It is not a rigid, step-by-step selling process that must be performed the same way every time by every salesperson—such processes are not practical or even realistic. I have cautioned you about process throughout the book because different personalities and styles all have different selling "tools" that they have come to prefer, and they will each utilize these different tools in their own way. Sales training, therefore, must impart new tools and ideas that are adaptable to *anyone*—to any and every selling style—and *SPIN Selling* very much is. *SPIN Selling* author and former Huthwaite president Neil Rackham himself said, "High-level selling never works successfully if you try to sell by a rigid formula. Flexibility is the hallmark of good selling."

In speaking with Professor Rackham recently, I asked which of his books I should ultimately recommend to my readers and he answered, *The SPIN Selling Fieldbook.* I think those of you who have not yet read the original *SPIN Selling* should read it first—the research and findings are fascinating and important. But to better *apply* its teachings I definitely concur with Neil. Read *The SPIN Selling Fieldbook.*

3. The Advising Process

By now you know what I mean when I talk about an adviser. Advisers are *closers.* There are polished, articulate, charming sales professionals who can mesmerize a room full of executives but who, at the same time, can never seem to bring the sale to a close—and then there are closers. Closers aren't always the most articulate. Or smooth. But they bring in the business. In their minds that's *all* they're there to do. They're not necessarily aggressive or abrasive, just fearless, self-assured, and assertive.

Why then do I use the word *adviser* instead of *closer*? Because there is one major difference between my closer and everyone else's. My closer doesn't ask; she *tells.*

Of all my surprising findings over the years, one of the most "contradictory" was the discovery that prospects do not want to be *asked,* they want to be *told*—and the reason I call this contradictory is because at this very moment there are countless sales training courses going on all over the world that are teaching participants to "ask for the business." It is one of sales training's most overused colloquialisms: *ask for the business.* As you read this, these sales courses are teaching all the "asking phraseology": "Do you think we should move forward on this?" "Is there anything else I can tell you before we move forward?" "Would you like this delivered Monday or Wednesday?" "Do you think we could earn your business today?"

The fact is, as long as the first two dimensions of influence outlined above have been conducted correctly, your prospects want to be *told.* That is to say, as long as there is good trust and rapport, and as long as the selling stage did in fact uncover that your solution will benefit the prospect, then your prospect wants his trusted adviser to advise him. *Telling* a prospect what you believe to be the right move for him rather than *asking* him what he wants to do is simply an extension of the trusted adviser relationship. And when you understand this relationship you come to realize how ridiculous a notion it is to be asking instead of advising.

Consider that you are sitting with Warren Buffett. Somehow you have been fortunate enough to nab him as your financial adviser. He asks you questions. He gets to know you. He starts to develop a picture of your current situation, your means, your goals, your risk level, and everything else he needs to know. During the latter part of his "interview process" his head begins to nod, and you suspect his strategy for you is solidifying in that brilliant investment mind of his. You're excited to hear his thoughts.

The conversation turns from him asking you questions to you listening to his explanations. He explains why a whole world of investment strategies that you have heard of and read about are *not* for you, and why these three strategies he's going to explain are the best options for you, and you find it all makes perfect sense. You feel an exhilarating confidence and a sense of real relief. Mr. Buffett explains the subtle differences between the three strategies. Then, as you're waiting for the climax to the whole wonderful experience, where you assume he is now going to tell you *which* of these three strategies will make you rich the quickest, he looks at you and says, "Which one interests you today? Which one do you think would allow us to move forward today?"

The only truthful answer out of your mouth would be, "What? You're asking *me* which one to choose? How do I know? *You're* the expert! You're Warren Buffett! *You tell me* which one is the best. . . . That's why you're here!"

As long as the "trust" part of "trusted adviser" is in place, and you have come to believe that the salesperson has your situation and your best interests ahead of his own commission, then it only makes sense that *he* be the one to advise you on the perfect solution for your situation (a situation he took the time to completely understand). There is nothing I appreciate more as a consumer than telling such a salesperson about all the research I've done on the product, and telling her what *I* think is the right choice, only to have her say, "No, I disagree with you." It shows she's thinking about *me,* and about her product's application to *my* situation. If she just wanted a sale today, and she was listening to me go on about a product that *I really like,* she would think to herself, "Well . . . he's going to buy that one for sure!" The fact that she would say, "No . . . wait a minute. Based on what you told me I'm not sure that's the right one," illustrates that she's listening, that she's thinking, that she cares about fitting me with the perfect solution for me. And that's what a buyer wants—to feel "taken care of" by someone who is more knowledgeable on the topic.

When I purchased a new telephone system for my office some years back, I called two different companies for the equipment. I was doing some sales training later that day on this very topic and the contrast between the two selling styles made my point so perfectly that not only did I use it in that day's training, I also told myself I'd put it in a book one day. The first company's salesperson launched into an explanation of one of today's "best models for my type of company." I don't know how he knew what my type of company was, because he really didn't ask me any questions at all, but apparently this was the best model for me. He talked about a whole lot of features that it had. Then he showed me two or three more choices—each a little less expensive than the last—and explained their features while I stood watching and listening, but definitely *not* participating. Then he asked me which one I'd like to have installed—that he could probably pull some strings and have it done *tomorrow*! Then I showed him where the door was.

The second salesperson asked me *all kinds* of questions: What type of usage did I have? Did I conference a lot? How much would I be expanding in the future? She listened intently. She asked me new questions based on my previous answers—as if she were actually *listening*, as if she actually wanted to prescribe the exact right system for our needs! Now it's obvious which approach is better and who I chose to buy from but my point is, being *told* what to buy rather than being *asked* is the only logical conclusion to the adviser sale. When my salesperson knew exactly what the perfect fit was for my needs, she *told* me, "buy this one." It was not pushy; it was not arrogant—it didn't even seem like she was a salesperson. She was the *expert in phone systems*—my trusted adviser in a purchase that was important to me. I was relieved to be told instead of being asked which one I'd like. It was one less thing for me to have to think about. And with her knowing so much more than me about these systems, can you see why I say it is ridiculous to ask me what the right choice is? I am paying for an expert opinion—the salesperson should *tell* me what the best solution is. *That's* an adviser.

It should interest you to know that Huthwaite's research determined that when the prospect senses you are transitioning into "closing mode" (and they all sense this—it's another primal throwback), the chances of a successful sale actually *drop*. Huthwaite measured a 9 percent reduction in successful sales when the prospect saw a closing behavior coming on. The prospects' emotional walls went shooting straight up.

When I learned this I was beside myself. Do you appreciate just how many sales courses are teaching all those standard closing techniques? The Ben Franklin Close, the Snooze-and-Lose Close, the Puppy Dog Close, the Alternative Choice Close. All are *reducing* the salesperson's closing ratio!

Your prospects and clients just want to believe that your salespeople know their stuff, and that they're honest. With that in place, it is the salesperson's obligation, their very *duty*, to advise their clients. Tell your salespeople this. Many of them have been poisoned with bad asking and closing techniques. Remember that if they lack the talent set for the adviser sale, the training won't do very much. But if they do possess adviser talents, teach them to *use* them by advising, not asking.

SALES TRAINING DELIVERY

In chapter 2 I pointed out that sales training is a form of *behavior* training and that altering habitual behavior requires reinforcement. If you want your salespeople to adopt their training and actually make use of it, here is the three-step training formula:

1. Classroom
2. Role Play
3. Field Training

1. Classroom

We discussed the actual curriculums for the three different dimensions of sales influence in the last section. The first method we use to teach those curriculums is the classroom. It does not have to be an actual classroom, of course; I call it this because it is a more one-directional setting than steps 2 and 3. In steps 2 and 3 salespeople will be *doing*. In step 1, they are listening and learning.

I only have one piece of advice to give you for this step but it's an important one. My advice is to *sell* your salespeople on the training. Many seasoned top producers are reluctant to receive sales training and there are some pretty good reasons for this. One is they don't like to take time away from *selling* time. Another is that so much of the training they have received in the past turned out to be a waste of their time. Many have become a bit jaded where training is concerned.

You must respect this. Any time I conduct sales training I begin by talking to participants about where the curriculum came from. They deserve to know what's in the food you'll be feeding them, and because I only impart training that has been substantiated beyond reproach, I want the salespeople to know that. I want them to *buy in* and the only way they will is if I tell them about all the research and all the ensuing success stories of those who have used these techniques. Tell them this training is being conducted not because everyone is doing poorly, but because it's such *good stuff*, because as a company you're dedicated to sharing what you have found to be world-class practices.

2. Role Play

Once the trainer has imparted the curriculum in the classroom, it must be practiced. You could learn all the postures and theories and techniques behind the perfect golf swing but you won't be able to implement any of that learning until you practice. And you golfers out there know that you'll need to practice a lot.

They say "practice makes perfect" but that's not why role play is important. This misunderstanding is why most role play sessions I have witnessed do not accomplish their intended goal. First, practice will *not* make perfect if you lack the talents needed for the task. You know this well by now so we are assuming in this chapter that only the correct talents are being trained. But practicing in order to "get better" at newly learned material is only one of the two reasons we need to practice. The second, equally important reason is to *reinforce new behaviors*. You can practice something until you feel you absolutely "have it down," but it does not mean that it will be your new habitual behavior from this day forward.

Replacing one habitual behavior with another requires reinforcement, but most companies don't appreciate what *kind* of reinforcement, or how *long* they must reinforce the new behavior. My research on the topic revealed three different time frames—21 days, 28 days, and 30 days—but my own tested application tells the true story: that different people require different amounts of time.

How many of you have made New Year's resolutions to eat better that lasted only a few days? How many of you have joined a gym and then gone twice? The fact is, if you had someone following you around for about twenty-eight days, making sure you stick to your new plan, the odds of this new behavior becoming permanent skyrocket. That's why rich celebrities are so successful changing their eating habits, or getting into shape. They have an entourage of trainers and chefs, who end up filling that reinforcement role.

An employee of mine used to work with mentally challenged children. We were discussing this topic when she told me of a child who used to grip her fork and spoon in her fist—the way we all do before we're taught otherwise. Katherine told me that for 26 days in a row she would take the spoon from the child and show her the "correct" way to hold it each time she ate. On day 27, and forever after, the correct posture was the child's new habit.

Neuroassociative pathways in the brain get deeper and deeper with repeated use—like any pathway does. When your new pathway reaches the point where it is deeper than the old one, *it* will be the behavior that presents when you're not paying conscious attention.

Most companies practice role play only until it is clear that trainees understand how to use the new material, but that should be a starting point, not an end point. Once the new material is digested and understood through role play, *the role playing should continue until trainees no longer have to consciously think about it.* Only then will a trainee be ready for field training.

The amount of time needed will depend on the individual and on the curriculum being digested, but the rule of thumb is that role playing should be done regularly—in a few smaller sessions rather than one long session. You cannot expect to conduct some classroom training, do some role playing, and then turn everyone loose to perform the new material flawlessly. If time permits, go ahead and move right into role play following classroom training. But plan to reconvene *at least* one more time to continue to practice. You will get to know how much time is required for each step after doing field training with each trainee.

Before we move on to field training, one more word about role play. Most sales people I know dislike role playing and most often that's because it isn't conducted properly. Too often role playing becomes a "stump the salesperson" game, as the mock prospect throws any and every possible objection at the mock salesperson. This is *not* role play's intention. Players need to play their roles realistically. If, as the mock prospect, you truly find that the salesperson is tweaking your interest, then go with it as if you were a real prospect. If, however, the mock salesperson is losing you, then so be it. Be real. Keeping it real is the only way role play will help.

3. Field Training

Field training is sales training's missing link. It is the reason why you have watched clever, capable salespeople enthusiastically devour a new training technique, role play it to perfection, and then never actually use it in real life.

In a training situation your trainee knows there is a teacher, other students, and a mock prospect; he knows that if he messes up, he can restart the clock. In short, your trainee knows that the situation is *not real*. In this way, his brain has applied all that practice (role play) to training situations only. His brain has not yet applied the training to real life situations and, like it or not, these are two different situations. It's like practicing your lines for the school play over and over, until you know your part inside out and backwards. You recite it perfectly to your parents, time after time. Why then do you forget some of those lines as soon as you step onto the stage in front of an audience? Because your brain knew the lines in the context of your bedroom, in front of your mirror, with no one watching. On stage in front of an audience is a context your brain had not yet practiced within—there was no association in your brain between the two settings. Proof of this is, once an actor has had some experience—perhaps with several different plays under her belt—she will no longer freeze that way. Once on stage, she will remember the lines she rehearsed in the practice setting, even for a first performance of a new play. Her brain has developed a connection—an association between the practice situation and the real life situation. Forgetting lines is not a case of nerves; most performers will tell you they still get nervous before a performance, as they always have. But they no longer forget their lines.

The only way to create this association in sales training, so that the techniques tried out in a practice setting will have relevance in a real life setting, is to have the trainer accompany the trainee right into the sales situation. The trainer might be an outside trainer or your sales manager or a coach—but she must be someone who knows the curriculum and who participated in the training to this point. I have joined my trainees in their real life sales situations countless times and in many industries, and it's always fascinating to watch those who were the stars in the classroom, and in role play, completely forget everything. The coach's job in this situation is to note instances where newly trained curriculum was *not* applied and should have been—or perhaps where it *was* well applied (positive reinforcement)—for discussion immediately following the sale.

You can introduce the coach to the prospect any way that you see fit. I have been introduced as a manager, a new salesperson in training—often the salesperson will say that I am needed on the next client following this meeting and, rather than sitting in the car, would it be all right if I join in . . . whatever you feel fits the situation. Sometimes I will participate during the meeting, albeit very casually, sometimes not—but it is never awkward.

In the nearest coffee shop following the meeting, when everything is still fresh, the coach must share the instances where the newly trained curriculum was *not* applied, and should have been. This usually sounds something like:

"Remember when the prospect answered your question and admitted they were losing production time because of their old software, and you began telling them about how your software solution would solve that?"

"Yes . . ."

"Remember in role play we advised against 'pouncing' on a discussion of the solution too soon, that we want to explore the ramifications of his lost production time a little further, to add some urgency to the purchase?"

"Oooh riiight . . ."

And you hear a big "click" inside the salesperson's head, as they see in a way that only field training can make them see, *the ideal real life application of a classroom technique.* The good news with field training is how surprisingly *quickly* the association builds, how quickly a bridge develops between practice situations and the real life situations. For the most part I only have to accompany a trainee into a handful of sales before all the classroom training becomes associated with real life sales situations. And then, training is complete.

HOW MUCH TRAINING?

I assume you train newly hired salespeople. You have to at least teach them about your product or service offering and certain details about internal procedures and such. Sales training should go last, after all these other details have been covered.

I worked for a company in 1994 that gave its salespeople sales training before they really had a firm grip of the benefits of the product, on why a prospect might choose this company's solution over a competitor's. But at this early stage, salespeople can't field any objections. You need to begin by "selling" to your new salespeople in exactly the same way you sell to your clients. Let them ask questions and test drive the products and finally come to the point where they would buy—just like a client. *Then* do sales training.

Sales training for new hires should go according to this chapter's formula. Role play and field training should continue until the coach sees during real life sales that the trainee has absorbed the training.

After the initial training, sales training should be a regular resource, something you all meet about, for instance, monthly. The best sales organizations in the world are *proud* to be good sales organizations. For these companies sales training is a much discussed topic and a regular event; however, it may not continue to be a performance enhancer past a certain point. I have worked with many top producers who embrace sales training every chance they get, even when it is not new curriculum. They enjoy, and feel they benefit from, a review of certain "basics," but we do not necessarily see a raise in performance after each training session. I know an equal number of top producers who do not have any desire to attend training after a certain career point. So here's the rule.

For salespeople who regularly sell *above quota*—which is the very model you are creating—training is not compulsory, but all are welcome to attend. It's their choice. We took great care last chapter to establish the "right" quotas for each selling position and, as we discuss more in the next chapter, your manager will manage to these quotas. This means as long as salespeople are bringing you the amount you all agreed they would, you have very little to say. I have often watched a sales manager insist—or strongly recommend—that all salespeople attend training, which will annoy some of them. Their feeling is, "I can understand why *John* needs training—he's not doing well! But I'm a leader here. . . . I shouldn't have to attend if I want to be out selling instead." And I agree with them. Some want to attend and others do not, so let them decide. Most often you will see that curious human thing happen when attendance suddenly becomes optional—people start attending.

For those who are not making quota, training is compulsory. You do this to be supportive and to try your best to get everyone up to speed. You also do this so that those who unfortunately will *not* make it cannot say it was for lack of training or company support.

When the training being conducted is for new salespeople, tell your seasoned, successful reps they are welcome to attend and share, even teach certain topics if they want to. It will benefit newcomers and it definitely helps to create a sales-centric culture when everyone is gathered talking about best practices.

Make your regular sessions fun and participatory. Find out from the salespeople themselves what training topics might interest them. Some companies like to form a training committee—just remember to include the salespeople in decisions like how frequently you will train and for how long. Remember that you're doing this to support and provide further resources to your valued sales team—not simply for training's sake, and not because they necessarily need it. Ultimately, if I had the entire team tell me, "We don't want to do this anymore," then as long as everything is where it should be performancewise, it's fine with me. When performance is on track and things are running the way they should, the manager's job is *to listen to what the team wants, and to support them.*

Which leads us into the management chapter. We're at a point where top sales talents are performing each stage of your sale, and doing so under perfect performance conditions. These people are clear of purpose, they are as motivated as they can be, and they have been trained in the world's best selling style. Unfortunately, nothing can blow it all up faster than the wrong manager.

FURTHER RESOURCES

SPIN Selling (McGraw-Hill, 1988)
The SPIN Selling Fieldbook (McGraw-Hill, 1996)

Further reading for Neuro-Linguistic Programming
- *The User's Manual for the Brain* (Crown House Publishing, 2001)
- *From Frogs to Princes* (Real People Press, 1979)
- *Neuro-Linguistic Programming for Dummies* (John Wiley and Sons, Ltd., 2004)

Neuro-Linguistic Programming Web Sites
- www.nlp.com
- www.nlpanchorpoint.com

BEST PRACTICE #6: RESULT-BASED MANAGEMENT

How many of you have had the privilege of working for a good manager? The kind who made you look forward to going to work every day? How many of you have worked for a bad manager? The kind who frustrated you so much you were kept awake at night? Employees will overlook almost anything—and continue to give their best—if there is a solid relationship with a really good manager. Conversely, the best pay, perks, and conditions in the world will not make working for a bad manager tolerable.

The role of the sales manager is an absolutely pivotal one and it has two sides to it. As always, if you have one in place without the other, you will not reach top performance levels. They are:

1. *What* the manager does
2. *Who* the manager is

If you abide by the five best practices previously elaborated, then in theory you are finished. You will have "built" what we set out to build; the changes that were needed have all been made. Sale types and sales stages have been identified. Talents have been cast. Pay and quota have been tweaked. Training is in place. If these sales pros are so talented and so autonomous and if they have been plugged into such a complete and synchronized infrastructure, we could ask why they need a manager at all.

The answer is because they're still human. As high functioning as they may be, and as clearly defined as their environment is, top salespeople still need guidance, feedback, arbitration, praise, reprimands, and support. The manager does not *build* the infrastructure; he maintains, nurtures, and grows the infrastructure that *management* built. Management builds the machine but the manager operates it on a daily basis.

A sales team is like any other team. In sports teams you start by getting the best talents for each position. You incentivize them well. The expected results are very clear. Training is ongoing. *But the coach is the key to everything.* Your sales manager is that coach. She has to keep everything on the rails and that can be quite a job at times. Your Perfect SalesForce creates the ultimate sales-centric environment and culture, but it's still manned by *people*. And people are far from perfect.

The right manager will maintain the harmony—or as close to harmony as is possible. I will describe the right manager in the second of this chapter's two sections. First we will cover *what* your sales manager should be doing any given day.

PART I: THE PRACTICES OF THE WORLD'S BEST SALES MANAGERS

We stated earlier that a manager's primary job is to get those in her charge to produce whatever it is she needs them to produce. That's it. If you were to walk by the sales manager's office and he was snoozing with his feet up on his desk, your reaction should depend on whether the sales team is bringing the agreed-upon deliverables. If they are, then you smile to yourself and shake your head, thinking, "How *does* he do it!?" If they *aren't*, it is of course another story.

In a result-managed environment, people are held accountable for fair, reachable, pre-agreed-upon results for each period; they are supplied with all pre-agreed-upon resources needed to get there; and then *they are not micromanaged*. This does not mean that salespeople are abandoned—far from it. Managing results does *not* mean looking at people's numbers once a month and then "reacting" accordingly.

The sales manager will fully support and develop her salespeople, each in his own way as you will see. Result-based management is simply an agreement between the manager and each salesperson. The salesperson has agreed that he can produce X if the company gives him Y in the way of resources and support. As long as he achieves X, there is no need to police *how* X is being achieved.

If I'm harping on this point throughout the book it is because as logical as this arrangement sounds, very few companies live by it. Micromanaging is an epidemic and while many of the guilty parties are aware that it is wrong, they don't know what to do *instead*.

A colleague of mine was a sales manager for a large consulting firm in the mid-nineties. Greg managed all the salespeople in the eastern half of the country. He was doing well; his numbers were always ahead of where they had to be each quarter. Greg did *not* have a good manager (the national sales manager); as a matter of fact he kept many things from Rob. Rob insisted that *everything* be done a particular way—his way. He ruled this way because he thought it was what a manager was supposed to do. He believed he was being supportive by telling his people how to do every little thing.

What Rob didn't understand was that many of Greg's salespeople had their own preferred (and proven) way of doing certain things. Many of them were uncomfortable making canned presentations, for instance, stopping to ask rehearsed questions only at those points his script allowed. So Greg taught his salespeople the right way to "interview" their prospects. Many didn't like the company's pre-scribed cold-calling approach and would ask Greg why they couldn't do it their own way if it brought the same results. He completely agreed with them. Greg found that some on his team were far better at opening doors while others could carry the sale to fruition more easily, so he changed the whole selling structure around. He also spent his allotted budget quite differently than his manager expected he would; he introduced a lot of short-term incentives. Greg im-posed result quotas—something this company didn't even have.

Greg's group was always ahead of the agreed-upon quarterly re-sults when many other regions in the company were not (they op-erated in many countries). Every salesperson in the company knew the practices and policies were skewed and antiquated; Greg simply did something about it, not because he was a troublemaker but be-cause it was the correct structure for the sale. He had in fact tried to discuss these topics with Rob many times, only to be told to stick to company policy. And when Rob found out how differently Greg was running things, he was fired. Greg managed a leading region and he was fired. From the national sales manager's point of view, he was breaking rules, because *all the rules were based on activities* rather than results. If instead he allowed—or better, *encouraged*—the input of the whole team, he would have continued to prosper and the model would have been applied companywide. Instead he lost many top people and replaced them with mediocre but obedi-ent producers.

The structure you have built to this point supports a result-managed environment, *not* an activity-managed one, so let's get to the two duties that should occupy the majority of a good manager's time. They are:

1. Enforce results, manage activities
2. Develop strengths, not weaknesses

As I have said, if results are there the manager's primary job is done and she should be developing the team further. These are the practices that the Gallup Organization found the world's best managers, from eighty thousand managers interviewed, did differently than all the rest. It is what *natural born* managers and leaders and sports coaches understand instinctively. Let's look at these two practices in more detail.

1. Enforce Results, Manage Activities

We have certainly extolled the virtues of this management style throughout the book and it is surely easy enough to grasp in concept. It is in *practice* where we see managers inadvertently getting too involved with activities. So what is the right mix? After all, results are not possible without activities; surely a sales manager has to deal with activities to some degree! Of course they do.

Activities are discussed, debated, tossed around, supported—they are simply not *enforced*. Every company I have worked with has top producers who break the mold, those salespeople who do *not* do things the way the company's rule book suggests but who sell exponentially more than everyone else. This alone illustrates that there isn't one perfect approach to doing things. I know a company whose salespeople have appointments written for them. These salespeople attend the appointments and close a cost-effective percentage of them. But within this company there is a small group who do not take these appointments, preferring instead to walk into unsuspecting prospect companies cold—with no appointment. This definitely monkeys with the internal workings, as this company is a high-functioning machine of about three hundred salespeople attending appointments written by three hundred internal appointment setters. But management at this company is wise; it allows these types of exceptions. Why? Because of *results*. Those peculiar salespeople above, who prefer to walk in off the street without an appointment, simply sell more that way. When they did things the "company way," they did not sell as much.

This is but one example of how a common result can be achieved via many different approaches. When I was young, a group of my friends and I drove from my native Montreal down to Florida—a fifteen-hundred-mile drive—to escape cold weather and hang around the beach. We all got to the designated meeting point, on the designated date and approximate time—but you can be sure we all took varying routes. Some reached I-95 via I-81, going through Pennsylvania. Others accessed I-95 via New York and I-87—a *very* different route to take, but we all arrived at the same destination at the same time for about the same cost.

Activities *do* need to be discussed, just not enforced. The most successful sales teams have regular meetings whose sole purpose is to openly discuss best practices (which is synonymous with activities). Their salespeople know that this is an open forum, that their ideas are heard and considered. It is a brainstorming session whose purpose is to share what's working—not to decide which way is *best*. New salespeople quickly see that this company supports many styles and encourages all input. During initial training, new people are taught what selling techniques work best (as discussed in the previous chapter) but are also told that these regular brainstorming sessions are an exploration of alternative techniques and styles that are working well for others. These sessions, which I have attended on behalf of many companies, ultimately end up raising the bar significantly, and are a huge contributor to the sales-centric culture you would hope to build.

When you were picking which results to attach quota to, you made a list of all the tasks associated with the sales job. You learned that we attach quotas only to *primary* tasks—those few tasks that actually *make money*. These are the results your sales manager is enforcing.

But what about secondary and tertiary tasks? How does your manager deal with bad attendance, late reports, terrible typing skills, bad research habits, messy desks, bad breath, and all the other human flaws that are a daily reality? She manages them. She *enforces* results and *manages* activities. This means that if John is regularly selling well above quota, and enjoying all the monetary benefits of that rewarding pay plan you introduced, but he is also notorious for arriving late and unprepared, your sales manager deals with it. She manages these typical annoyances by asking what she can do to help John get to meetings on time, by telling John that it's not fair to the others at the meeting, and so on. She does her best to manage what is probably a weakness, and she knows that trying to improve a weakness is near futile.

Knowing what you now know about natural born talent—and the lack thereof—reread that last statement. Understand that managing a group of human beings becomes infinitely easier when you realize that certain behaviors are inherent; they are derived from the presence, or absence, of talent. We refer to the absence of talent as a *weakness* and—just as you have come to understand that certain salespeople can impact a room full of executives while others cannot, or that certain salespeople can quickly close business while others simply cannot—you must also understand that the degree of neatness, organizational skills, and social skills are also part of everyone's DNA. If you try to teach something that is *not* a part of someone's genetic makeup (a weakness), you will have little success in raising performance.

Knowing this, the world's best managers address issues that affect the rest of the group, or that affect the client, but with the understanding that they will not likely be very effective in correcting this behavior. This is why it is so important to have a clear understanding of primary, secondary, and tertiary activities for each job, *before* you set your quotas. You are actually deciding which things *must* be performed to a certain standard versus which things are allowed a little human lenience. It would be terrific if all your top producers were also neat, punctual, and perfectly groomed but it's just not realistic. It's up to management to make it crystal clear what gets *enforced* and what gets *managed*.

2. Develop Strengths, Not Weaknesses

The very same human dynamic is applied to the manager's second duty, developing strengths instead of weaknesses, and it is arguably as rampant a management practice as enforcing activities. This one, however, I can sympathize with. I am quite guilty of having catered to weaknesses in my past, instead of to strengths. It seems only natural; a salesperson is having trouble closing, so we train them how to close better. If prospecting is a weakness, we get them some prospecting training. It just seems supportive, as if *not* doing so would be unfair to the salesperson. Well, it might *seem* supportive certainly, but now that you have a better understanding of skills, knowledge, and talent, how much will performance increase after you get that weakness some training? Remember, new skills and new knowledge *can* be acquired but talent *cannot*, and weak performance is almost always an indication that the talents needed for the job are simply not there. Training, therefore, though seemingly supportive, is most often futile.

It certainly seems backward, the idea of not training a weakness. Most companies are deeply rooted in the notion of assessing employee performance and then offering training "where needed." They never consider developing a *strength* further; it is after all already a strength! This is why I am such a fan of properly executed real world testing. It provides reassurance when we are asked to stray from popular thinking, and the data provided by the Gallup study is difficult to question. Gallup proved that when training a weakness, the improvement is marginal at best—if there is any improvement at all. But when the very same resources are applied to further developing a *strength*, the rise in performance is significant. And when you think about it, it makes perfect sense.

The world's best managers do not spend their time trying to develop their employees' weaknesses. They understand what can and cannot be trained and if training will indeed raise performance, then they train. But when there is a clear and obvious lack of the talent needed for the task, they know that training is futile. If the task in question is a *primary* task—those tasks that typically generate revenue and that you have attached a quota to—then you have a problem. The employee will not likely be reaching quota. If, however, the task is a secondary or tertiary one, then performance will not be affected and the manager should *manage* the weakness, *but not try to correct it.*

Let me illustrate with a case history. Sylvia and George are two salespeople I worked with in a distribution company. They epitomized how two people can reach desired sales levels via different methodologies. George was a strong adviser who did not like to prospect new business very much. He did not have a particularly great work ethic but he always made his numbers—and a good living—because of his relationships and his high closing ratio.

Sylvia was only a quasi-strong adviser but what really hurt her closing ratio was the absence of the **Explanation** talent and to a lesser degree the **Need** talent. She could not explain concepts, only straightforward products. So when she had a prospect's attention she could *demonstrate* her products, but not explain the application and benefits to the prospect's situation. Top performance in this sale type required **Need** to be created by getting a prospect to visualize the product's application to his own situation, which Sylvia could not do.

But here's the interesting part. Sylvia always sold above quota and she too made a good living. Although her closing ratio was nowhere near George's, her work ethic put his to shame. She made appointments with not fewer than two new prospects every day—which you must note is a sales stage that does *not* require the **Explanation** or **Need** talents.

If we look at these two salespeople through conventional sales department eyes, we would be speaking to Sylvia about her poor closing ability. We would tell her how pleased we are with her work and then, to be a supportive company, we would train her in closing skills. And nothing would change. Likewise, we would pat George on the back and tell him what a great job he does, and then speak to him about seeing more prospects. But if George was to be honest he would tell his manager that he *hates* prospecting with a passion (something he told me in confidence, but which was obvious when you understand talent-based interviewing). Any discussion or training in this area would accomplish nothing.

The owner of this company was not displeased with these two salespeople; both made their numbers. But until I advised him differently, he continued to pour resources into training their weaknesses. I told him that if improvement were possible, it would have happened by now.

What we did instead was to *develop strengths instead of weaknesses*. George was a strong adviser; when he talked about the application of his products, you felt absolutely compelled to buy them *right now*. So we got George in front of more prospects. The company began sponsoring product information sessions where many prospects would attend a free luncheon seminar to discuss relevant best practices and industry solutions. George got to do his thing in front of many prospects at once.

The company also sent George to public speaking training. Think about that. How many companies can you name that send their employees to be trained in something they're already good at? George raved about the training. He told me that he knew he had the gift of gab, and that he led people pretty well, but he had no idea how much there was to learn. He told me how he was taught to use stories and metaphors—something he never had done before. He learned how to use his body more when he spoke. And he explained all this to me with more enthusiasm than I had ever seen before from George. How much enthusiasm do you see when people are being taught to do something they don't do well, or even like?

We played to Sylvia's strengths as well. Sylvia's glaring strength was her ability to pick up the phone and get an appointment with almost everyone she spoke to. What we did, therefore, was to have Sylvia begin making appointments for George, for his one-on-one appointments and for his group sessions. And she just swamped him. This would later become my client's new model, and Sylvia became the head of the appointment-setting department. Both Sylvia and George were more productive, made more money, and were definitely happier—all of which benefited their employer. Not only did the employer shift from training their weaknesses to developing their strengths, he restructured the sale to exploit more of their individual talents (Best Practice #2: Sorting Sales Stages for Talent).

You can see how this type of individual development quite contradicts the model of enforcing one consistent, companywide selling methodology. Top managers get to know each of their salespeople's unique strengths, and they develop those further.

Spend More Time with Your Best

A spin-off application of the very same theory is to spend more time with top producers than with those who are struggling. This too was found to be a practice of the world's best managers, and if you think it sounds harsh, it's not. Those who need help, get help. They are not ignored or left to flounder. Actually, as far as those who are struggling goes, nothing really changes managementwise.

What changes is the attitude toward your *better producers*, who are typically left alone. The thinking once again is that they don't need help. Why work with those who are doing so well? The people who need help are the weaker performers. But the data collected from eighty thousand managers in four hundred companies contradicts this thinking.

Once again it was clearly illustrated that when resources are spent on weaker producers, the improvement is nowhere near that of the same resources applied to the top producers. And again I would suggest that this makes perfect sense when you stop to think about it. So don't ignore your weaker people; just stop ignoring your top people. See what they might want. Ask what you can do to further develop their preferred approach and style (as we did in the last section), and then *do it*. Involve them more; they'll appreciate it. Far too many top salespeople have said to me—with no small amount of what I can only call *hurt* in their voices—that they do not feel a part of the company.

PART II: WHO TO SELECT FOR THE SALES MANAGER POSITION

I mentioned in the last section how important it is to have the right immediate manager. The following is a synopsis from every poll I have been privy to, every company I have worked with, and every salesperson I have ever known. Not surprisingly it also represents what we all know in our hearts about good managers.

The best sales managers are part salesperson, part disciplinarian, part friend, part boss, part trainer, part mentor and part psychologist. They are at once a respected colleague and a down-to-earth member of the group. They lead by example and are never intimidating.

Top managers always put their team members ahead of themselves. They know that their job is about getting their people to produce, not about shining themselves. They are not the kind of people who need to have all the good ideas all the time just because they are "the manager." Conversely, they look to award praise for good ideas and effort to team members rather than themselves.

Top managers genuinely care about their people and frequently become friends with many of them. They look out for their people. Top managers have told me that they do not think of themselves as the salespeople's boss per se. They think of their job as more of a *guide* or a coach, providing salespeople with whatever they need to succeed. A good manager fits perfectly halfway between management and the salespeople, and yet is completely loyal to both. Salespeople know that their manager is accountable for results just like they are, and that he will fight management to the death for his team if he feels the cause is just, but he will *defend* management with equal passion when they are right. Top managers praise and reprimand with equal ease and, when they do have cause to reprimand, it is received without resentment. Although not necessarily demonstrative, they are almost always very passionate about what they do, and they expect 100 percent from the team in return. They are not always great orators who offer inspiring speeches to rally the troops; we often find such leaders to be in it only for their own glory. Top sales managers are in it for their people.

In terms of expertise the sales manager does *not* have to be the best salesperson on the team—it is common to have salespeople who beat their manager's track record—but he does have to know the industry and, in most cases, he needs to have been a successful salesperson himself in the same industry. It is also not necessary for the manager to be a gifted trainer, although it helps. Training can always be outsourced. The manager does, however, need to understand the training material, participate in training sessions, and walk the talk every day.

The best way to understand what a good manager is, is to ask her salespeople. Because of my consulting practice, I have had candid conversations with many hundreds of salespeople about their managers. About the good ones they say things like:

- "She'll always go to bat for us."
- "He has no ego. The best idea is the best idea—no matter who thought of it."
- "He looked at me and apologized for being wrong. I gained a lot of respect for him that day."
- "I felt slower than all the others, I just didn't get it. But she never made me feel that way. She sat with me and took all the time that was needed."
- "I trust him completely. If he tells me I should do this—even though I may not agree—I'll do it. I know he has my best interests at heart."
- "She actually lent me money once . . . told me not to say anything to anyone."
- "I really needed it for that new account and management was saying 'no.' He stayed on them until he got it for me."

- "Yeah, he chewed me out pretty good that day. But he was totally right. And he did it properly . . . in private. And then it was over—back to business."

As I have said, a sales manager is like the coach of a sports team. Like the players, he must produce; he is accountable. He focuses on the bigger picture: *winning.* With this kind of perspective, ego is rarely a problem. He will jump right into the game at any time. He is passionate about everything he does and genuinely cares about the players, and he can praise and reprimand with equal ease.

Promoting from Within

I have found no grounds for ruling for or against promoting someone to manager from within your organization. I have seen the wrong person get promoted from within as often as I have seen the wrong person hired from outside. I have also seen the right person come from inside or out—it really depends on available talent. This is a good thing, as you are not restricted to only one source.

What I do see with disappointing regularity is the right person being passed over. This is due to the rampant misunderstanding of the duties and accountabilities of the sales manager position; too many executives attach unrealistic qualifications and expectations to this position. The sales manager's job is simply to generate the agreed-upon results from the sales team, and to grow it further. For this you need the salespeople's respect, certain industry knowledge and experience, and *natural management talents*—not too much more.

A very common error worth mentioning is the assumption that a great salesperson will make a great sales manager. I know that many heads are nodding as I tell you that this is not necessarily true. It's also not necessarily untrue. Hiring (or promoting) your sales manager is the exact same process as hiring salespeople. If the candidate possesses the talents needed for the position, then she will do well. If your top salesperson happens to possess sales manager talents—and I have seen this on occasion—then he is a candidate for the position. The mistake I see being made very often is the assumption that the top salesperson can teach everyone else to just do what she does, and this never works. Let's look at the talents of top sales managers.

Sales Manager Talents

The talent interview you learned in chapter 5 identifies repeated patterns of behavior in your candidates, which are your best indicator that the associated talents are likely present. Using this process, the talents I look for in a sales manager are:

- Empathy
- Diplomacy
- Leadership (basically the adviser talent)
- Amiableness
- Humility and a lack of ego
- Fearlessness

As always, talk about past jobs to start the interview, going over positions the candidate liked or disliked. Experience is not necessarily required (talent is still talent with or without experience) but it is preferable. Look for patterns of standing up for what she believes in, of going to bat (leadership, fearlessness). She should ask you many questions as well—about how things are done at your company, what the management style and criteria are. She should want to know these things to know if your ideals are in line. I would not want to hire someone who was prepared to accept the position without having *asked me* enough questions about the company. Asking these types of questions shows maturity, leadership, and fearlessness.

Here we do not necessarily need a great speaker, but we do need a great listener. You should feel easy and comfortable with this person before long; it should not be difficult to like them.

Just as we did when looking for adviser talents, don't always agree. Offer alternative and conflicting opinions to see what the candidate does. We don't want a "yes man"; we want someone who knows how to diplomatically disagree, and present another opinion. Yet we want someone with enough humility to respect that you have your own opinion.

Here are some good interview questions to start you off (these too are available at www.theperfectsalesforce.com/tools):

- What will you do if a salesperson has their own way of doing things? (*The best managers know instinctively that everyone has their own style. You hope they answer, "It's really about results."*)
- What will you do if a salesperson is lagging?
- What will you do if you know someone just isn't going to make it? (*We don't want to hear, "I never give up." We want the manager to do what is necessary if it's inevitable.*)
- What will you do if your people are doing well? (*We want, "Praise! Party! Encourage!" We don't want, "Leave them alone."*)
- How involved do you get in your salespeople's daily activities? (*We don't want a micromanager.*)
- How involved do you get in your salespeople's personal lives?
- Would you ever have a salesperson, or the team, to your house? (*For these last two: the Gallup Organization found that the world's best managers do not find it inappropriate to be this friendly and personal—and their teams appreciate it.*)
- Tell me about a time you had a disagreement with management. (*Looking for leadership, diplomacy, and courage.*)

- Tell me about a time you had a disagreement with someone you managed. *(Top managers often have "heated discussions"; they do not fear or avoid it; they do not see it as negative—just a means to an end. They invite different opinions; it's a typical part of their day.)*

Remember to probe answers; ask *why* they feel that way, and what exactly they mean.

Managing with PIC

There is really no better way to manage than with an understanding of behavior analysis. In chapter 7 we learned the power of *positive, immediate,* and *certain,* and all managers should write these three words on the back of their hand and read them before and after every exchange with an employee. The greatest impact on an employee's performance—by far—is the relationship they have with their immediate manager. And the most impacting tool a manager has to work with is *reinforcement.*

The One Minute Manager has sold ten million copies since its release in 1981 and continues to sell ten thousand copies every month. The book's simple message is one of clearly communicated deliverables, and immediate and frequent reinforcement—both positive *and* negative.

The sales manager should try to catch his salespeople in the behaviors desired, and then praise. As simple as it may sound to you, these associations (behavior → praise) are strong motivators. Most managers wait for something to go wrong before they step in. Top managers step in when things are going right, and praise. This is the *positive* part of the PIC formula.

The *immediate* part of the formula refers to how soon following the desired behavior the acknowledgment comes. Employee reviews, for example—whether annual, biannual, or quarterly—are a ridiculous management practice. Employees should know at any (and every) moment exactly how they are doing, and exactly how pleased or displeased their manager is with their performance. To praise infrequently is to ignore the most powerful management tool available. Praising (reinforcing) desired behavior creates more of that behavior, and must be done *immediately following* the behavior.

This type of reinforcement must be the norm, not the exception, and it must be from the heart. Employees know when praise is sincere, and when it is not. This is why it is so important to have the right manager in the position; if praise is used only as a management technique—without real sincerity—it will not work. This is the *certain* part of PIC. Salespeople will very quickly come to *expect* positive reinforcement from their manager, because that is her way. Quite subconsciously, they will look forward to it, and do what is necessary to get it. We think we are complicated creatures but, in truth, we are still very primal. We gravitate to positive things and away from negative things, and the more "doses" per day (of positive *or* negative reinforcement), the more effective.

Goals

We have not yet talked about goals. This is because they are fairly overrated as a management tool. We have quotas that serve to commit salespeople to a "guaranteed" level of productivity, and a pay plan that motivates as much as a pay plan can. Goals are a practice that most managers believe they are supposed to be setting but the fact is, I have never seen it enhance performance.

Goals are personal. Every high achiever I have ever interviewed or worked with reached the levels that they did for their own reasons—not because their manager had a goal discussion with them. It was because they had *their own goal.*

Knowing this is important. There is nothing wrong with discussing goals with each salesperson (individually and privately) but they should know that it's just a talk—not something that is enforced or even necessarily expected. The only thing *enforced* is quota, and the pay plan amply rewards the ambitious and the greedy. During an informal, unscheduled chat, I will ask a salesperson, almost humorously, "What are you going to do with all the money you'll make this year?" Or, "Do you mind me asking what your personal goals are? How much would you *like* to make this year?" But it is conversational, not official. Some salespeople do not even consciously make goals! I like to chat about it to point out the value I have found in personal goal setting, and to get people thinking about high earnings. But I do so as a friend and a coach, to offer my experience in the matter. Goal setting is not a formal part of *The Perfect SalesForce* curriculum for the recurring reason that dominates this book—simply because it has not shown to be tied to a sustained increase in performance.

NOW THAT WE have covered each best practice, let's finish the book with a look at how to properly make use of what you have built. It would be a shame to build a high-performance vehicle and then never learn how to shift it into high gear.

GROWING THE PERFECT SALESFORCE

H ow would you describe *The Perfect SalesForce* in a nutshell? After implementing each best practice, what would you say it is that you built? How is it different from most?

I have personally come to refer to it as an "autonomous growth machine." This chapter's message is, if you have invested the effort and indeed built a high-performance vehicle—an autonomous growth machine—*then let it run.*

There is something in our nature that makes it difficult to "let go" of something we are invested in. Whether invested personally, financially, or emotionally, it is difficult to trust any system to the point where we won't pounce on every little bump that may occur along the way, and swoop in to fix it. We are all very much invested in our children and so, when they reach an age where they begin to find their own way of doing things, most parents swoop in and make the mistake of policing activities. The lessons I learned from the wonderful best-selling author Barbara Coloroso in her book *kids are worth it!* (HarperCollins rev. 2002) about policing my kids' *results* rather than *activities*— and how to establish the clear parameters and conditions that are first required—taught me more about generating desired behavior

without having to micromanage than any business course I have
ever attended.

Being emotionally invested is just fine. But if you don't learn
the appropriate behavior—what your role is in that investment—
you will likely sabotage your performance machine. The majority of company owners, execs, and managers I have met need a
lesson in letting go. The good news is letting go does not mean
turning as blind eye; it does not mean letting go *completely*. It
means trusting in your system, trusting in the talents you hired
and in the environment you created with the 6 best practices. It
means establishing short-term deliverables (or quotas) with your
department heads, providing all resources needed to reach these
quotas, and then *allowing each of them to do so*. It is this last part
of the sentence that most companies struggle with: the allowing,
or *letting go*.

The practices outlined in this book need not apply only to the
sales force. They are a model that applies to every department,
every team, every person—they are quite simply the natural laws
of human behavior, applied in the workplace. As such, they should
be applied companywide. They should become a company mind-
set. You cannot have a sales manager who manages the *results* of
her salespeople (as this book advocates), who in turn is micromanaged by *her* boss.

The top sales forces that I have been privileged to work with
have all figured this out; they have found a way to stifle that natural urge to micromanage. They set correct results and expectations, put the right people in place, create the right conditions, and
then trust the logic of that system enough to *let it run*.

Having been involved with so many implementations of the 6
best practices—both successful *and* nonsuccessful—is what led to
the disturbing observation that when implementation of these
practices is not successful, it is due to the owner's activities and

his lack of understanding of what his daily role should be. Years of trying to boil it all down to a succinct, common behavior have led to these observations:

- Owners and execs of high-growth companies focus on the sales they get.
- Owners and execs of slow or nongrowth companies focus on the sales they don't get.

I worked with a teleconferencing company that had, for the most part, a pretty talented team of salespeople. There was a mix of inbound calls from prospects and outbound sales calls to be made, as well as tremendous opportunity for growth through account penetration. These three different sale types—and the stages of each—very much needed to be arranged according to talent (Best Practices 1 through 3), and performance conditions then needed to be put in place for this revised structure (Best Practices 4 through 6)—a pretty straightforward mandate.

It is the experience of working with the owner of this company that crystallized exactly why some *Perfect SalesForce* rollouts are successful and why others are not. The term "micromanaging" is too vague—owners and execs need to know what they should be doing in place of micromanaging, rather than only being told what they *shouldn't* be doing. My teleconferencing owner made me think of an episode of "Survivor," where each team needs to gather water from the ocean in a small bucket, and then pass it from one person to the next—assembly-line style—up the beach to the last team member who pours that water into a larger container. The first team to fill their container wins.

It takes many repetitions of this process, many buckets of water before the large container is filled. Obviously there is much spillage along the way. The point of this analogy is my client focused almost entirely—to the point of near obsession—on all the spillage. He focused on all the water that *didn't* make it to the container. Winning sales teams—winning companies—focus on filling containers as quickly as they can, as often as they can, and, yes, with as little spillage as possible, but their *primary focus* is on the filling, not on all the drops that get away.

I tell you here and now, as I told my client, that *this single mindset* is what kept them back. I pulled out files of past clients and those of the two thousand owners I had interviewed and sure enough—the common denominator was an inability to let go of the drops that get away.

GROWTH EQUALS LOWER RATIOS

Because I am suggesting that you let go so as to enjoy greater autonomous growth, you deserve to know the whole story. There is an odd, slightly disturbing but natural byproduct of growing: *there will be more spillage.* It needn't be disturbing but it does seem to bother many owners and execs. It is also not difficult to understand; with all the money spent on marketing and lead generation and such, you don't want those leads slipping through the cracks.

Understand, therefore, that I am by no means suggesting that you turn a blind eye. You must continue to explore better practices and methodologies related to your machine's efficiency, but you must do so with the understanding that *growth equals lower ratios.* It is a bit of a paradox; you will continue to explore ways to spill as little as possible, simultaneously knowing that you will likely spill more as you grow. I have followed the growth of many companies—companies that run tight ships, mind you—and as they grew their various closing ratios diminished: the ratio of calls needed before an appointment is set, the ratio of appointments to sales, the average number of products purchased by each client.

A bigger machine will have more parts to fix and replace than a smaller machine. It will spring more leaks. There are more daily fires to put out. To continue my "Survivor" analogy, the more teams you have on the beach moving water, the more spillage you will have. And so let me share the two facts that offset this disturbing growth anomaly, the two reasons that you *want* more spillage: *because it means more money,* and *because you have no choice.*

You cannot change a natural law, which is why I say you have no choice. A bigger machine has more parts to fix and more leaks to patch. You cannot fight the natural byproduct of growing larger. But if you learn to focus on the *sales*—as the top sales-centric companies do—instead of on "the ones that get away," then the growth machine that you build with *The Perfect SalesForce* will kick into high gear. And if your closing ratio happens to drop from 25 percent to 15 percent over a five-year period, you should be okay with it for the two reasons cited: because it is an inevitable part of being bigger and, more relevant, given the choice, you would rather close 15 percent of five thousand prospects visited than 25 percent of one thousand prospects!

Fast-growth companies learn to focus on the machine—the bigger picture—rather than "those that get away" and this philosophy carries through all levels. Salespeople know full well they will not close everyone, and yet they still try. Sports teams know they cannot win every game and yet they still enter every game fully intending to win it. This is the mind-set of growth: the ability to focus on the sales instead of the ones that get away. The ability to focus on a steady hiring and training regimen instead of fixating only on your current producers. The ability to focus on the whole machine instead of obsessing on any one part—the *managers* are there to work the parts and fix them when needed.

THE PERFECT SALESFORCE
COMMITTEE

To aid you with that focus is your committee. People sing the praises of *The Perfect SalesForce* to me often—and that is certainly gratifying—but these same diligent disciples themselves break the rules, and they do so very unintentionally. With the best of intentions people make errors in talent judgment, or they pick unrealistic quotas, or they introduce short-term incentives that do *not* respect behavior analysis and PIC the way they should, or any number of other human misjudgments. And for this reason I recommend to any company that wants to implement the 6 best practices in this book that they form a *Perfect SalesForce* committee.

Depending on your company's size, the committee will typically include at least one executive (e.g., VP Sales), a human resources person, the sales manager, *at least* one salesperson (several is better, ideally top people), and the company owner(s) if appropriate. The committee has only one purpose: *to stay on track.* The above are realistic examples of how companies can unwittingly get bumped off track and then, before long, you're back to policing activities and focusing on the drops that get away. The committee will give you confidence in decision making, in creating new policies and quotas and pay plans. More heads are better than one when you are venturing into new practices. Assemble a good crew and listen to them all.

Such a committee will have two phases: the changes that you will choose to make *now* (after digesting this book's teachings) and then the ongoing, daily operational phase. This latter phase is where companies can go off track; everyone is too close to the daily grind to step back and see things objectively. It is here that your committee best serves. If you meet regularly (monthly, perhaps bimonthly) you will be able to assess whether all the typical daily choices are respecting the laws of natural talent and behavior analysis (PIC). You will catch things that might otherwise have slipped unnoticed through the cracks and poisoned the performance formula.

CHANGE

I will end with a word about making changes in your company. People like to say that change is scary, that most people fear and resist change. This is absolutely not true. People fear the unknown.

If you walk up to an employee right now and tell them you are changing their pay plan, there will likely be fear. But it is not the change they fear, only the fact that they do not yet know what the new pay plan will be. If you tell them in the next breath that the pay change is simply a 20 percent raise across the board, is there still fear? Does the employee fear making 20 percent more income? Of course not. People fear the unknown, not change itself.

This is a very important and powerful management lesson. *Keep your people informed.* Let them know why you are doing things, involve them in planning it, get their buy-in (which happens naturally when you involve them and listen to their ideas), and not only will there be no fear, there will be excitement!

That said, the fact is you can't please everyone. There are always the exceptions, those who like things the way they are. Let me tell you therefore how top companies deal with this. They do their best to inform and include everyone—as stated above— knowing that there will be those few who resist. You must explain the reasons for any changes; that after much deliberation you all feel this is the best thing for the company, and that the health and well-being of the company is, after all, your primary responsibility. (Don't ever let someone suggest that an owner's first responsibility is to her people; it is to build and grow a healthy company. That is what best serves the people.)

Having properly announced and discussed the upcoming changes, your secret weapon is *time*. You cannot be held hostage by a few employees who may not want to change. As long as your committee is in agreement, and everyone but a few agree that the proposed changes will benefit the company, you must move forward. Time will fix everything.

I have witnessed the reaction to change a great deal (change is my primary function) and the most gratifying thing to observe is the postchange phase. I love to watch practices align, and talent gel, and the machine begin to purr (to everyone's amazement), but as far as those who resist go, I can tell you that time is a sneaky ally. By nothing more than the passage of time, people acclimatize. You turn around one day and notice that everyone is once again on the same page. Never allow the few who fear new things to prevent you from implementing better and better practices in your company. The only true constant in life, after all, is change.

I WISH YOU the greatest success with your sales team, with your company's growth, and with your new understanding of these 6 best practices. Assemble your *Perfect SalesForce* committee, get everyone to read this book, and get started. Peter Drucker once said, "Wherever you see a successful business, someone once made a courageous decision." I wish you the courage to stray from the safety of what everyone else does, to do what actually works.

ACKNOWLEDGMENTS

T he *Perfect SalesForce* program would not exist without my clients. I thank each of them for their dedication to better management practices, for having the courage to step outside the box, and for letting me hang around to observe as long as I have.

My thanks to everyone at Portfolio and most especially to my editor, Jeffrey Krames, for caring about the quality of the program right from our first meeting and for restructuring my scribbling. It is a far better book for his participation. I thank my agents, Michael Larsen and Elizabeth Pomada, not only for bringing me to the likes of Portfolio, but for Michael's tireless badgering to produce a superior product. *Merci vous deux.*

I'd like to thank Neil Rackham for his support and for taking the time to write the foreword despite three other all-consuming writing projects and, perhaps most of all, for inspiring me by continuing to care about good content more than money.

A big thanks to Dale—as always—for pre-editing the entire book, and to my partners Robert and Gary for helping bring it to life. Thanks to Courtney Young at Portfolio for artfully juggling one million details but, moreover, for that cool pencil sharpener.

Thank you to my creative confreres Peter, Lawrence, Laurie,

and Susan for all the late nights of brainstorming and support (and wine).

Finally and most especially I must acknowledge three phenomenal women without whom I would not be here: my mother Olive, who continues to go above and beyond; my sister Dale, who never stops believing; and my wife, Linda, who quietly and tirelessly rides the roller coaster at my side.

APPENDIX: CASE STUDY

This section is a detailed case history. If it reads a bit like a story, it is because this is an account of an actual company, right from the time I first began working with them. It is intended to be an exercise more than a before and after story; you can "practice" on this company and see if you would have made the same changes I did. It will illustrate how I assessed the company's existing situation, how we all decided what things should be changed and why, the implementation of the new approach to the 6 best practices, the immediate reactions and ramifications of the changes, and finally, the results one year later. Only the names have been changed.

The implementation of any such changes in a company will always follow these four stages:

1. Assess the current situation (including strengths, weaknesses, good and bad systems and processes, good and bad employees and managers, etc.)
2. Obtain agreement on what to change, and change it
3. Announce "the changeover" to the company; explain the thinking
4. Train the staff in any new systems, processes, and procedures

I received a call from the owner of the Dilan Ink Company one afternoon several years ago. Dan was frustrated with the lack of performance from his salespeople. We talked for a while, had a more detailed meeting several days later, and I was hired to conduct the assessment that begins each of my consulting engagements (#1 above).

It is worth noting that I learn 80 percent of what I need to know about a company from its salespeople. I interview a great many of them—all of them if it's feasible. If some are located in other cities, we speak on the phone. I meet managers. I hang out and observe. I often accompany salespeople into sales calls. The whole point is to see the company and the daily jobs through the eyes of the employees, not management. Too many consultants have meeting after meeting with management; they formulate a plan of action, and then go about implementing it—without ever speaking to a salesperson or sales manager.

The same is true (and I think even worse) when companies make their own changes. They so rarely confer with salespeople and sales managers. These are the people who not only do the job every day; they are the ones who are in front of your clients every day. Their feedback is invaluable.

Yes, you have to filter out a lot of complaining and petty issues. But once they're filtered, and after you've spoken to a large enough demographic, the observations and recommendations made by the salespeople are usually right on the money. If company executives had better and more regular lines of communication with their foot soldiers, there would be far less need for outside consultants.

The Dilan Ink Company was thirty years old and had three locations in two states. They are primarily a manufacturer of ink that is sold to commercial printers. They also supply their clients with ink-related equipment and parts, and many accessories that they buy and sell as a convenience to clients. These products have a very different profit margin than the ink that Dilan itself manufactures.

When I began my assessment Dilan had eight salespeople, one sales manager, a total of about eighty employees, and annual sales of about $9 million—down from $9.5 million the previous year, and $9.8 million the year before that. Dan was understandably concerned.

STEP 1: THE ASSESSMENT

During the assessment stage, the ultimate goal is to see how a company "measures up" to the 6 best practices, to see how close (or far away) they are to perfect alignment and application of these practices. To this end I form my opinions two ways; I ask *many* questions, and I observe for a long enough period of time to give me a realistic feeling of what it is like to work at the company. It is risky to blindly believe what people say in these cases. Observation and time will confirm any details that need clarification.

I will share my findings about Dilan momentarily. First let me give you the list of criteria I bring with me. This is a guideline of questions that must be answered, and they are available to download at www.theperfectsalesforce.com/tools. As you know the 6 best practices serve to create a culture of pinpoint talent casting and ideal performance conditions. The following questions therefore are divided into these two categories. There is no order in which they must be answered, and some will be answered by people, others by observation.

Assessment Questions

Pinpoint Talent Casting

- What sales are each of the salespeople producing? Are some salespeople selling a lot more than others?
- Are there different sales positions that require very different work ethics?
- Are there different sales positions that require very different tolerance levels?
- Do some positions require more of an adviser, others more of a pleaser?
- Is the prospect or client always the same executive level?
- Do the products or services require detailed, abstract explanation?
- Is need established or must it be created? Is it a mix of both?
- How long is the sale cycle? Are there different cycles for different products or services?
- Is the solution a commodity or does it have benefits that are unique to the company? Is it a different answer for different products or services?
- Are people being asked to perform multiple sales stages that would ultimately be better performed by separate talents? Is such a structure feasible or would it be disruptive to the prospect or client?
- Has the company ever experimented with different sales stages assigned to different people? What happened? Was this approached from a *talent* perspective?
- How many different marketing channels are there for generating leads?
- Is there cold-calling or prospecting?
- Is there ongoing servicing?
- What is the hiring decision based upon (i.e., sales experience,

industry experience, university or accreditation, any special skills, talent, personality)?

- Do some salespeople appear to be miscast?

There are times when the work sheet can be helpful, but it is not generally needed at this stage. The work sheet should always be used when your management team wants to brainstorm the idea of assigning different sales stages to different salespeople and such things but at this point we are assessing the current situation; we are not making changes just yet.

Ideal Performance Conditions

- Are salespeople (and sales manager) paid on the sales revenue or on profit?
- Is the same remuneration plan available to everyone or are there factors that salespeople consider unfair or inconsistent (i.e., different base salaries for those who were hired with more experience)?
- Does the pay plan fully capitalize on PIC (*positive, immediate, certain*)?
- Does the pay plan respect the following rule? The base salary is just high enough to hire the caliber of salesperson needed, but the real earning potential is in the commission plan.
- Would a sliding-scale commission plan better incentivize here?
- Are short-term incentives being used?
- Do top-producing salespeople earn enough? Do they earn significantly more than average producers?
- Would "career levels" apply here?
- Is there a quota?
- Is quota a short enough period (in relation to the sales cycle)?
- Are quotas primary activities only?

- Are quotas *"the results that a properly cast individual can regularly accomplish with reasonable effort"*? Or are they fairly unreachable?
- Are quotas enforced? How?
- How frequently do salespeople sell above quota? How about well above quota?
- Are there any different quotas for different people? Does that make sense?
- Are quotas mentioned in the salesperson's contract? Is there a contract at all?
- Is the pay plan in the salesperson's contract?
- Do salespeople work in teams? Are there situations where an individual's pay is affected by the performance of another team member?
- Is there sales training? Is it only for new hires or does it continue?
- What is the curriculum taught in sales training? Is it consultative or "old school"?
- Is there role playing and reinforcing of the sales training? For how long?
- Is there field training?
- What other training is being done?
- Are activities or results being managed? If results, do they correspond to the quotas as they should?
- Does the sales manager try to correct (train) salespeople's weaknesses or develop their strengths?
- Does the sales manager spend more time with top performers or weaker ones?
- Do the salespeople like the sales manager? Do they respect him or her?
- Is the sales manager paid based on performance like the salespeople are?

- Does the sales manager have a quota? How long is that quota's period (e.g., annual, quarterly)?
- In general do the salespeople feel supported, appreciated, and part of a team culture?
- Do salespeople feel micromanaged?

As you can see, these questions follow the 6 best practices, and if it seems like an awful lot to discuss, keep two things in mind. First, it's worth the effort. Remember, we are not talking about selling "a little more" with *The Perfect SalesForce* structure; we are talking about building a sales force of people who sell four times more than everyone else. Second, every hour spent *before* changes are implemented (assessing, planning, brainstorming) will save you many, many hours *after* implementation. Undoing and rethinking and backpedaling are very costly and disruptive to morale.

Assessment Results

Having examined all these details, the following is a synopsis of the findings.

There were indeed many different sale types in this company, requiring various combinations of selling talents. Most products, for instance, did not require need to be created—the need for ink was already established when a salesperson visited a commercial printer. A printer knows he needs ink; he does not necessarily need Dilan's ink but he must buy ink. However, Dilan also sold an ink recovery system—something that had great value but that a client did not *have* to have for core business. Naturally Dan wanted his salespeople to sell this system as well, but most were not equipped with the talents needed to create need.

This recovery system also required the **Explanation** talent for concept sales, which some salespeople had and others did not.

Although Dilan's clients were companies of all sizes, the executive level of the contact at each company was the same throughout. Salespeople sold to buyers and shop foremen, not to owners or top executives, so this particular selling talent was not an issue.

Most of the products were commodities (clients felt they could get similar ink most anywhere else), but others were unique to Dilan (as in the ink recovery system). As such, different salespeople gravitated to selling different products and not others. This frustrated Dan. He wanted account penetration.

The sales stages were a major talent issue and a big influence on performance. This was a sale that required salespeople to manage a territory of existing clients (whose needs required an almost full-time commitment) while also bringing in new clients. As you might imagine, the amount of new business being brought in was nowhere near what the owner would have liked. Furthermore, there was virtually no marketing and hence no leads were supplied. Salespeople had to "go find" new commercial printer prospects, develop a relationship, and try to bring them on board. In terms of sales stages, this sale consisted of:

- Finding leads
- Prospecting them (either by calling to try to make an appointment or by just walking in off the street)
- The entire selling process
- Ongoing servicing

As you now appreciate, this is the equivalent of several jobs from a perspective of the talents required. It's a little like asking your architect to please take on the additional roles of land surveyor, building engineer, and general contractor. Because these jobs are related, your architect would likely not do a terrible job.

But he would certainly not perform at top levels in all categories. It is for this reason—as well as the other selling talent reasons mentioned—that performance at Dilan was sporadic. Every salesperson gravitated to the sale type, the sales stages, and the products that each of their talent sets instinctively directed them to. Let's move on to the performance conditions.

The pay plan had quite a high base salary; it varied from $50,000 to $75,000. Dan justified this variance as recognition of the different levels of industry experience that each salesperson had when they came to the company. The commission component was a straight 5 percent of all sales. A pay plan like this is fraught with many negatives for the company. It is not necessarily negative for the salespeople, mind you—many of Dilan's salespeople do very nicely—but such a pay plan does not serve management.

First, if a salesperson was to sell a $100,000 piece of equipment, she would get $5,000 in commission. If she instead sold $100,000 worth of ink, she would still make $5,000—despite very different profit margins on these two products. Salespeople were (understandably) motivated to sell the higher-priced equipment for the larger commission—a perfect illustration of how the conditions you create dictate what actions salespeople will take—but Dilan made almost no profit on the equipment they distributed.

Second, salespeople were resentful of the variance in salary. It is pretty difficult to explain to a salesperson how he can be selling 25 percent more than someone else, but earning a smaller annual income. Because Armand had less industry experience than June, his annual salary was $18,000 less than hers. And although he sold $300,000 more than she did one year, the 5 percent commission still had him earning less. These variances in base salary put a huge damper on morale—it's simply not right. When Armand approached Dan about this, Dan gave him a bonus at the end of the year—a sincere gesture but one that wound up annoying other salespeople. The conditions associated with such a bonus are completely random.

The high base and low commission are another problem. Salespeople were simply not as motivated as they could be. Most had reached their complacency point; they were comfortable. There were no short-term incentives of any kind. PIC did not score well at Dilan.

As for quota, there was virtually none. Dan and his sales manager would periodically chat with salespeople about prospecting more new business, upselling other products, getting referrals, and so on, but you and I know such talks accomplish nothing. Conditions do.

With good intentions Dan would engage the services of a local sales training company several times a year. I was told that several of the salespeople told Dan to save his money but I believe Dan thought it was his duty to support his salespeople, and this was the only way he knew how. The training produced no increase in performance.

The sales manager was a well-meaning, senior salesman named George. He had a territory of his own to service, his duties were never elaborated beyond "help the salespeople," and he earned a higher base salary because of the title. The salespeople liked George and he did in fact have the right talent make-up and personality to be a manager. Like many managers, he worked almost entirely with the new salespeople and with those who were weaker performers. The only time he ever really "helped" a weaker producer was when he accompanied that salesperson on a sales call and, basically, made the sale for them. Though well meaning, this was the extent of George's influence on sales. He led the weekly sales meeting, which was mostly a recap of what selling activities each salesperson had done in their territories the week before. Dan would occasionally attend these meetings and give his "we need more new clients" talk, or sometimes the "why aren't you up-selling more?" speech, while George sat quietly.

STEP 2: OBTAIN AGREEMENT ON WHAT TO CHANGE AND CHANGE IT

As unstructured as some of you may see Dilan Ink to be, this is not an uncommon setup. Dilan's owner Dan is a well-meaning man who simply didn't understand how to structure performance conditions or how to cast talent. He had built a $10 million company—an admirable feat—but revenue had stalled there years ago which, sadly, is all too common. The structure that is needed to go from $10 million to $50 million in revenue is very different from the structure that drove the company from zero to $10 million. An autonomous growth machine needs to be built and installed. The number of daily details that need to be managed have surpassed Dan's capacity. The passionate and well-intended micromanaging that is so commonly used by an owner (and probably needed) in order to go from a start-up to a $10 million company, only works to a point. With eighty employees, Dan's only hope of exploding out of the $10 million paradigm was to relinquish his hold on the activities, learn how to build the new structure needed for autonomous growth, and then change his own job description to one that oversees that growth machine. Dan needed to make the change from working *in* his business to working *on* his business.

Dan took this suggestion well but then most owners do at this stage of things. It all sounds quite logical so I generally get enthusiasm and a hearty, "Let's get started!" The moment of truth comes later, when we see if that enthusiasm can override the urge to micromanage.

Dilan's agenda for deciding exactly what to change looked like this:

1. Establish a *Perfect SalesForce* committee
2. Brainstorm with the committee and ultimately agree upon the optimum talent structure, addressing:
   - whether salespeople should continue to work all sales stages or whether we should assign different stages to different people
   - the possibility of different salespeople selling different products and services (in accordance with the 10 selling talents)
3. Once all selling positions have been agreed upon, create quotas for each position, as well as a suggested list of primary, secondary, and tertiary duties
4. Create new pay plans for each new selling position, and brainstorm the idea of "career levels" for salespeople

These four steps would create the foundation of the new sales machine. Following this, and equally critical, is educating everyone about the new structure, their new roles, and *why* changes are being made, which we cover in Step 4: Training.

It was agreed that Dilan's *Perfect SalesForce* committee would consist of Dan (the owner), George (the sales manager), Norman (the office manager and controller), Eva (human resources), two senior salespeople, and me (my role would be a temporary one, to facilitate the change process). We got down to it one Thursday afternoon.

We began with the whole issue of talent. We discussed the idea of assigning different sales stages to different people, different products that required different talent sets, how disruptive this might be for clients (if at all—often the new structure *benefits* clients), and so on. One predominant issue was immediately obvious: that salespeople are not visiting enough new prospects. The salespeople all claimed that the majority of their time was needed to service existing clients, which we all agreed may well be the truth. This then made us consider a model consisting of an entry-level, clerical position whose main accountability would be sourcing and compiling leads, and appointment setters who would write appointments for salespeople to visit new prospects. "Force feeding" appointments in this way would assure that salespeople always visited a certain minimum number of new prospects each month, alongside their current servicing duties.

The next question that this begs is how many new prospects can salespeople comfortably manage, given that they do spend the majority of their time servicing existing clients. This created a new thought: the idea of having hunters and farmers—one group that brings in new business and another that services that clientele ongoing. In chapter 4 we addressed this type of situation, and I explained how to decide whether or not hunters and farmers are the way to go. I called it the long sales stage factor: if any one sales stage will take so long that a relationship of trust and rapport develops, then it could be detrimental to the sale to switch players midway. In Dilan's case, appointment setters would not need a very long time to get salespeople in the door to have a brief chat. We all agreed it would not take a great many calls, so this appointment setter can be a separate job.

However, the next sales stage *can* take a long time. In this type of sale, a salesperson might well walk in a new door and come out with a small order—a way for the prospect to "test" Dilan's products and service level—but in most cases this does not happen. The salesperson will likely need to stop back to visit this prospect regularly and often, and eventually that first order may well materialize. In these cases a relationship definitely develops between prospect and salesperson and we all agreed that it would just be a bad idea to try to tell this new prospect that, now that an order has been placed, he is officially a client and a new salesperson will be taking over.

This then brought to light how different the ink sale was from the ink recovery system sale—not just from the talent perspective, but from a sales *process* perspective. The process described in the last paragraph applies to a commodity sale; the prospect is already buying ink from a competitor and perceives Dilan's ink to be of comparative quality and price. In these sales the salesperson usually woos the prospect away from his current supplier and over to the Dilan camp—something that usually takes a period of time. When the product in question is not a commodity, however, as with the ink recovery system, its unique value and benefit may attract the prospect to buy immediately, or at least much sooner. We parked that fact for the moment.

This was already good progress. We had identified that an appointment-setter position would benefit, as well as a lead-sourcing position, and that the "seller" should also continue to be the "servicer." Notice that work sheets have not been used up to this point. The work sheet's purpose is to identify what talents are needed for any given product or marketing channel or sales stage. But Dilan's lack of prospecting activity had more to do with the time constraints of servicing a client base than talent casting. In other words, even if a Dilan salesperson had the perfect talent set for prospecting—and was indeed itching to go visit new prospects—he or she would still not have enough hours in the day to prospect as much as Dan wanted.

The fact was that some salespeople did have more time for prospecting than others—those who were newer to Dilan and therefore had a smaller client base to serve. This led our thinking of course to the topic of career levels (as discussed in the territory-building sale in chapter 6). New salespeople have very few clients to serve and therefore a lot of time to prospect new business. That balance tips in later years as the servicing of a larger number of clients takes up more time.

Everyone liked the career level idea, as it addressed other issues as well, like pay, quota, and salesperson retention. Salespeople could now be supplied with appointments by the appointment setters, distributed daily, perhaps by a "head appointment setter." The number of prospect appointments given to any salesperson would depend on their career level, which of course is designed in accordance with how much time there is for prospecting at that level. This design also reduced the number of different talents a salesperson would need to have, since prospecting new appointments would no longer be a duty for salespeople. Given that it is much easier to find top-producing salespeople when you are asking them to be "top" at fewer sales stages, this was a good thing. We would no longer be asking salespeople to wear all the different hats; they would just *sell*.

It was still not yet time for work sheets. Brainstorming the sales "structure" in this way can change direction on a dime. One moment you can be talking about two groups of people needed for a particular thing and the next moment you've discovered that it won't work and that one group is better. This of course is the whole purpose of the exercise, and you won't typically want to use the work sheets to identify the talents needed for each position until those positions are certain. That said, I know some people who find it helpful to just go ahead and fill out lots of work sheets; it's up to you.

A framework was developing, but nothing would be written in stone until we had addressed everything. The next issue we discussed was the different talents needed for different products, specifically the ink recovery system where need had to be created.

There were really only two options here: either the same salespeople sell everything, or we have some salespeople selling ink and others who specialize in the recovery system. Everyone agreed it was a good time for a work sheet, to see what we were up against in black and white. The first one we did (see opposite) was for an ink salesperson, with the assumption that they are no longer writing their own new prospect appointments. Their job, therefore, is to bring a new prospect on board with Dilan, provide top-notch service into the future, and then upsell as many relevant products as possible (account penetration). We decided that, just for the moment, we would not establish the amounts and time frames that we usually do in the *Desired Result* column of the work sheet. We would fill those in when discussing quotas for each position.

A few points about this work sheet. Sales stages 1 and 2—even 3—might sometimes happen during the same appointment. Remember that sales *stages* are not necessarily sales *appointments;* they are simply different stages in the sales process that might possibly require different talents. This is why it is better to list more stages if you are not precisely certain how to define them. You may well need more than the four rows my work sheet provides. If so, you can download longer work sheets from:

www.theperfectsalesforce.com/tools

Notice that the talents needed for the first three stages are the same, but different from those needed in the fourth stage. This was not surprising, as we have always acknowledged that it is a different talent set that excels at closing business, rather than servicing clients long term. Despite this fact, the Dilan committee (including me) had decided that the same salesperson should carry out all four of these sales stages, since a relationship develops with the prospect throughout the selling stages. Remember also that finding a top producer who possesses all of the talents needed here is by no means impossible—only a bit more time

Sales Stage Work Sheet for:

Product Inks

Marketing Channel Attending appointments supplied by appointment setters

Step 1 ⟶ Step 2 ⟶ Step 3 ⟶ **Talents**

Sales Stages	Desired Result	The 10 Selling Talents	Talents Needed

1

| First meeting with a new prospect; learn about his ink needs and situation | Build rapport; establish Dilan's credibility (and salesperson's); gain permission to start a dialogue (return visits) | **1 Work Ethic** Quality vs. Quantity **2 Tolerance** High vs. Low **3 Persuasion** Adviser vs. Pleaser | 1 50–50   6 Obvious
2 Low to Mid   7 Medium
3 Adviser   8 Commodity
4 Mid level   9 Many
5 Established   10 Few |

2

| Identify areas where Dilan solutions are a smart alternative (i.e., better quality, cheaper, delivery…) | Get prospect to a point where he agrees Dilan products have a place in his company, either now or one day | **4 Executive Rapport** High vs. Low **5 Need** Create vs. Established | 1 50–50   6 Obvious
2 Low to Mid   7 Medium
3 Adviser   8 Commodity
4 Mid-level   9 Many
5 Established   10 Few |

ENGAGEMENT

3

| Continue all of the above (selling stage) to close; bring product samples where possible | Get first order | **6 Explanation** Obvious vs. Concept **7 Sale Cycle** Short vs. Long **8 The Solution** Unique vs. Commodity | **ENGAGEMENT**
1 50–50   6 Obvious
2 Low to Mid   7 Medium
3 Adviser   8 Commodity
4 Mid-level   9 Many
5 Established   10 Few |

4

| Develop account; interest client in additional relevant products | Grow territory (according to career level quotas) | **9 Products** Many vs. Few **10 Decision Makers** Many vs. Few | 1 50-50   6 Both
2 Low to Mid   7 Medium
3 Pleaser   8 Both
4 Mid level   9 Many
5 Both   10 Few |

consuming (we were already ahead of the game, having removed the need for those talents associated with the whole prospecting function).

Did you notice in the *Talents Needed* column that we wrote "50–50" for the first talent? Where the **Work Ethic** talent is concerned (quality versus quantity), not every sales job will be either 100 percent quality or 100 percent quantity. Many sales jobs require a mix of a pretty diligent work ethic and that star-quality-performance talent. The point is the committee should identify, in its own words, what mix of quality and quantity is needed for the job, firstly so they can hire accordingly and secondly so they can compare this mix to the other sales stages in the work sheet exercises.

Having completed the work sheet for the ink products, Dilan's committee then did one for the ink recovery system (see opposite).

As we were aware, a very different talent set is needed to sell the ink recovery system. The question was what should be done about it? Should we be looking to hire salespeople who can sell both or go with two groups of salespeople? We discussed the implications of both scenarios.

On the issue of the same salespeople selling everything, remember that those who do *not* possess the **Need** and **Explanation** talents necessary for selling the ink recovery system *will not sell at high levels* and, furthermore, cannot be *taught* to sell at high levels. The flip side, however, is a viable option: a salesperson who does have the **Need** and **Explanation** talents needed for the ink recovery system will be able to sell the ink as well. The only downside to this scenario is the **Solution** talent of unique solution versus commodity, which states that all salespeople strongly prefer one over the other. I reminded the committee, however, that this talent fell in the preference section of the 10 selling talents table; it does not mean that the unique-solution salesperson is incapable

Sales Stage Work Sheet for:

Product Ink Recovery System

Marketing Channel Attending appointments supplied by appointment setters

Step 1 ⟶ Step 2 ⟶ Step 3 ⟶ Talents

Sales Stages	Desired Result	The 10 Selling Talents	Talents Needed

1

First meeting with a new prospect; elaborate benefits of recovering and reusing ink that used to be discarded

Get prospect interested in starting a dialogue about the system

1 **Work Ethic**
Quality
vs. Quantity

2 **Tolerance**
High
vs. Low

3 **Persuasion**
Adviser
vs. Pleaser

1 Quality	6 Concept
2 Low	7 Medium
3 Adviser	8 Unique
4 Midlevel	9 Few
5 Create	10 Few

2

Bring in a sample recovery system; leave it for a week or two for a "test drive"

Get prospect attached to the system by using it and seeing monetary benefits firsthand

4 **Executive Rapport**
High
vs. Low

5 **Need**
Create
vs. Established

1 Quality	6 Concept
2 Low	7 Medium
3 Adviser	8 Unique
4 Midlevel	9 Few
5 Create	10 Few

ENGAGEMENT

3

Continue selling stage to close

Sell the system

6 **Explanation**
Obvious
vs. Concept

7 **Sale Cycle**
Short
vs. Long

8 **The Solution**
Unique
vs. Commodity

ENGAGEMENT

1 Quality	6 Concept
2 Low	7 Medium
3 Adviser	8 Unique
4 Midlevel	9 Few
5 Create	10 Few

4

9 **Products**
Many
vs. Few

10 **Decision Makers**
Many
vs. Few

1	6
2	7
3	8
4	9
5	10

of selling a commodity—only that she prefers to sell unique solutions. These salespeople thrive on the challenge of creating need—creating a genuine desire to own a product that the prospect didn't even know existed a half hour ago. By comparison, selling a commodity is quite boring to this group.

It was time to examine the other option: a separate group of ink recovery system specialists whose sole job would be to sell these systems, both to existing Dilan ink clients and to new prospects. Pondering this approach immediately got the committee's creative juices flowing. For those prospects who would tell Dilan's appointment setters, "Thanks but our ink needs are all taken care of right now," salespeople could then switch to the topic of the unique recovery system. That immediately led to the idea that the recovery system should always be the appointment setters' opener: "Let us show you how local printers are reusing ink that used to be thrown away." Whether the prospect buys the system or not, he would then be told about Dilan's ink line.

The committee liked this structure. It felt more professional; it would prevent unique-solution salespeople from becoming bored with commodity sales, and it seemed more scalable (any time you can assign different products to different groups, you can influence each group's behavior more effectively since you can now create performance conditions specific to each group). At this time I remember George frequently asking who from the current group would be selling which product. The advice I gave to George and the committee has already been mentioned throughout the book, and always seems to come up during these planning sessions. You cannot let the current salespeople or the current structure or pay plan or anything else affect the process that will create your company's ideal sales department model. Pretend that you are starting over and designing the department from scratch—your current team does not exist. Do things in order: the ideal talent structure first, followed by the conditions for each of the new positions. Remain completely objective.

Thinking that we liked the proposed structure for the time being, we moved on to the task of defining the right quotas for each position. You certainly may well go back and rethink the structure you just created at any point; attaching the conditions to each position often shines new light (and raises new issues) on the proposed structure.

The discussion of establishing quotas should be in tandem with company growth discussions; however, many companies need to rethink their growth-forecasting process. I have seen many a company commit to a particular revenue increase by year's end, then simply divide that increase by the number of salespeople they have, look at those salespeople, and say, "Okay . . . go!" without really knowing whether the increase was a realistic one for the sales team. Many companies embrace such an approach, thinking that an aggressive goal will motivate everyone to rally and step up to the plate and ultimately produce more than they normally would. Their company goal isn't necessarily a true goal; if they fall short but have a decent increase over last year, they're happy.

Unfortunately this is not controlled growth, and furthermore, it's not fair to the sales team. *The Perfect SalesForce* allows for a slightly different but far more reliable formula to forecast growth: one that comes as a result of knowing far more accurately, and certainly, what each salesperson will produce. This is the key piece of information missing from the growth formula that most companies use: they don't know how much each salesperson will really sell. Although it may seem a fantasy to some, imagine that you know for certain what each salesperson—current and future—will produce in the coming year. As long as you believed it was for certain, you would make informed decisions about how many new salespeople you should hire, what that would cost, and exactly how long it would take for each new hire to produce a return.

Right now these decisions being made in most companies are not informed decisions, they are guesses. Making a forecast means estimating. It means take your best calculated guess, and the only reason that anyone ever needs to guess about something is because they don't have all the information; there is a piece missing. And where forecasting sales is concerned, that missing piece is almost always related to how much each salesperson will produce—particularly those yet to be hired.

Growth costs money and produces negative cash flow for a time. If you know for certain what every existing salesperson and new hire is going to produce, you can approach growth very differently. With no more missing information, you can calculate exactly what it will cost to grow at whatever rate you choose, how long you will be in the red from new hires, how long cash flow will be negative, and so on. Most companies deal with new hires very emotionally. They do not know how well these new salespeople will do so they fear (understandably) a hiring regimen that is too aggressive.

If you were asked to make a buying decision on a piece of equipment you needed for production without knowing its output level, your decision would be nothing more than a guess. Without knowing how much the machine is capable of producing in what time frame, you could never calculate your return on investment. I have watched many companies spend millions of dollars on new equipment because of how much it will increase their productivity. Growth-oriented companies understand that such a purchase is not an expense, it is an investment. The new machine allows these companies to produce (and hence grow) at rates they would not otherwise be able to, making the investment an intelligent one.

If you could look at hiring salespeople the very same way, your growth rate would be as fast as you would like (and can afford). There would be no risk. The risk that is currently associated with aggressive salesperson growth is the complete uncertainty of their future productivity.

Of course, no group of people will ever perform with the same level of certainty as a piece of equipment, no matter how much we've raised the bar. Predicting human behavior just isn't as exact a discipline as mechanical engineering, but the point I'd like you to take from the analogy is still a valid one. The 6 best practices in this book will build a machine that is far more predictable and reliable than it used to be, and the companies that I have worked with that grew at record-breaking rates treated their salesperson growth machine like any other machine—they measured output religiously, thereby establishing the realistic expectations of each position so as to choose, and financially plan for, whatever rate of growth they wanted. Which brings us back to the Dilan Ink Company's quotas.

With this mind-set, we began discussing what everyone felt were the "right" results for each sales position. We were working with the three positions that we had all agreed were "the model to beat" to this point—appointment setters, ink salespeople, and ink recovery system salespeople. While these were new positions, their constituent tasks had been measured by Dilan management for many years—things like how many calls it took to make one prospect appointment, the company's overall closing ratios for ink and for the recovery system, upsell percentages and account penetration details, and so on. These tasks were not going to be new, only the arrangement of who does which ones.

I had to be careful with what data we chose to use. Understand that much of the measured results and ratios that George offered up included certain selling tasks that the new sales positions would not. In other words, when George told the committee that it took the average salesperson one year and nine appointments to sell an ink recovery system, his data was not detailed enough to tell us whether these were existing ink clients, new prospects, or a combination. Another example was how many calls it took to make an appointment with a new prospect; if the data happened to be mixed with other calls being made by a salesperson—a service call to an existing client perhaps—then the resulting ratios are not trustworthy.

We had a lot of good data upon which to estimate what the results would be from each new position, but I offered the following very important caution. In the quota chapter we acknowledged how important it is to set the "right" quotas—that you don't want to be changing them all the time. So what happens if a position is so new that you really don't know what it will or should yield? The answer is sometimes you have no choice but to make an adjustment to a quota, and how you do it is very important.

Remember our definition of quota is *"the results that a properly cast individual can regularly accomplish with reasonable effort."* Remember too that salespeople who are clearly miscast according to this definition will be replaced. Managing to this definition— enforcing it universally and fairly—is absolutely essential. If it is not enforced it is no longer a quota; it is no longer something the salespeople believe *must* be done. After we teach the sales manager this rule, and train him in the correct way to enforce it, he will have a load of misery if he comes along one day and tells the sales team that management has decided to alter a particular quota. What if certain salespeople had been promoted—or *released*—based on that quota?

As usual the answer to this potentially disastrous situation is nothing more than good communication. If it is a new selling position, salespeople will understand that an exact quota cannot yet be attached to it. As a matter of fact, if management tried to do so, the sales team would rightly question where the number came from. The logical thing to do is to postpone setting an official quota, incentivize the position well, and measure results for a long enough period, and from enough salespeople, that you feel confident that the number you plug in to that quota definition is the right number. In other words and as always, communicate your plans, and the reasons behind them, to the salespeople. Let them know the goal is to identify deliverables that each selling position should yield if the person in it is properly cast. Include them and they will help you. Keep them in the dark and they will feel everything from fear to resentment.

It was time to plug some estimates into the *Desired Results* column of the work sheets. We would not announce these as official quotas but use them as a working model to continue brainstorming. We needed to complete three such work sheets, one for each new position. We started with the appointment setters, and as soon as we began to discuss just how many new appointments they should write per salesperson (our first official *Desired Result* column), the point came back about how different salespeople, who are at different points in their careers with Dilan, will be able to manage a different mix of new prospects to existing clients. We realized that the number of appointments this new position (or department) should produce will depend on how many salespeople there are at each different career level—something that would constantly be changing. We all agreed therefore that a discussion of the career level plan for the ink salespeople was in order: those who would visit new prospects more heavily in the early part of their career with Dilan, and do more ongoing servicing (and less prospecting) as time went on.

We talked about what that plan might look like, how people would be remunerated at each level, where the break between levels should be and, since the usual starting point is to establish how much of the pie there is to split among the sales team, it was time to address the very different profit margins between Dilan's manufactured ink products and distributed equipment. We simply could not continue to pay the same commission on all of these different products. The group felt it was a pretty straightforward solution to assign two different commission percentages, but I reminded them that this was also a good opportunity to address the in-the-moment pricing that Dilan salespeople inevitably have to do. When a commercial printing prospect is asked to buy a product like ink, he is being asked to move away from his usual ink supplier, over to Dilan. On a commodity product this will always involve competitive pricing, since it is quite unlikely that the prospect would leave their usual supplier if Dilan's pricing was higher. Dan wanted his salespeople to talk more about Dilan's service, its reputation, the ink recovery system—things that might differentiate Dilan. He wanted the salespeople to stop instantly dropping the price without at least trying to illustrate why there was value in paying a little more.

This is an age-old issue between owners and salespeople where a commodity sale is concerned. It must be acknowledged that if there are no positive or negative motivators associated with dropping the price, salespeople will drop it to get the sale, especially when they believe that fighting for a slightly higher price might blow the deal. It should also be acknowledged that the salespeople are usually right; more often than not the prospect will *not* switch suppliers if all conditions appear to be the same. As much as most owners believe their company provides a better product and better service, the decision maker doesn't see that as enough reason to go through a change. This is different of course if there is a problem with the current supplier, but by and large salespeople usually need to offer a better price to win the business.

That said, it still makes perfect sense to use our knowledge of positive and negative motivators to motivate the salespeople to at least attempt to sell higher wherever possible. I proposed paying them based on the profit margin—a matter of adding another field to the commission calculation. I had created such plans before, adding a profit consideration to the sliding-scale commission. This meant obtaining new software to track all of this. While the software wouldn't be an excessive expense, Dan decided to wait, since Dilan was already considering changing their entire enterprise resource planning (ERP) software—a big upcoming project. We tossed around various alternatives and finally decided to create the usual sliding-scale commission plans for each career level based on revenue, not profit, but only for the ink products Dilan manufactures. The distributed equipment would pay a lower, flat commission, not a sliding scale. These distributed items were available as a convenience to clients, not to mention as a deterrent to the client shopping elsewhere and being wooed away. But we all agreed that these higher-priced items should not count toward sales that would get salespeople to the next sliding-scale payout level.

Finally, to address the pricing issue, we agreed on the following positive and negative motivators. We would add a minimum acceptable price (MAP) level to the salespeople's ink catalog. This would halt the never-ending calls to George and Dan when a prospect requested special or lower pricing; it gave pricing control back to the salespeople, but with clear parameters. They could negotiate price wherever they deemed necessary, but only down to the MAP. If that didn't get the deal done, the salesperson could always call George to request a larger discount if he wanted to, but he would make no commission. That minimum acceptable price level truly was as low as Dilan could profitably sell ink. This was the negative motivator to price dropping, and the salespeople understood it perfectly when we explained it. It simply doesn't make sense to sell at a loss.

The positive motivator to selling as high as possible came in the form of a quarterly profit margin bonus to those who had the highest average markup in the quarter. When one of the senior salespeople on the committee came up with this idea, it was first conceived as a bonus awarded to one "winner" annually. While certainly on the right track, it didn't adhere to our PIC (*positive, immediate, certain*) rule. Paying one salesperson only once a year is not nearly as effective a motivator as paying several salespeople as many times as possible per year, so we decided to reward the top 25 percent of the sales force who sold at the highest profit margin. We would establish just how much to give them as we further developed pay plans, but we were making significant progress arranging all the pieces.

We came up with the following career level idea for ink salespeople shown on the opposite page.

As discussed in chapter 6, the first decision when creating pay plans is how much of the pie can be shared with the sales team. Dan told us that in the manufactured ink products, the company could part with a maximum of 24 percent (of sales).

Let's look at the Welcome Level. Here new salespeople are supplied with ten new prospect appointments per week (by the appointment setters). These salespeople start with a client base of $100,000 in sales per year, which I will explain in a moment. As the average Dilan client spends about $50,000 per year on ink, servicing this small client base does not take a lot of time, and leaves new salespeople the majority of their time to bring in new business. Quota in Q1 is $25,000, which is the amount that the salespeople "inherit" when they start. There are actually no sales expectations in the first quarter when salespeople are undergoing a lot of training. Quota then rises by $10,000 a quarter

Welcome Level	Silver Level	Gold Level	⭐ President's Club
			• Club membership • President's biannual meeting in Europe ⇧
		• Annual Meeting in Bahamas • Increased expense account • Increased clerical assistance ⇧	• Annual meeting in Bahamas • Increased expense account • Increased clerical assistance • Company car
	• Company car ⇧	• Company car	
Appointments Supplied 10 per week	**Appointments Supplied** 6 per week	**Appointments Supplied** 3 per week	**Appointments Supplied** None
Quota Q1: $25,000 in sales Q2: $35,000 Q3: $45,000 Q4: $55,000 Q5: $65,000 Q6: $75,000	**Quota** Increase of 10% per quarter	**Quota** Increase of 6% per quarter	**Quota** Maintain min $1,000,000, annually
Pay Plan • Base of $45,000 for max 12 months • $1,000 bonus when less than 3 months to next Q level (above) • Self-generated sales bonus • Eligible for profit margin bonus	**Pay Plan** • Sliding-scale per Silver Plan • Self-generated sales bonus • Eligible for profit margin bonus • Short term incentives	**Pay Plan** • Sliding-scale per Gold Plan • Self-generated sales bonus • Eligible for profit margin bonus • Short term incentives	**Pay Plan** • 20% of Sales • Self-generated sales bonus • Eligible for profit margin bonus • Short term incentives

Annual Sales ⟶ $300,000 $600,000 $1,000,000

for the next eighteen months—something that everyone agreed was extremely doable, especially with appointments being supplied.

The pay at this career level was guaranteed to be no less than $45,000 for a maximum of eighteen months—the amount that the committee agreed was necessary to attract the sales candidate needed for this job. As soon as the salespeople built their client base to $300,000 in annual sales they moved on to the Silver

Level, whose sliding-scale commission plan started at 15 percent, the equivalent of the $45,000 the salesperson was used to, and increased from there.

The significantly greater earning opportunity at the Silver Level was not the only motivator to reach it as quickly as possible. To further motivate Welcome Level salespeople to reach the Silver Level sooner, we would pay a $1,000 bonus every time a salesperson's sales increased by $10,000 in less than a quarter's time. In other words, as you see in the quarterly quotas at this level, sales should rise by $10,000 per quarter. If the salesperson achieves this amount in less time than a quarter, she will get a $1,000 bonus.

Notice the profit margin bonus is included for every career level, including the Welcome Level. The top 25 percent of the sales force who sold at the highest profit would receive quarterly bonuses relative to their sales volume and profit margin. This would never be less than $1,000. You will also notice a "self-generated sales bonus" at each level. This was to motivate salespeople to continue to prospect their own leads and appointments. Just because they were being supplied with appointments from the appointment setters did not mean that ambitious salespeople could not prospect on their own as well. Any new client who came from a salesperson's "self-generated sale" came at a savings to Dilan, since the appointment setters did not need to be paid their share for the deal. That savings would be shared with the salesperson in the form of the self-generated sales bonus, and served as yet another motivator for the ambitious.

The sliding-scale commission plans in the Silver and Gold Levels (see opposite) were structured just like the examples in chapter 6, the intention being to motivate salespeople to reach each new "jump point"—that point where the commission paid on all sales that quarter jumps to a higher percentage.

SLIDING-SCALE COMMISSION:
SILVER PLAN

Quarterly Sales	(Equivalent in annual)	Commission
$75,000–$99,999	($300,000–$399,999)	15%
$100,000–$124,999	($400,000–$499,999)	16%
$125,000–$149,999	($500,000–$599,999)	17%

This plan would have salespeople striving to reach the Gold Level sooner than a consistent commission rate would. If it is nearing the end of March (Q1)—when the commission rate is assigned to my quarter's earnings—and my sales are around the $115,000 mark, the monetary motivation for me to reach the next level ($125,000) before March 31 is about $1,400 ($124,000 commissioned at 16 percent = $19,840; $125,000 commissioned at 17 percent = $21,250). The thinking that goes on at quarter's end is "I'm going to reach this next sales level shortly anyway; I might as well give a little extra effort to reach it a bit sooner, and see $1,400 extra dollars on my paycheck at the end of the month."

The Gold Level plan was similar.

SLIDING-SCALE COMMISSION:
GOLD PLAN

Quarterly Sales	(Equivalent in annual)	Commission
$150,000–$183,333	($600,000–$733,333)	18%
$183,334–$216,666	($733,334–$866,666)	19%
$216,667–$250,000	($866,667–$1,000,000)	20%

You may have noticed that the gaps between career levels are not even. There is a gap of $200,000 between the Welcome Level and the Silver Level (remember, salespeople inherit $100,000 in sales when they start), a gap of $300,000 between the Silver Level and the Gold Level, and $400,000 between the Gold Level and the President's Club.

When new salespeople are making $45,000, they are naturally pretty motivated when they look at, for instance, a Gold Level salesperson who has $185,000 in sales on the board for the quarter—the equivalent of $140,600 in annual income. Rather than splitting the career level gaps equally, you will better capitalize on that early career vim and vigor if your people can reach the next levels sooner.

Note that at each level certain working conditions change and more perks are added. There are myriad short-term daily and weekly incentives at every level (paid for by the 24 percent that Dan said he could pay on all sales—note that our pay plans all slide between 15 and 20 percent, leaving the rest for other incentives). At the President's Club level, no appointments are supplied and there is no growth quota—only the mandate to maintain a minimum of $1,000,000 in sales. Salespeople at this level can and should continue to sell more to their existing accounts, and are welcome and encouraged to bring in new clients. If they do, they receive the usual self-generated bonus, since the sale was self-generated. Twenty percent commission on the President's Club required $1,000,000 in sales makes for a nice living, and once the obligatory "get more" atmosphere is taken out of the equation, we see salespeople, even at these earning levels, strategically looking to make even more. Which brings back the topic of that $100,000 in sales that each new recruit inherits.

A win-win arrangement that I have used several times in the territory-building-sale consists of President's Club salespeople "weeding" their client base. We don't want to create the impression that when you reach President's Club, you're done. We don't want a "coasting" mentality. Remember the management lesson of focusing on your top producers rather than leaving them alone because they are doing well. We want them to know that they are valuable and that we still try to find creative earning strategies for their group.

When a salesperson is new and aggressively building their client base, signing up a "small" client is as thrilling as any other. But as time passes the focus (and the training) will tilt more toward territory management and time management. Any seasoned salesperson knows the lopsided and unfortunate truth that you often spend as much time on a $20,000 account as you do on a $400,000 account. Many of Dilan's senior salespeople managed client bases where 80 percent of their revenue came from 20 percent of the clients—those big ones. However, these salespeople usually spent more than half of their time with all those smaller clients, who make up only 20 percent of the revenue.

Again, this is not a concern in early career levels. But at the million-dollar level, where a salesperson would like to go get more *big* clients, he often has no time. In *The Perfect SalesForce* this problem is management's, not the salesperson's. Here we have a top-producing salesperson who wants to go get more big clients but can't. Enter the win-win arrangement, where a President's Club salesperson can weed her garden and transfer any smaller accounts she no longer wants over to the new recruits (as orchestrated by the sales manager). This typically represents a reduction in earnings of anywhere from 5 to 20 percent for the top salesperson, but also an opportunity to free up half her time to get bigger clients, and potentially more than double her income.

This is obviously a choice each salesperson will make individually. At this point some of you may be thinking about those clients who are transferred to a new salesperson—a very valid thought. It is arguably disruptive to announce to the client that they now have a different sales rep, but no more so than when a salesperson leaves your company and they are replaced. If the change is handled properly it is more than worthwhile. Your top people should be working with top clients, not little ones. Obviously, this is not the way you will word it with your smaller clients, but it is what serves your company best. Have the President's Club salesperson bring the new salesperson with her for a few of the regular sales calls to these smaller clients. When the time is right the top salesperson can simply tell the clients that her position and her duties in the company are changing—something that happens at companies every day. Having the familiar rep introduce the new rep is professional, respectful, and kind. And again, revenuewise, this model is superior.

At this point we had a structure for career levels and for pay plans and quotas at each level. This progress had taken several short meetings and a total of about six hours, and I can tell you that everyone was pretty excited about the proposed structure— especially Dan. I believe he very much understood how these clear parameters and well-constructed positive and negative motivators could generate the results he was after. It was time to address the other two positions, starting with the ink recovery system sales-people (now known as the IRS salespeople, which everyone found quite amusing).

Having gone through the previous position's brainstorming pro-cess already, I can tell you that on this round I spoke less and lis-tened more. This stuff isn't difficult once you understand the basics of talent and of what conditions produce what actions, and the committee covered a lot of ground with only the occasional bit of guidance from me. They opened with the question of whether the IRS salespeople should visit existing clients or new prospects or a mix of both. They decided both to be a good idea since the ap-pointment setters would probably get in some new doors every day based on talk of the ink recovery system rather than ink itself, and because they felt that many existing clients were great IRS candidates that had never even been introduced to the system—a case of their salespeople not being talent equipped to talk about a create-the-need product.

Regarding existing clientele, the committee felt it logical that the ink salesperson—who already has a relationship with the client—should announce the recent addition of an ink recovery system "specialist" and that Dilan would send him over to anyone interested. I disagreed. In a create-the-need sale it is illogical to leave prospects to assess their own needs—the salesperson needs to *create* the need, and we had already established that many of the ink salespeople lacked the talents to create need. And left to self-assess, a great many clients would decide they don't need such a system without knowing very much about it! This is why it's called a create-the-need sale.

The committee agreed that the appointment setters should systematically call all clients and make complimentary appointments with Dilan's new specialist. The appointment-setter position is one where all the training is geared toward making an appointment at all costs. We agreed that this person would make the most of Dilan's client list. We decided the IRS salesperson would start with two new appointments per day, since much of their day would soon be occupied with callback appointments as well.

As for a quota, past sales statistics associated with the recovery system suggested that one in every eight prospects bought the system. We were uncertain as to how accurate this data was and decided to tell the IRS salesperson that, since it was all new, we would be implementing these parameters in the near future. It was time for the pay plan.

We went with a higher "base" for this position. I put the word "base" in quotations because it's not always a true base salary, as in the ink salespeople's pay plan. As soon as the ink salespeople are selling enough that the commission generated exceeds that base amount, the "base" is irrelevant. It's really a 100 percent commission plan but with the added security of a guaranteed minimum. These pay plans take advantage of the 100 percent commission mentality, and allow for a more vivid effort-to-earnings reward system.

We chose a "base" of $55,000 for this sale because, to put it bluntly, this is a harder sale and it requires a better communicator and persuader. Dilan's core-business ink sale is a territory-building sale, for which the required primary talents are relationship building and a decent work ethic. The create-the-need sale, however, requires concept explanation talents, need creation talents, abstract thinking, higher-level leadership, and strong persuasion talents. Top salespeople with these talents are simply a little harder to come by. They also know they're talented and will likely cost you more, which is fine. They're worth it.

The average ink recovery system sale was around $70,000 with all the machinery, equipment, and supplies. Dan said he could share a total of only 10 percent of that with the sales team; Dilan did not manufacture this equipment itself and the profit margin was lower. So we had $7,000 per sale to work with. We also felt that the right individual should have no problem selling a system to one in every ten prospects. (We try to use conservative estimates, not aggressive ones. If we can make the numbers work with conservative estimates, it's a safer bet everything will work out in real life.)

Given the number of prospects we identified among Dilan clients, as well as the number of nonclient prospects there were to visit, there was no real danger of saturating a territory too quickly. Nonetheless we decided to test this position with just one salesperson. We would work out kinks before expanding this sales position. We came up with the following pay plan.

INK RECOVERY SYSTEM PAY PLAN

Quarterly Sales	(Equivalent in revenue)	Commission
2 to 3 units	($140,000–$210,000)	7%
4 to 6 units	($280,000–$420,000)	8%
7 to 10 units	($490,000–$700,000)	9%
		9%
11 + units	($770,000+)	Plus a $1,000 bonus for every unit

If you do the math on this plan you will see the type of living the right individual can make. You will also see the usual dramatic increase in quarterly earnings from one commission percentage to the next, motivating the salesperson to close that extra deal or two that might be in the pipeline, in this quarter rather than the next.

The additional $1,000 bonus for any sales over ten units would actually exceed the 10 percent that Dan said he had to share with the sales team (remember, there would be appointment setters to pay from this 10 percent as well), but he told us that if he was selling this number of units, he could get a good volume discount from the company that manufactured them.

We would also use the usual short-term incentives for this position. Although we had agreed to see some results before establishing the quota, the group feeling at the moment was somewhere between two and four units per month.

The issue of ink sales came up. It certainly stood to reason that if an ink recovery unit was sold to a new prospect, Dilan may also end up selling its ink to this new client. The ink sale should certainly be attempted after every successful IRS sale—even if the IRS did *not* sell, for that matter—but who would then service this ink client? This prompted a discussion of what to do about existing ink salespeople who might sell an ink recovery system. The issues were: who should be allowed to do what, and how would Dilan remunerate?

The primary goal is always harmony within the sales team—the company must always "do the right thing." If certain ink salespeople happened to gravitate toward the IRS sale (which was in fact the case—a couple of ink salespeople had create-the-need talents), then they should certainly not be penalized by being told they can no longer sell it. And if an IRS salesperson goes on to open an ink account, he certainly deserves a piece. On this latter scenario we quickly acknowledged that the IRS salesperson should not continue to *service* ink if he were to introduce the core ink products—that decision was covered way back when we decided to make IRS its own position in the first place. We had separated these two sale types. But certainly some sort of spiff or commission should be paid.

This is where we must always use our knowledge of PIC. If the reward isn't worth the effort, we will not generate the behavior we want. For the IRS salesperson (who will be making a good living) to be motivated to try to upsell some ink, or to even get an ink salesperson in the door, the incentive must be there. It should, however, be a one-time commission, not an ongoing one; the ink salesperson will be doing all the ongoing work and frankly, it wouldn't be right for the IRS salesperson to make an ongoing piece of the pie.

The obvious starting point was the piece that is usually paid to the appointment setters to get our ink salespeople in a new door. In this scenario, the IRS salesperson has performed this door-opening function and can receive this commission. We couldn't immediately say if this would be enough of a motivator, since we hadn't yet worked on the appointment-setter package. We agreed that after establishing the appointment-setter pay plan, thereby identifying the "ink referral commission" for the IRS salesperson, we would revisit this. If it wasn't enough of a motivator we would simply raise it. After all, it was a much warmer lead and well worth paying for.

On the topic of the commission for ink salespeople who might sell an ink recovery system, we couldn't very well have a different payout than the IRS salesperson's. The same IRS commission plan would therefore apply. Someone raised the question, "What if an ink salesperson begins selling too many recovery systems and not enough ink?" The answers to this question are a great illustration of some of the benefits of *The Perfect SalesForce*, so I sat back to watch the group toss it around. I simply said, "So what?"

George offered that this person is supposed to be selling ink primarily. Norman said sales are sales, who cares? It was Dan who hit the nail on the head when he asked the group, "You asked what happens if the ink salesperson is so preoccupied with the ink recovery system that he doesn't sell enough ink. What do you mean by enough?" Everyone thought for about two seconds before saying, "Quota." Dan continued, "And what happens if the salesperson starts to miss quota?" He looked at me as if to say, "Right?"

I told them Dan was right. We establish clear parameters for just this kind of reason. We have identified what the "right" amount of ink is that should be sold in that sales position. More important, every salesperson knows what that amount is and they understand why these things are identified in the first place. Without this clarity, a salesperson could sell "some" ink and "some" recovery systems, and no one would be able to say whether it was a good thing or a bad thing. The answer in this case is, as long as the ink salesperson maintains at least their quota in ink sales, they can do whatever they want. However, if they start selling so many recovery systems that quota is affected, I hope the choice is obvious—this is clearly an IRS salesperson, not an ink salesperson, and a change should be discussed with this salesperson. Remember that one of the sales manager's primary duties is to develop salespeople and the sales team. It is not at all uncommon for a salesperson to cross over this way; it is management's job to pay attention to the things each salesperson gravitates to. Finding each person's ideal fit is what best serves everyone involved.

Sean, one of the two senior salespeople on the committee, rightly pointed out that there might be an issue with calling existing clients in order to introduce the ink recovery system. He suggested that the ink salespeople may feel, "This is my client. *I'll* sell him the IRS." Dan almost jumped to his feet. He pointed out—quite emotionally and quite correctly—that the IRS had been available for the last two years. He had tried everything he knew to get the ink salespeople to sell these systems to their clients. This is a typical element in what I call "the changeover." When it is time to explain all these changes to the staff, and announce new positions and pay plans, there will be some emotion. Even though all of this is for the better—for salespeople as well as management— we all know that change can be disruptive. That's why "the changeover" is its own step: how it is handled is very important.

I told the committee that when we have the company "changeover" meeting and explain everything, we should explain to the ink salespeople that a decision has been made to create a separate sales position for the ink recovery system. When we share with them the measured closing ratio of this system companywide, followed by the number of potential IRS clients Dilan has, that math will help them understand management's frustration at how terribly few have been sold. However, some will still complain.

George suggested that we ask all ink salespeople to produce a list of clients with whom they may already be discussing this system— a list that would be protected from the new IRS salesperson. I intervened. I have participated in many changeovers, and this is a common suggestion. What would inevitably happen is every ink salesperson would produce a large list—whether they were actually in the process of discussing the IRS with the clients on the list. A salesperson's instinct is to protect his "property," and right or wrong, he thinks of his clients as his property. I suggested that George was on the right track, but what had worked well in the past was to establish a time period that all ink salespeople had to close up any outstanding IRS sales. This way, any sales that *were* in fact in the pipeline for the IRS would get closed, and no one could complain that it wasn't fair. We would even go so far as to offer any ink salesperson the services of the IRS specialist salesperson "free of charge" to help close any outstanding prospects.

By this point the committee felt much empowered. Once you have participated in such an open and creative brainstorming process, you realize that it is a little like looking into a crystal ball. When a handful of experienced employees sit and brainstorm a future situation, the stumbling blocks that are inevitable to that situation and that would have surfaced down the road are identified and dealt with, without having to live through them in real life. If you were to reread the last ten pages, you would see just how many ideas were proposed, dissected, challenged, thought through—and then either agreed upon or vetoed. When you have gone through this process a few times and witnessed the benefits, you realize that such open brainstorming sessions should be a regular, mandatory process. To not do so is to not take full advantage of the talent you have around you. I am told that many of the world's most innovative companies have regular—often weekly—brainstorming sessions.

It was time to address the appointment-setter package. Quota would be a minimum acceptable number of appointments produced each day (or each week), and the pay plan would of course incentivize a higher number. We weren't certain how many appointments an appointment setter would be capable of scheduling in a day so we decided to brainstorm the framework and then plug in numbers later. We would get a properly talent-cast appointment setter up and running, measure results, and then fill in the pay and quota numbers as soon as possible.

I was pleased when several committee members voiced concern about incentivizing the number of appointments. They wondered if the quality of the appointment would suffer if we incentivized quantity of appointments only. This showed that everyone was beginning to appreciate the power they had sitting in this room creating conditions; they were very conscious of how the conditions they would create today would directly translate to the actions the salespeople would take.

This brought about a discussion of what constituted a "good" appointment; was it with a particular executive level in the prospect company? Should the prospect be warm to the product before an appointment? What if the salesperson arrived and then the appointment got cancelled? All valid thoughts. Here's what was decided:

- **The appointment should be with a decision maker.**
  After a brief discussion of who the decision maker was, we quickly acknowledged that it varied depending on many factors. In a large company it might be the plant manager or purchaser; some printers had ink managers. In a smaller company the decision maker might well be the owner. We would have to train the appointment setters how to determine such things in the moment.

- **The appointment had to "sit."**
  The appointment had to happen. The prospect did not have to be warmed up or, for that matter, even fully understand

what the salesperson was there for. We agreed that it was the salesperson's responsibility to quickly establish the validity of the appointment's subject matter, to quickly create engagement and, ultimately, need. The appointment setter's only responsibility was to get the salesperson in front of the right person. If the appointment got postponed or the salesperson was stood up, it would not count as a "sit." The appointment setter could, and should, try to reset any of these anomalies.

- **Dilan would share a piece of the selling commission.**
  The issue of commission was well discussed. It was agreed that the only real way to ensure that the appointment setters would care enough to get the right decision maker in each case (instead of writing an appointment with a junior pressman—who has no authority—just to get the appointment commission) was if she received a good-size commission for deals closed on her appointments. This would address the quality-of-appointments versus quantity-of-appointments concern; we agreed it would incentivize quality appointments but at the same time it would also incentivize quantity—the thinking being the more you write the more of "yours" will ultimately close.

We set out to create the incentive plan but we found an immediate hiccup related to the fact that appointment setters would be writing appointments for both ink salespeople and IRS salespeople. While the IRS side was not difficult to calculate (the average system sold for a pretty consistent $70,000), the new ink clients were all over the board. Some placed large orders right off the bat, but most started small and grew over time. If we gave appointment setters a small commission of a small initial purchase, it would not be nearly PIC enough to motivate the desired number of appointments—as a matter of fact it would motivate appointment setters to gravitate to writing only IRS appointments. We had no desire to get into paying appointment setters a percentage of ongoing ink purchases. And finally, if we were to raise the ink commission to a larger, one-time payout, there was no guarantee the brand-new client would make enough future purchases to justify it.

We looked back through statistics of existing clients to get a feel for how many of them make an initial purchase but do not go on to buy very much more; we also looked at average revenue per ink client. These are times when the old adage "If you can't measure it, you can't manage it" proves itself. You should measure everything.

We decided there was no way around the "risk" associated with the one-time payout and, after analyzing the data, very few clients bought so little from Dilan that we felt it terribly risky anyway. We then came up with the following commission framework. As stated, we would tweak these numbers as needed after people had settled into their new positions for a while.

APPOINTMENT-SETTER PAY PLAN

Sales per quarter	Commission	(Equivalent Annual Income)
2	Quota—no commission	$30,000
3–4	$500 for every sale in the quarter	$36,000–$38,000
5–7	$750 for every sale in the quarter	$45,000–$51,000
8–10	$1,000 for every sale in the quarter	$62,000–$70,000
11+	$1,250 for every sale in the quarter	$85,000+

We would make the commission the same for a new ink client as a new IRS client—again, so that appointment setters would not gravitate to one over another. Yes, we could control this with quota but only to a point; once quota was attained, appointment setters would spend the rest of their time in whatever activity paid more.

In this position Dilan would pay a salary—a true base salary—of $30,000. Commissions would be paid on top of this salary. We felt it wrong to tie 100 percent of the position's earning potential to sales, since this employee's primary activity was not sales, it was appointment setting. To some degree, their sales commission was in the hands of the salesperson, and depended on his or her ability to sell—something we knew would be an issue. Still, it was the only way to assure quality appointments.

To address this issue I shared a practice I had learned at a high-performing and very sales-centric company. The appointment setters would all want to write appointments for the best salespeople, so we agreed that the *best* appointment setters would write for the *best* salespeople. In turn the best salespeople would end up getting the best appointments. Dilan would also win in such a scenario. This arrangement motivates both parties—appointment setters and salespeople—to be as good as they can be. And if anyone thinks this unfair to the weaker producers, it is not. Everyone is working under the same conditions and has the exact same opportunity. It is no more unfair than the fact that better salespeople earn more commission. It is in keeping with any logical business hierarchy: you don't get promoted for mediocrity. Higher producers get promoted.

The committee felt comfortable with the structure they had conceived. They felt it was 100 percent better; they understood how it better catered to behavior analysis, how it would be an easier model to manage and to grow. We knew that we would tweak a few details in the coming months, but the sales team would be told this in the changeover meeting. It was time to move on from pay and quota and talk about what there might be to change in the areas of training, the sales manager, and the current salespeople. We began with the salespeople.

The hope is always that if someone is indeed miscast—and is currently in a sales position that they do not possess all the talents for—that there exists another position that their talent set *does* fit. Once the appropriate staff members had been trained in the talent-based interview, we would interview the sales staff and determine who belonged where. We conduct these interviews covertly, as chapter 5 suggests. We tell each salesperson that we want their input on things—given the changes we are in the midst of implementing—and then we conversationally assess them, just as we would in a talent interview. You simply cannot tell an employee that you need to interview them to see if they have the talents for the job they've been doing for four years.

Such interviews rarely reveal surprises. If someone is perfectly cast in their position they will be doing well. If they are not well cast talentwise, they are not likely breaking records. If a conversation is needed following these interviews to discuss a possible position change, don't be surprised if the candidate embraces the idea of the change. Everyone agreed that following the changeover meeting, interviews (conversations) would begin and we would see where Dilan stood regarding talent and the new selling positions.

As for the topic of training, there were two different categories: the designing of the training that Dilan salespeople should receive, both initially and throughout their career and then training that the Dilan staff would need soon, in order to pilot the vehicle they had just built. The latter would consist of:

- **A result-based management course.**
  This should be attended by not only the sales manager, but other key management staff and Dan. It is critical that every-

one is on the same page with the concepts of result-based management discussed in chapter 8. When this is *not* the case I have watched sales managers doing exactly what they should be doing, only to have the company owner begin asking how many calls were made today and a plethora of other activity questions. When the sales manager informs him that they don't police activities anymore—they only police results— the owner intervenes. Everyone has to understand how a result-managed company runs, what everyone's role is, and why it works.

- **A talent-based interview course.**
  The sales manager, Dan, Eva (the human resources coordinator), and a few others will need to learn how to conduct a talent interview.

- **The changeover meeting.**
  All Dilan employees should understand not only what changes are taking place, but why. They should be exposed to the very same evidence and philosophies that initially led management to embrace these 6 best practices. This will ultimately create more companywide buy-in.

The training that Dilan salespeople would receive—initially and throughout their career—would follow exactly what was covered in chapter 7: rapport skills training (mirroring, etc.), *SPIN Selling* sales training, and an understanding of the adviser approach to closing.

All that was left was the topic of the current sales manager, George. Was he the right person for the job? Remember the two equally important pieces to the sales manager formula: *who* the manager is and *what* the manager does. If the right sales manager is doing the wrong things, he can be trained. But if he lacks the personal criteria elaborated in chapter 8, he cannot be trained.

I discussed this privately with Dan in his office; this is not a topic for open committee discussion and, ultimately, it's not their decision—the decision should be most influenced by the salespeople. I had covertly assessed George throughout the time I had been working with him, but for all I knew he might behave differently with the salespeople than he did with the committee and me. Since the respect and cooperation of the salespeople is the critical component, their opinion of him counts most. We know this of course and so the topic of George, his management style, and his personality were a big part of the initial interviews I had conducted with each salesperson during the assessment stage.

The salespeople liked George just fine but did not particularly think of him as their leader. They did their own thing and did not often call upon George. While it is true that George's role had not been well designed or even defined, the question was whether the salespeople would respond to him now, after he had his management training. After all, their relationship had been a certain way for a long time.

It is at these times when you must remember to pretend the current structure and the current people do not exist. You must ask yourself what you would do—knowing what you know now—if you were starting the department from scratch. I reminded Dan of this and asked him to answer this simple question. I asked him to pretend he was hiring a sales manager for the first time to lead the current sales team; I asked him to imagine that George was just another salesperson on the team. Knowing what he knows now about *who* the perfect manager is and *what* this manager should be doing with the group, I asked him if he would immediately promote George to manager, or would he likely consider other candidates. Without any hesitation Dan said, "If he wasn't already manager, I would look for someone who better fits your description, maybe someone younger, dynamic, a leader they will all respect and follow."

I told Dan that he had his answer; the only remaining question was what to do. I also reminded him that the relationship between a salesperson and the manager is the single largest influence on performance. Different people will make different decisions at this point, and it is indeed a personal choice. George could remain as manager and perhaps things would be fine. But Dan didn't want "fine." He told me the whole reason he had hired me was to create awesome, not fine. It was time for a few options.

To be very blunt, some of the obvious choices were:

- Leave George where he was
- Fire George
- Ask George to return to being a salesperson; he had his own territory after all
- Offer George an early retirement

Dan said the first two were out. He wanted a different arrangement certainly, and a new manager, but the man certainly did not deserve to be fired. I agreed. We also felt it would be quite a slap in the face to simply ask George to return to his salesperson duties and then give the manager job to someone else, although Dan said if it was the only option, he would do so. A little creative thinking, however, produced an additional option.

George was sixty-one years old. It was a realistic assumption that before too many years Dilan would be facing the issue of a new manager anyway. We felt that in a private chat George would appreciate that fact and see the logic in discussing the situation now, since the company was about to go through so many changes anyway. We believed it a logical and respectful suggestion to begin to groom someone new, a sales manager in training

who, for the moment, would report to George. Both would receive the result-based management training and both would understand that the "balance of power" would gradually shift over
time.

The beauty of this arrangement was that a gradual shifting of
power would not actually occur. When a great manager is suddenly present, his or her impact is felt immediately. George would
appreciate the logic and the respectfulness of this approach, and
the new manager would begin to influence right away. The discussion turned to the new candidate.

I had identified the needed talents and personality in two of the
salespeople I had interviewed. During sales meetings, these two
naturally led and others naturally followed (while George usually
sat quietly). What I did not know was whether either one had any
management aspirations. I asked Dan about these two as well as
the idea of looking outside the company. After discussing it for a
while we agreed that it was something to revisit when the time
came. We had found the right approach to the situation. Plugging
the right individual into the position would not be a difficult process. Dan would have a chat with George before the companywide changeover meeting, which suddenly had become the very
next step. Our new structure was complete.

STEP 3: ANNOUNCE THE CHANGE-
OVER TO THE COMPANY; EXPLAIN
THE THINKING

Dan invited the salespeople, George, and all senior staff to a local
hotel for a daylong meeting. I had suggested we get off site and
make a day of it. Dan read a lot and had tried many different management ideas on for size. This can cause the employees to think,

"Okay . . . what's next? What are we trying now?" This is why it is important to include employees in these decisions, rather than announcing a change you have already decided upon. If an employee questions a particular change that management is proposing, that employee may well have a better idea, which serves everyone. If no better idea is offered, then the proposed change is deemed accepted.

Dan opened the meeting by explaining who I was, how he had found my company, and why he was attracted to these philosophies. As I told him to be sure to do, he explained that we all had some ideas that we thought were good ones and that had worked well with other companies, and we would like the input of the sales team. Dan gave it the feel of "We want your feedback and advice. We will listen," rather than, "Here's what we've decided to do." This was met with slightly less than the usual skepticism, which was fine. Skepticism or not, a better way is a better way. The whole trick is to stay on the new path, to avoid a return to the way everything was before.

In this setting we want people to question. Every change being proposed has a valid reason behind it. If people question, there will be a good answer, which serves to convince them that this is at least a good direction. And if someone has a better idea for a particular detail, so much the better. I actually hope for such occurrences; nothing builds rapport better than an employee saying, "What about this way instead?" followed by management answering, "Good idea. Let's do that."

Dan explained the proposed changes to the sales structure. He did not mention any changes to pay and quota, just the new sales positions. The immediate question was who would fill which positions, to which Dan answered, "Whatever you guys tell me." A great answer. He explained what he had learned recently about natural talent, about how it cannot be trained and how we may well have people currently being asked to carry out too many sales stages. Everyone liked the idea of appointment setters.

Throughout the meeting I would assist with certain explanations. My answers always included the research behind the thinking, as well as testimonials and results of past clients. It is important to "sell" the program to your people. They must buy in and the changeover meeting is as much about obtaining buy-in as it is about providing information.

Lunch was filled with questions and casual talk. Salespeople tend to adapt more quickly than other employees and they were already participating. It helped that management was listening to their ideas. When we covered the proposed pay plan changes after lunch, the usual frozen faces appeared. Then the questions came—many questions. They were answered one by one and after several hours, everything was just fine. Everyone understood the concept of quota—some even suggested it was too low. Everyone immediately loved the idea of policing results rather than activities, but openly voiced their skepticism that Dan would live by this rule. Dan gave a short, sincere speech about how hard he would try, and that everyone's help would be appreciated. He also told them of the new committee, which included two senior salespeople. This committee's purpose was to keep this program on track.

There are owners, managers, and consultants who have told me we needn't approach change with such sensitivity. They suggest you should be a strong leader and just announce that this is the way it is. Take it or leave it. And they are dead wrong. These are the consultants and clients I get hired to clean up after. The strongest leaders listen. They do not always go ahead and do what is being proposed but they always listen and consider. Then they choose which direction they think is right. Leadership is listening to the people you have hired and then going with the best idea. If there are conflicting ideas, a leader's job is to choose a direction after having heard and considered every option equally.

As usually happens, many suggestions from the salespeople were suggestions that the committee had already considered in order to arrive where we had arrived. We were careful not to constantly say, "We already thought of that." To build a team atmosphere everyone must feel they are being heard. We explained the thought process and invited opinion, stating that maybe we had indeed missed something.

In the latter part of the afternoon we began openly discussing which salespeople would like to explore any of the new positions. When a few hands shot up for the IRS sales position, we congratulated these people and then reminded them that talent would ultimately decide. One of them suggested that in this new result-managed environment, we should try several people and let the results decide. Since no one could find a reason to disagree, we didn't. Dan was already "getting caught" doing exactly what he said he was going to do—a great thing for morale.

Over the following weeks new positions were discussed and finally assigned. One salesperson wanted to run the appointment-setter department. Dan told him that he could start as an appointment setter and then Dan would review. The employee understood when Dan told him that not every great salesperson makes a great manager—that a separate talent set is needed. Dan also said that any department manager must be good at that department's actual sales job, so the first step was to be an appointment setter. The man agreed and became Dilan's first appointment setter. We ran ads and hired two more.

In the months to come everyone was trained in all positions, including Dilan's brand-new sales manager, Andrea (sales manager "in training"). Andrea was one of the two internal salespeople who I believed had what was necessary, and she was very enthusiastic to manage. Everyone liked Andrea and was thrilled for her.

ONE YEAR LATER

I said this wasn't a before and after story, but you certainly need to hear how things were going following the changeover. Remember that Dilan's sales had gone down over a three-year period, from $9.8 million to $9.5 million to $9 million when I was called. One full year after the changeover, sales had increased by $1.1 million to $10.1 million. They have continued to increase dramatically every year.

The year following the changeover was not without its ups and downs, but every business has daily challenges. I stayed on board to coach the committee. This book's final best practice advice is about your *Perfect SalesForce* committee. Do not let the daily fires keep the committee from its regular meetings. Do not allow your committee to fall apart. Set regular meetings and stick to them— even if they are nothing more than a five-minute checkup. Continue to brainstorm and test better approaches, new ideas, and new training, and measure all results. You won't know what's working without good measuring in place.

Remember that the best idea is the best idea no matter who thought of it, and remember to include, regularly communicate with, and listen to those who I believe are the most important people in your company—your salespeople.

PERFECT **SALESFORCE**
ONLINE SUPPORT

ecause this book stresses the importance of correct implementation of
each best practice, all owners of this
book are entitled to one month at my exclu-
sive Members Community Web site. There
you will find articles, training videos, tools,
and resources, my daily personal blog, and a
members' forum where we all discuss and
share these best practices in real time and
on a daily basis. Whether you choose to participate or simply observe, you will find a
wealth of assistance to and support of everything in this book. Details can be found at
www.theperfectsalesforce.com/trial. This offer expires on December 31, 2009.

INDEX

Pages with illustrations/figures are listed in *italics*.

Ability. *See* Talent, natural

Account penetration, 20, 50

Activities
  defining, 68
  sales manager managing, 185–88

Advisers (closers), 42–44, 167–71
  interview and identifying, 88–90,
    95–96
  questions for identifying, 95–96
  sales stages and, 56

Advising, 161, 167–71
  trust and, 169–70

Antecedent, 105–7
  reinforcement of, 109

Assessment, case study, 213–21
  questions for, 214–17
  results of, 217–21

Awaken the Giant Within (Robbins), 163

Base salary, 130–33. *See also* Pay plan
  commission blended with, 133
  sales manager, 155

Behavior, 105–7. *See also* Sales
    behavior training

conditions altering, 112
  interviewing and identifying
    recurring, 79, 82–93
  reinforcing, 110–11, 173

Behavior analysis
  ABC in, 105–7
  performance influencers and,
    104–12
  workplace application of, 13, 104

Bonuses, 130
  as consequence, 107–8
  team, 154

Brainstorming
  case study, 251
  employee involvement in,
    74–75
  sales managers and, 186–87
  sales stages and, 74–75
  work sheet process and, 70–71

Career levels
  case study, 225, 238–44, *239*
  pay plan and, 150–53
  quotas and, 125

Change, implementing, 207–8
  case study, 221–60
  stages of, 211
Changeover meeting, case study, 257,
    260–64
Clear parameters, 102–3
"Client engagement," 59–60
Closers. *See* Advisers
Closing, 20
  techniques, 171
Cold calling, 66
Commission, 130, 134–38. *See also* Pay
    plan
  base salary blended with, 133
  100 percent, 131–33
  quotas and, 137
  sliding-scale, 135–37, *136*, 146–47
  sliding-scale, case studies, *136*,
    136–37, 240–43, *241*
  team, 154
Commodity, 49–50, 236
Complacency, 135–37
Concept sales, 47–48
  sales stages and, 56
Conditions, 13–18
  behavior altered by, 112
  ideal performance, case study,
    215–17
  intolerable, 101
  logistical influencer, 14
  performance influencer, 14, 101–2
  productivity and, 27
  psychological influencer, 14–15
  talent operating under specific,
    9–18, 26
Consequences, 105–7
  dimensions of, 107
  motivator, 107–8

  NIC, 109
  PIC, 107–8
Consultative selling, 28, 166
Contracts, salesperson's, 126–27
CSR. *See* Customer service reps
Customer service, 20
  pleasers as, 43
  quotas, reaching and, 124–25
  training, 160
Customer service reps (CSRs), 160

Daniels, Aubrey, 105
Decision makers, many v. few, 51
Drucker, Peter, 208

Engagement, 59–60
Executive rapport, 38
  high v. low, 44–45
  interview questions for identifying,
    96
  sales stages and, 56
Experience, hiring and, 77
Explanation, 38
  interview questions for identifying,
    97
  obvious v. concept, 47–48
  sales stages and, 56

Firing, 128–29

Gallup Organization study,
    3–4
  sales managers in, 185
  top performance and, 23
Goals, 199–200
Growth, 204–6
  case study, 231–32
  Perfect SalesForce and, 201–8

Hoarding sales, 138
Huthwaite study, 4
    closing and, 171
    sales performance and, 27–28
    solution and, 166

Incentives
    selling positions and, 144
    short-term, 108, 130, 138–39, 148–49
International Profit Associates (IPA),
        16–17
Interviews
    answer file from, keeping, 98–99
    behavior patterns and, 79, 82–93
    controlling, 84–85
    dialogue examples, 86–90
    dividing your mind during, 97–98
    guiding, 98
    level of detail in, 79–80
    listener in, 51–52
    performance potential revealed in,
        7
    process, steps for, 79–93
    questions, 78, 84–85, 93–97, 197–98
    sales manager, 196–98
    speaker in, 51–52
    structure, 82–93
    talent-based, 30, 77
    ten selling talents identified in, 52,
        82–83, 86–90
    tips, 97–99
    vague, 79–81
In-the-moment decisions/judgments
    salespeople's ability for making,
        8–9
    selling process and, 8
IPA. See International Profit
        Associates

Job ads, 79–80
Job description, 127

Lead generation, 20
    preengagement stages and, 60–61
Leads, warm, 68
Listener, 51–52
    interviews and identifying, 84

Management structures. See also
        Result-based management
    group performance, 15–16
    IPA, 16–17
    pay plan and, 17
    results and, 17
"Marketing channels," 60–61
    exercises for, 64
    sales stages in, 62–64
    work sheet for, case study, 67
Micromanaging, 183, 202
Microsoft employee productivity
        survey, 103–4
Mirroring, 84
    rapport, attaining and, 162–65
Motivators
    consequences as, 107–8
    negative, 111–13
    pay plan as positive, 112–13
    positive, 111–13
    quota as negative, 112–13
    sales managers as, 109

Need, 38
    created v. established, 45–46
    creating, case study, 225–26
    developing, 20
    establishing, 45–46
    interview and identifying, 91

Need (*continued*)
    interview questions for identifying,
        97
    sales stages and, 56
Negative, immediate, certain (NIC),
    109
Neurolinguistic programming (NLP),
    163
NIC. *See* Negative, immediate,
    certain
NLP. *See* Neurolinguistic
    programming

Objective, work sheet and being,
    70–73
Online support, 265

Pay plan, 15, 130–57
    base salary in, 130–33
    building, three-step process to,
        140–49, *141*
    career levels and, 150–53
    case studies, 219–20, 245–49, *247*,
        253–55, *254*
    commission in, 130, 134–38
    generating, 20
    incentives, short term in, 138–39
    management structures and, 17
    motivation and, 21
    performance-based components,
        146
    as positive motivator, 112–13
    pricing and, 143
    profit-based, 143–44
    sales-based, 143
    salesperson's contract and, 126
    sliding-scale, 153, *153*
    territory-building, 149–54
    transitioning, 155–57

Perfect SalesForce, 3, 5–18
    case study, 211–64
    committee, 206–7, 222
    firing in, 128–29
    growing, 201–8
    6 best practices of, *19*, 19–31, 29,
        202–3
Performance
    base-line, 119
    behavior analysis and influencers
        on, 104–12
    conditions, case study, 215–17
    conditions influencing, 14, 101–2
    group, 15–16
    Huthwaite study and, 27–28
    interview and revealing potential
        of, 7
    logistical influencers on, 14
    management, 13
    pay plan components based on, 146
    preferences and, 49
    psychological influencers on, 14–15
    sales training and, 3, 6, 159
    talent as predictor for future, 78,
        91–92
    territory-building levels of, 150–52,
        151
    workplace, 101
Performance-based remuneration,
    130, 133. *See also* Commission
Perks, 14, 130
Personality
    groups, 162
    talent v., 92
Persuasion, 38
    adviser v. pleaser, 42–44
    interview questions for identifying,
        95–96
    sales stages and, 56

PIC. *See* Positive, immediate, certain
Pleasers, 42–44
  customer service and, 43
  interview and identifying, 88
  interview questions for identifying, 95–96
Positive, immediate, certain (PIC), 107–8
  managing with, 198–99
  quotas, 121–22
Postengagement stages, 61–62
Preengagement stages, 60–61
Preferences, 48–49
Price change request, 143
Pricing
  case study, 236–38
  pay plan and, 143
"Process-izing," 7–8
Productivity
  conditions and, 27
  levels of, 135
  Microsoft employee productivity survey, 103–4
Products, many v. few, 50–51
Prospecting, 20
  case study, 223–25
  defined, 36–37
  preengagement stages and, 60–61
  talent and, 37
  tolerance and embracing, 41
  training skills for, 41
Prospects, telling, 168–69

Quality v. quantity, 39–40
Questions
  asking, 20
  assessment, case study, 214–17
  interpretation of, 85

interview, 78, 197–98
  control with, 84–85
  sample, 93–97
Quotas, 15, 101–57
  cap, 124
  case study, 220–21, 234–35
  commission and, 137
  components to definition of, 115–21
  customer service after reaching, 124–25
  defined, 113
  firing and, 128–29
  generating, 20
  increasing, 122–23
  meeting, 118–19
    effort for, 120–21
  missing, 127–30
  motivation and, 21
  as negative motivator, 112–13
  new hire, 127
  period, 120
  PIC, 121–22
  properly cast individuals and, 119
  purpose of, 114
  ramifications of not making, 127–30
  results and, 114–19
  rewards for going over, 120
  sales managers and setting, 187–88
  salesperson's contract and, 126
  tasks, job and, 115–19
  territory-building, 123–26

Rackham, Neil
  Huthwaite study, 166
  sales performance research of, 27–28
  SPIN Selling, 28, 166–67
  SPIN Selling Fieldbook, The, 167

Rapport, attaining, 161–65
  mirroring and, 162–65
Ratios, growth and lower, 204–6
Reinforcement
  antecedent, 109
  behavior, 110–11
  management and, 198–99
  negative, 111
Result-based management, 20, 22–29,
    181–200
  case study, 256–57
  sales force, 29–30
Results, 68
  assessment, case study, 217–21
  defining, 68
  exercise for picking, 115–16
  incentives and desired, 144–45
  management structures and, 17
  quota and, 114–19
  sales manager enforcing, 22,
    185–88
  sales stages, 62–64
  talents for, 69
  tasks, job and, 115–19
Revenue levels, 136
Robbins, Anthony, 163

Salary. See Base salary
Sale characteristics, 33–34
Sale cycle, 49
Sales, focusing on, 205
Sales behavior training, 20, 21,
    159–80
  altering behavior and, 13
  classroom, 171–72
  delivery, 171–77
  field training, 171, 175–77
  role play, 171–75
Sales force, 29–30

Sales manager, 15
  activities managed by, 185–88
  behavior reinforced by, 110–11
  best salespeople and time spent
    with, 192
  brainstorming, 186–87
  feedback from, 212
  Gallup Organization study and, 185
  goals and, 199–200
  interviewing potential, 196–98
  micromanaging, 183
  as motivator, 109
  PIC and, 198–99
  practices of world's best, 182–92
  promoting from within for, 195–96
  quota setting and, 187–88
  results enforced by, 22, 185–88
  role of, 181
  salary, 155
  selecting, 192–200
  strengths developed by, 188–91
  talents, 196–98
  telling by, 104–5
  training, 194
Salespeople
  approaches, different of, 9
  contract for, 126–27
  feedback from, 212
  hiring, 5–6, 77–78
  in-the-moment decision-making
    ability, 8–9
  natural born, 1, 5–6, 7
  quality v. quantity and, 39–40
  sales stages performed by, 55
  specifications for perfect, xi
  stages and multiple, 72
  switching, 72–73
  trained v. untrained, x
Sales process, x, 8

Sales stages, 19, 53
  assigning, 56–57
  case study, 218–19
  defined, 59–62
  duration of, 71–73, 223–24
  integration in, 73–74
  long, 71–73
  objectivity and, 70–73
  results identified for, 62–64, 68
  salespeople, multiple for different,
    72
  salespeople performing, 55
  sorting, 20–21, 55–75
  structural changes in, 73–74
  talent and sorting, 20–21, 55–75
  testing arrangement of, 73–74
  work sheet, 63
  work sheet, case studies, 64–69, 67,
    226–30, 227, 229
Sales training, ix–x, 12–13, 15. See also
    Sales behavior training
  amount of, 177–79
  approaches to, 3
  behavior altered by, 13
  case study, 220–21, 256–57
  compulsory, 178–79
  curriculum, 159–71
  customer service and, 160
  delivery, 159
  flexible, 12–13
  money spent on, 3
  new hire, 159, 177–78
  performance and, 3, 6, 159
  "process-izing" and, 7–8
  prospecting and, 41
  sales manager, 194
  talent and, 12
  top-performing salespeople and,
    6–7

Sale types, 5–6
  talent and, 6, 7, 11–12, 24
  top-performing, 6
Selling stage, 61
  engagement and, 59–60
Service, 50. See also Customer service
Servicing, 62
Shaping, 111
  incentives, short-term and, 139
Skills, hiring and, 77
Solution, 161, 166–67
  unique v. commodity, 49–50
Speaker, 51–52
  interviews and identifying, 84
"Specializing," 58
Specific knowledge, hiring and, 77
Spillage, 204–5
SPIN Selling (Rackham), 28, 166–67
SPIN Selling Fieldbook, The (Rackham),
    167
Spitzer, Dean, 102
Supermotivation (Spitzer), 102

Talent-based hiring process, 20, 21,
    24–25, 77–99
  interview in, 30, 34–35, 82
  methodology, 44
  resumé volume and, 80–81
  sales manager, 196–98
  tolerance level and, 41
  training, case study, 257
  work ethic and, 40
Talent, natural, xi–xii, 10–12
  hiring and, 77
  identifying, 10, 34–35
  as performance indicator, 78,
    91–92
  sale characteristics, different and,
    33–34

Talent casting, 10–12, 66, 128–29
  pinpoint, case study, 214–15
  quotas and proper, 119
Talents. *See also* 10 selling talents
  cold calling, 66
  common, 36
  key, 36
  personality v., 92
  prospecting, 37
  results and, 69
  sales, 25
  sales manager, 196–98
  sales stages sorted by, 20–21,
    55–75
  sale types and, 6, 7, 11–12, 24
  specific conditions and, 9–18, 26
  training and, 12
Tasks, job
  primary, 116–17
  quotas attached to, 115–19
  results and, 115–19
  secondary, 117
Team remunerating and bonuses, 154
Technical support, 61–62
Telemarketing, 37
Telling
  prospects and, 168–69
  sales manager, 104–5
10 selling talents, 19, 33–53, *38*
  identifying, 52

interview and identifying, 82–83,
    86–90
sale and arrangement of, 20
sales stages results and, 62–64
Territory building
  pay plan for, 149–54
  performance levels for, 150–52, *151*
  quotas, 123–26
Tolerance, 38
  defined, 40
  high v. low, 40–42
  interview and identifying, 91–93
  interview questions for identifying,
    95
Top-producing/performing
    salespeople, 1
  Gallup Organization study on, 23
  hiring, 6–7
  studying, 6
  talent and, 10–12
  types of, 6–7

Unlimited Power (Robbins), 163

Work environment, 13, 101
Work ethic, 38
  interview and identifying, 91
  interview questions for identifying,
    94–95
  quality v. quantity, 39–40